TOBIAS SMOLLETT

PLATE I—Professor Lewis M. Knapp.

TOBIAS SMOLLETT

Bicentennial Essays
Presented to Lewis M. Knapp

Edited by
G. S. ROUSSEAU and P.-G. BOUCÉ

New York
OXFORD UNIVERSITY PRESS
1971

ACKNOWLEDGMENTS

THIS collection gathers essays in celebration of the two-hundredth anniversary of the death of Tobias Smollett (1721–71) and pays tribute to his most dedicated student in the twentieth century, Professor Lewis M. Knapp. It originated one afternoon in the summer of 1966 when its two editors were wandering along the Embankment in Chelsea, not far from a quiet spot that Smollett would have known well. During the last four years the collection has acquired too many friends to list them here. We hope that many of these friends on three continents will understand what its editors mean when they write that the book could not have come into being without the unfailing support of Professor James L. Clifford of Columbia; without the generous assistance of D.M. Davin, John R.B. Brett-Smith, and Whitney Blake, all of Oxford University Press; Carroll Camden, Geoffrey Carnall, David Foxon, John Price, the late Sir George Clutton, Walter Anderson, Mrs. John Butt, and the services of the Reading Room and North Library of the British Museum; and without the research assistance and secretarial aid of Roger Hambridge, Jane Flick, Ellen Cole, and Betty Baker. And James L. Clifford wishes to thank Lillian McCue for her invaluable help with the tribute to Lewis M. Knapp. For permitting us to reproduce "The Pineapple Picture" (Plate V) we are indebted to the Marchioness of Cholmondeley, Houghton Hall, King's Lynn, Norfolk, England. The late Professor John Butt's essay was originally written in 1964 as a chapter for the eighth volume of the *Oxford History of English Literature: The Mid-Eighteenth Century,* in which it will be published, and appears here for the first time in print by kind permission of Mrs. John Butt and the Delegates of the Clarendon Press, Oxford. Professor Knapp's Clarendon Press edition of *The Letters of Tobias Smollett* appeared after this volume had gone to press.

G.S.R.

October 1970   P.G.B.

NOTE TO THE READER

All references to Smollett's novels are to the Shakespeare Head Edition (Oxford, 1925–26), with the exception of the *Travels through France and Italy,* which is not included in that edition.

For the reader's convenience we have referred to pages in *Humphry Clinker* by date of the letter rather than volume and page number.

TABLE OF CONTENTS

Lewis Mansfield Knapp   3
    JAMES L. CLIFFORD, *Columbia University*

Smollett's Achievement as a Novelist   9
    JOHN BUTT, *Edinburgh University*

Smollett the Historian: A Reappraisal   25
    DONALD GREENE, *University of Southern California*

The Pilgrimage and the Family: Structures in the Novels
                 of Fielding and Smollett   57
    RONALD PAULSON, *Johns Hopkins University*

Pineapples, Pregnancy, Pica, and *Peregrine Pickle*   79
    G. S. ROUSSEAU, *University of California, Los Angeles*

Smollett's Picaresque Games   111
    PHILIP STEVICK, *Temple University*

The Two Worlds of *Ferdinand Count Fathom*   131
    T. O. TREADWELL, *Columbia University*

The Economy of *Humphry Clinker*   155
    BYRON GASSMAN, *Brigham Young University*

Smollett as a Caricaturist   169
    GEORGE KAHRL, *Elmira College*

Eighteenth- and Nineteenth-Century Biographies   201
    PAUL-GABRIEL BOUCÉ, *University of Paris, The Sorbonne*

Smollett's Traveler   231
    ROBERT D. SPECTOR, *Long Island University*

PUBLICATIONS OF LEWIS M. KNAPP   247

INDEX   251

LIST OF ILLUSTRATIONS

PLATE

I Professor Lewis M. Knapp FRONTISPAGE

II Title page of James Augustus Blondel's *The Strength of Imagination in Pregnant Women Examin'd . . . By a Member of the College of Physicians, London.* London, 1727.

III Plate illustrating the abnormal cravings of pregnant women. From George Alexander Stevens, *The Dramatic History of Master Edward* (London, 1763).

IV Plate illustrating the abnormal cravings of a pregnant woman. From George Alexander Stevens, *The Dramatic History of Master Edward* (London, 1763).

V The Pineapple Picture. By Henry Danckerts (*c.* 1625–79?).

VI Table of Contents for *Les Caricatures de M.* [Arthur] *Pond, publiées par Jean Boydell, graveur, Rue de Cheapside, à Londres, 1740–42.*

VII Pier-Leone Ghezzi, "Le Docteur Tom Bently."

VIII Raymond La Fage, "Carnacci, acteur du théâtre du Vallon dans le Tems du Carnaval de l'Année 1738, que tout Rome alla voir en Foule, à cause de son Jeu & sa Voix."

IX Raymond La Fage, "Polichinelle attaqué de la Goutte."

X Annibale Carracci, "Deux Philosophes."

XI Karl Marcus Tuscher, "Vieillard qui n'est pas trop réchauffé."

XII Pier-Leone Ghezzi, "Bernardino Luchesini Bolognese."

XIII Pier-Leone Ghezzi, "Il Sig: Dottore che tasta il Polso."

XIV Pier-Leone Ghezzi, "Il Sig: Abbate Napoletano."

XV Pier-Leone Ghezzi, "Cercante Cappuccino."

XVI Pier-Leone Ghezzi, "Decano."

XVII Pier-Leone Ghezzi, "Petruccella."

TOBIAS SMOLLETT

Lewis Mansfield Knapp

———— •◆• ————

JAMES L. CLIFFORD

IT sometimes happens that a figure of the past so engages a modern scholar that the two become inextricably connected in the reader's mind. "Lefty" Lewis, for all intents and purposes, is Horace Walpole; Frederick Pottle stands for James Boswell. Similarly, Lewis Knapp is the twentieth-century representative of Tobias Smollett. For any problem connected with this novelist, if there is an answer Knapp will have it; if not, he will know why. He towers over Smollett studies like his own Pikes Peak.

Back in the early 1930's, when I began graduate work myself, I was an unrestrained Smollett enthusiast and vaguely hoped to make him the subject of my dissertation. But when I tentatively proposed the idea, my adviser at Columbia said that was impossible. "Smollett has been thoroughly divided up at Yale," he said, "and there is nothing left for outsiders. One is going to edit his letters, another write his life, and others are working on his novels." So I turned instead to the Johnson circle, with whom I must say I have been as happy as any Yale man with Tobias.

At that time I could never have guessed that the man who was at work on the Smollett biography would later become one of my best friends. It was in the 1940's that I first met Lewis Knapp, and I enthusiastically reviewed his volume when it appeared in 1949. During the following years, though usually far apart, we have kept up a steady correspondence, and I turn to him constantly for advice. We have been always in touch, whether because of something connected with the forgery of Smollett letters, or a question con-

3

cerning some London geographical problem, or something having to do with the relations of Johnson and his Scottish contemporary; and even now we both find ourselves on the Advisory Board of the Bicentennial Edition of the Works of Tobias Smollett. When a few years ago, in a nostalgic mood, I agreed to edit *Peregrine Pickle* for the Oxford English Novels series I counted on Lewis for continual advice and help. He did not let me down. The close association we had then has further reinforced my great admiration for the man and the scholar.

Lewis Mansfield Knapp was born at Groton, Massachusetts, on March 4, 1894. Growing up there and attending the local schools, he entered Amherst College in the fall of 1912. In 1916 he graduated *cum laude*, a member of Phi Beta Kappa, and winner of various prizes. For a year he was at Bishop's College School in Lennoxville, Quebec, teaching English, physics, and Latin, and playing the school organ. Then for two years he was in an ambulance unit of the 5th division of the U.S. Army, and at the end of the war attended the University of Clermont-Ferrand in France.

After a year and an M.A. (1920) at Columbia University, he became a teacher at the Hopkins Grammar School in New Haven, Connecticut, and at the same time began his association with the Yale Graduate School. From 1922 to 1925 he was Instructor in English at the University of Colorado, but then returned to New Haven for work on his Ph.D. With a Sterling Fellowship at Yale, and with some part-time work at the Hopkins Grammar School, he speedily completed the requirements and received his doctorate in 1928—the topic for his dissertation, "A Study of the Final Period of Tobias Smollett: *The Expedition of Humphry Clinker*, and Contributions to the Biography of Tobias Smollett and Ann Smollett." The die was cast. From this time on Tobias was to be the governing influence of his life.

During the next ten years he threw himself exuberantly into college teaching, first as an Instructor and then as Assistant Professor at Williams College. In 1936 Louise Ansley, whom he had married in 1922, died. Two years later Knapp married Helen June Heath, an ordained minister and a talented amateur actress. They have a daughter and a son and four grandchildren. The son, Hugh, is, like his father, an eighteenth-century scholar and has recently christened his second son "Tobias Lewis Knapp." In 1939 Knapp moved to Colorado College in Colorado Springs, where he has been ever since. He retired in 1962 and served for a year as Carnegie Visiting Professor of English at the University of Alaska. In 1966 he was awarded an honorary degree of Doctor of Letters by Colorado College.

Through the years there have been two compelling urges in Lewis Knapp—his teaching and a determination to write the definitive life of Smollett. For too long this writer had come down to us in distorted legends and half-truths: as the opinionated medical man who was a failure at his profession, the cynical traveler who saw nothing good in Continental manners and customs, the misanthropic and irascible journalist always at odds with his contemporaries. It was not Knapp's method to make a frontal attack on the old legends or to argue with the unsympathetic critics of the past. Instead he patiently assembled all the available facts and allowed the reader to make up his own mind about Smollett. And Knapp turned up ample evidence by which to judge. Here, for example, was the actual bill for clothing purchased in June 1739 when young Smollett was preparing to go to London, which showed that he had been much better equipped than was his fictional counterpart, Roderick Random. From wills and documents in Jamaica there was ample evidence concerning the financial status of his wife, Ann Lassells; in seldom-consulted London Rate Books were details about Smollett's various residences and the rent he paid; and in the Public Record Office were important facts about his business affairs and his various lawsuits. A thorough survey of the public prints and the discovery of obscure manuscripts in the British Museum made clearer the reasons behind Smollett's admiration for his friend Daniel MacKercher. There was even a careful transcript from the manuscript diary left by the Italian doctor who attended Smollett during his last days at Leghorn. But none of this was put in merely for display; everything was pertinent to an understanding of a difficult personality of the past.

Knapp surveyed Smollett's literary work with the same thoroughness. Never interrupting the narrative with long critical digressions, he gives the reader what is necessary for an understanding of the way the writer's career developed. When the book finally appeared in January 1949, as *Tobias Smollett: Doctor of Men and Manners* (Princeton University Press), there was for the first time a trustworthy, full-scale biography of the man and the writer. Here was a superb modern biography, in the best possible sense, which can never be rendered obsolete, filled out only in spots by the occasional discovery of some hitherto unknown bit of evidence. The results of Lewis Knapp's devoted labors will continue to be the cornerstone of all subsequent work on Tobias Smollett, especially for the scholarly Iowa edition now in progress.

One need only mention a few of Knapp's subsequent works— his admirable edition of *Humphry Clinker* in the Oxford English Novels series and his fully annotated volume of Smollett's letters recently published by the Clarendon Press, or the many valuable articles that are listed at the back of this book. Nor is Smollett his only literary interest. What may surprise some readers is the amount of creative work Lewis Knapp has published as a poet. Active for years in the Poetry Fellowship, he reads at times his own sensitive verses in a clear, emphatic voice. One of his former students, Thomas W. Ross, now Chairman of the English Department at Colorado College, when presenting Knapp for an honorary degree, said, he has given us "exquisite poetry—controlled, passionate, civilized." Very fitting are these lines from Pope's *Essay on Criticism*, quoted at the time:

> [He] judged with coolness, though he sung with fire;
> His precepts teach but what his works inspire.
>
> (ll.659–60)

A dedicated teacher, Lewis Knapp has inspired generations of undergraduates at Williams and at Colorado College. One former student testified, "We loved him for his gentle, but at the same time very tough, teaching." It was this "respect-with-love" that made its mark on hundreds of young people. There was never any compromise with scholarly truth. Nor ever any acceptance of shoddy thinking or slipshod workmanship. But his love of books, his devotion to great literature, and his sheer goodness of heart were passed on to all who came within his orbit.

Tall, broad, with features rough-hewn of White Mountain granite, and an emphatic New England twang that thirty years among the cowboys could not alter, Lewis Knapp gives the impression of entrenched integrity. To quote one of his friends, "He meets life with a kind of unworldly innocence that can hardly even recognize sharp dealing and downright dishonesty in the world about him. His own dealings are effortlessly upright, and incorruptible. His friendship is true and steady, his domestic affections benevolent and happy. He has something of the broad humane viewpoint of his tutelary saint, Tobias, and nothing at all of the latter's waspish irascibility. His sunny good will shines alike upon the deserving and the undeserving." There is not an ounce of malice in his nature. Torn between amusement and indignation over an attempt to promulgate fabricated letters which would settle various Smollett problems, he refused to engage in nasty recriminations. Instead, to keep the record straight, he has put a confidential account of the exposure of the forgeries in several appropriate libraries.

In politics his stand is independent. A New England Republican, he joined the Democratic party after coming to Colorado. Always on the side of the angels, he is ready to stand and be counted in all good causes. His humor shows itself not in grotesque wit or savage irony, but in gentle delight at human foibles. There are no stories of Lewis Knapp's bitter in-fighting or of his engaging in cruel gossip. What one remembers best are the times when his joy in life runs over.

When asked for descriptions of the man, his closest friends will gladly pour out their most prized recollections. Fellow actors will recall Knapp the amateur Thespian, sailing into Ibsen, or wearing tartan trews in *Brigadoon,* or type-cast as "Editor Webb of Grover's Corners, New Hampshire" in *Our Town.* Team-mates remember Knapp on the bowling alley, spinning strikes and spares to the applause of on-lookers. Colleagues picture him among the faculty poker players, "as wild as the one-eyed Jacks, champing a frayed cigar, essaying desperate bluffs, raking in chips with abashed apologies when one improbably succeeded, laughing with rueful glee when one failed."

Perhaps most characteristic of all is Knapp the dedicated book collector. Lillian McCue describes him engrossed in his favorite reading, rare book catalogues, or digging through stacks of apparently worthless dog-eared volumes in second-hand book shops and coming up with some long-lost rare edition, or impatiently waiting for the arrival of some precious item he has ordered from abroad, or gloating over some sixpenny purchase of long ago that has since the 1930's appreciated in value more than Xerox stock. He lends his dearest book treasures with open-hearted trust. Often he will find and give away scarce pamphlets out of sheer delight in tracking them down. He is always thrilled by the feel, the smell, the look of old books, as well as the feats of discovery they bring, and he generously rejoices over the triumphs of others as well as his own.

To all his friends—and they are countless—Lewis Knapp embodies the gentleman and scholar *par excellence*, and the happy man. For those of us represented in this volume it is a joy to extend our thanks to him and to all he represents.

Smollett's Achievement as a Novelist

———•◆•———

JOHN BUTT

SMOLLETT, like Fielding, reached the novel after trying other forms, though his attempts at tragedy and at verse-satire were neither instructive to him nor significant to us. *The Adventures of Roderick Random* (1748) was the work of eight months' interrupted writing in the summer and autumn of 1747. It was hastily written; but the preface shows that Smollett had given some thought to the question of form. He recognized that distinction between the novel and the romance, which Johnson was to draw so clearly in *The Rambler*, and he seems to have believed that the novel as an anti-romance had not yet been attempted in English. *Pamela* he might justly regard as something different in kind, a quite unsuitable model for his purpose. *Joseph Andrews* would have served him better; but it is not surprising that this solitary example of an English anti-romance did not make so powerful an impression upon him as Lesage's *Gil Blas*, that massive work of the greatest living French novelist. His purpose would have been served equally well by either model, for each provides a suitable opportunity of representing "familiar scenes in an uncommon and amusing point of view"; in each the reader is permitted to "gratify his curiosity, in pursuing the adventures of a person in whose favour he is prepossessed; [to] espouse his cause, [and to] sympathize with him in distress"; and in each, "the vicissitudes of life appear in their peculiar circumstances, opening an ample field for wit and humour": these are Smollett's stated intentions. But whereas the pattern of *Joseph Andrews* would have confined him

9

to a single journey along an English highway, the looser pattern of *Gil Blas* gave the perhaps illusory freedom of a whole lifetime's adventures.

But though Lesage had shown how the knavery and foibles of life might be described "with infinite humour and sagacity," the extravagance of some of the situations and the ludicrous disgraces to which Gil Blas is subjected prevent "that generous indignation which ought to animate the reader, against the sordid and vicious disposition of the world." Smollett, in short, had no use for the *picaro*, the rogue whose exploits keep him moving from place to place; but he would retain the scenes of the *picaro*'s adventures, since his reader will

find entertainment in viewing those parts of life, where the humours and passions are undisguised by affectation, ceremony, or education; and the whimsical peculiarities of disposition appear as nature has implanted them.

The center of his stage is occupied, not by the *picaro*, but by a young man of good birth and sound education exposed, as an inexperienced orphan, to the "selfishness, envy, malice, and base indifference of mankind." He has come from a remote region (Scotland), where manners are simple, to make his way in a society where men and women, of both high and low degree, are marked by affectation and deceit. He is an innocent whose character will be toughened by experience of the world. The time was yet to come when a novelist could make a child of virginal innocence the hero of his adventures, as Dickens was to do in *Oliver Twist* and *The Old Curiosity Shop*, and as Kafka was to do in *Amerika*, imagining that child holding his solitary way "among a crowd of wild grotesque companions, the only pure youthful object in the throng." The opportunities latent in this situation were doubtless beyond Smollett's power to seize: opportunities not merely for pathos, but for enlisting the reader's generous sympathies on behalf of the defenseless beset yet uncontaminated by evil. His aim was essentially similar to those of Kafka and Dickens; but he seems to have thought that our sympathies would be most readily enlisted for the ordinary sensual man, sanguine in temperament and of "an amorous complexion," quick to defend himself with his fists, or to revenge an insult, or to dally with a wench who took his fancy; but loyal to his friends, generous with his purse whenever it was full, and practical in relieving distress. The type has not lasted well: it was already too gross to appeal to Scott; but the blend of inexperience and impulsiveness serves to motivate a wide range of adventures. Such a man is likely to be often down on his luck, but his resilience will ensure that he takes the momentary advantage in any turn of the wheel of fortune; and this permits Smollett's observation to take an extensive view of mankind, if not as widely as from China to Peru, at least from Jamaica to Bath, and from the battlefield of Dettingen to the quarter-deck of a man-of-war in a sea fight.

In his observation of mankind Smollett was not concerned to make subtle discriminations. He introduces us once more to the well-established types inherited from Latin comedy, the bully, the braggart, the old miser, the proud coquette, and the honest whore; and he assists our recognition in the traditional manner by giving them allegoric names, Banter, Chatter, Bragwell, and Cringer. He also takes a hint from Shakespeare's *Henry V*, and brings together in a ship's cabin typical representatives from England, Scotland, Ireland, and Wales; and perhaps it was Ben in Congreve's *Love for Love*, who revealed to him the humorous possibilities of the sailor on shore. The hint once taken, he could supply from his own experience as a ship's doctor material for his imagination to shape into Lieutenant Bowling in *Roderick Random* and Commodore Trunnion and his associates in *Peregrine Pickle*.

But though he worked in an inherited tradition of types, he made them, or many of them at least, his own. He possessed the eye of a caricaturist, which by grossly exaggerating a feature or two converts the human form into a gargoyle. One of Roderick's employers, a French apothecary, was a little old withered man, "with a forehead about an inch high, a nose turned up at the end, large cheek-bones that helped to form a pit for his little grey eyes, [and] a great bag of loose skin hanging down on each side in wrinkles like the alforjas of a baboon"; and the body of his former master Mr. Launcelot Crab, a surgeon, was no less distorted in an opposite direction:

This member of the faculty was aged fifty, about five feet high, and ten round the belly; his face was capacious as a full moon, and much of the complexion of a mulberry: his nose resembling a powder-horn, was swelled to an enormous size, and studded all over with carbuncles; and his little grey eyes reflected the rays in such an oblique manner, that while he looked a person full in the face, one would have imagined he was admiring the buckle of his shoe.[1]

It is doubtful whether any reader could retain the impression of such a figure throughout the episodes in which the character appears. Nor need he try. It is enough if he responds to the description with delighted astonishment, and is conditioned to expect extravagant manners from such extravagant deformity.

For it was manners rather than men that exercised Smollett's attention. The vicissitudes of his inexperienced hero provide the opportunity of extending the polite reader's experience by showing him aspects of life which he knows to exist, but with which he is probably not acquainted at first hand. He has passed stage-wagons on the road, but he does not know what it is like to travel that way; Smollett tells him. He has heard of the press-gang, he may have seen a gang at work; Smollett tells him of the victim's fate. He has read about recent battles at sea; Smollett tells him how the sailor lives and describes how, when he is ill on board, he must lie suspended in his hammock with fifty other wretches,

so huddled one upon another, that not more than fourteen inches space was allotted for each with his bed and bedding; and deprived of the light of day, as well as of fresh air; breathing nothing but a noisome atmosphere of the morbid steams exhaling from their own excrements and diseased bodies, devoured with vermin hatched in the filth that surrounded them, and destitute of every convenience necessary for people in that helpless condition.[2]

Or the reader may have wondered how the down-and-out feed; Smollett takes him to a cellar, and shows him:

. . . descending very successfully, [I] found myself in the middle of a cook's shop, almost suffocated with the steams of boiled beef, and surrounded by a company of hackney coachmen, chairmen, draymen, and

1. *Roderick Random*, ch. vii.
2. *Ibid.*, ch. xxv.

a few footmen out of place, or on board wages, who sat eating shin of beef, tripe, cowheel or sausages, at separate boards, covered with cloths, which turned my stomach.[3]

The sense of physical repulsion in such passages as these is forcibly conveyed. The vividness of the reporting might almost seem to be its own justification: it might seem almost enough that Roderick Random, endowed with his creator's nervously irritable sensibility, should pass from one scene to another and record what he observes. But Smollett was not content with a "documentary," however vivid; he must devise some means of deploying his characters. Thus as Roderick surveys the scene in the cook's shop, he is followed by his man Strap, who misses his footing on one of the steps, tumbles headlong into the room and overturns the cook, as she carries a porringer of soup; the hot soup scalds the legs of a customer, who roars with the pain, and the cook strips off the customer's stocking to empty the contents of a salt-cellar on the wound. This misadventure, like Roderick's subsequent misadventure in the ship's sick-bay, is of a sort which today we associate with newspaper comic strips designed for children. The episodes are mostly short and violent: they are more or less ingenious variations on the booby-trap by which inexperience is started, or dignity is humiliated, or arrogance and conceit are revenged; but a few, such as the barbarous "roasting" of Dr. Wagtail and Roderick's vengeance upon the Lavements by a design expounded by Chaucer's Reeve, extend to a complete chapter.

The Reeve's Tale exists both in its own right and as part of a larger pattern of story-telling; but no such co-ordinating design can be discerned in the jests and tales which make up *Roderick Random*, except in so far as all are part of Roderick's manifold adventures. We might be reminded of the Merry Tales of an Elizabethan Jest Book, if it were not for the inclusion of narrative material of a different kind. Thus the history of Miss Williams, the reluctant and repentant prostitute (chs. xxii and xxiii), belongs to a recognizable literary type; and many of the episodes on board ship are as old as the Greek romances; while the account of Roderick's

3. *Ibid.* ch. xiii.

shipwreck off the coast of Sussex (ch. xxxvii) is modeled directly upon the wreck of *The Wager* as described in George Anson's *Voyages*. Other episodes are more or less strictly autobiographical, notably the account of the Carthagena expedition, and the experience of Melopoyn the dramatist with patrons and actor-managers. The reader's attention is not kept by watching the unfolding of a plot, but he is bustled along by the author's gusto toward a conventional ending, Roderick's happy discovery of a long-lost father and his eventual reunion with the colorless Narcissa.

In *The Adventures of Peregrine Pickle* (1751) the change of scene is no less frequent and little less diversified; the merry tales, in still greater profusion, are more carefully staged; the character-types are even more numerous, and so, alas, are the booby-traps. Peregrine himself is engineer-in-chief, and he exercises his barbarous powers of invention at the expense of his uncle, his tutor, his traveling companions, the physicians of Bath, and ladies in high society. "The wild and ferocious Pickle," so Walter Scott described him, "who,—besides his gross and base brutality towards Emilia, besides his ingratitude to his uncle, and the savage propensity which he shows, in the pleasure he takes to torment others by practical jokes resembling those of a fiend in glee—exhibits a low and ungentleman-like tone of thinking, only one degree higher than that of Roderick Random." Scott's castigation is morally justifiable, but it overlooks a difference in function between the two heroes, which points to a difference in purpose and structure between the novels, similar as they appear to be in their dependence upon picaresque adventure. Roderick's responses are violent but they do not affect his role as a victim of a cruel society; and though his new-found father at the end of the novel blessed God for his son's adversities

which, he said, enlarged the understanding, improved the heart, steeled the constitution, and qualified a young man for all the duties and enjoyments of life, much better than any education which affluence could bestow; [4]

the reader is not permitted to observe this improvement, since his attention is directed entirely to Roderick's misfortunes. Peregrine,

4. *Ibid.* ch. lxvi.

however, received the best education "which affluence could bestow"; but it clearly and totally failed to qualify him "for all the duties and enjoyments of life." He is represented as a young man remarkable for his wit and high spirits, with a fund of good nature and generosity in his composition, and liberal to profusion; but so vain of his parts, so passionate, and so ungovernable, that neither Winchester, Oxford, nor a private tutor could restrain his irregularities. Though his foreign tour was less futile than the young rake's in Pope's *Dunciad*—for he was not deficient in spirit and sense—it yielded ample opportunities for display of folly and obstinacy, which were to land him in the Bastille and to require the British Ambassador's skill to extricate him. His behavior on his return to England is directed by no higher principle than self-conceit. His conduct towards his Emilia, which Scott so sternly censured, is not excused by Smollett, who invites the reader to witness

this degeneracy in the sentiments of our imperious youth, who was now in the heyday of his blood, flushed with the consciousness of his own qualifications, vain of his fortune, and elated on the wings of imaginary expectation. Tho' he was deeply enamoured of miss Gauntlet, he was far from proposing her heart as the ultimate aim of his gallantry, which (he did not doubt) would triumph o'er the most illustrious females of the land, and at once regale his appetite and ambition.[5]

As to the fortune of thirty thousand pounds, inherited from his uncle, this

did not at all contribute to the humiliation of his spirit, but inspired him with new ideas of grandeur and magnificence, and elevated his hope to the highest pinnacle of expectation.[6]

These warning notes may sound a little muted amid the *brio* of Smollett's horseplay; but it should be clear enough that Peregrine is riding for a fall. He loses his mistress, his fortune is dissipated in imprudent political adventures, and his attempt to revenge himself in political journalism brings him to the Fleet Prison, where he

5. *Peregrine Pickle,* ch. lxvi.
6. *Ibid.* ch. lxxiii.

languishes, relieving so far as he is able the distresses of others, and
where he is metamorphosed from a sprightly, gay, and elevated
youth into "a wan, dejected, meagre, squalid spectre; the hollow-
eyed representative of distemper, indigence, and despair." [7] Peregrine has learnt his lesson, and it is time for Smollett to effect his
rescue and to possess himself both of Emilia and of "a fortune more
ample than his first inheritance, with a stock of experience which
would steer him clear of all those quicksands among which he had
been formerly wrecked."

I

Thus *Peregrine Pickle* can be seen to conform to a theory of the
novel which Smollett was to formulate in the preface to *Ferdinand
Count Fathom* (1753):

A Novel is a large diffused picture, comprehending the characters of
life, disposed in different groupes, and exhibited in various attitudes,
for the purposes of an uniform plan, and general occurrence, to which
every individual figure is subservient. But this plan cannot be executed
with propriety, probability or success, without a principal personage
to attract the attention, unite the incidents, unwind the clue of the
labyrinth, and at last close the scene by virtue of his own importance.[8]

Yet as he (or an associate of his) admitted in an article in the *Critical Review* (in January 1763), "a romance writer may slacken the
reins of his genius occasionally, without fear of offence, and sport
with his subject in a careless manner." [9] All need not be pointed to
the primary issue; and we are not required to search for the bearing upon Peregrine's career of such an elaborately staged episode as
the feast in the manner of the ancients (ch. xliv), or the baffling of
the bailiffs (ch. xcvii), still less in the "Memoirs of a Lady of Quality" (ch. lxxxi) inserted in the novel to oblige Lady Vane. Smollett
cannot resist a good story: he can even turn aside in the penulti-
mate chapter, when Peregrine is hurrying to a reconciliation with
Emilia, for a jest at the expense of a country squire who was so in-

7. *Ibid.* ch. ci.
8. *Ferdinand Count Fathom,* p. 3.
9. Vol. XV (1763), p. 14.

censed at Van Dyck's portraits of his ancestors "with a parcel of loose hair hanging about their eyes, like zo many colts," that he employed "a painter vellow from Lundon to clap decent periwigs upon their skulls, at the rate of vive shillings a head."

With the reins held loosely in his hand, Smollett always had time to indulge us with such tidbits. But there are two dangers: the reader loses sight of the main issue, and the author impoverishes his estate. Dickens had begun to write with the same generous expenditure of his resources, and we are told by his biographer John Forster that by the time he reached the end of *Nicholas Nickleby* he was already beginning to feel the strain upon his fancy. The course he took to relieve the strain was to adopt a more economical mode of writing. It seems probable that Smollett felt the strain too. In the early 1750's he had begun to turn to those works of translation, compilation, and synthesis which were to occupy so much of his time, and which were eventually to ruin his health. He began work on his version of *Don Quixote* in 1748; he signed an agreement in 1753 for a new collection of voyages and travels to be completed in seven volumes; from 1756 till 1762 he owned and edited the *Critical Review*, though this, as he explained to an inquiring friend, was but "a small branch of an extensive Plan which I last year projected for a sort of academy of the belles lettres"; and throughout this decade he was engaged upon his *Complete History of England*, the first four volumes of which he finished late in 1757. With these prodigious enterprises on his hands, not much could be expected of the two novels which belong to this period of his career, *The Adventures of Ferdinand Count Fathom* (1753) and *The Adventures of Sir Launcelot Greaves*, published serially in the *British Magazine* in 1760 and 1761. In fact he failed to escape from the problems posed by his conception of the novel. His "large diffused picture" of life involved him in stories of multifarious adventures, but his stock was depleted. In purposely choosing the principal character of *Ferdinand Count Fathom* "from the purlieus of treachery and fraud," he was turning his back upon the resolutions which had guided him in *Roderick Random* and attempting the true picaresque. This certainly enabled him to widen his range. The reader is accordingly introduced to the arts of the cardsharper, the quack-doctor, and the quack-connoisseur, aspects of life which the scope of *Roderick Random* and of *Peregrine Pickle* had not given him sufficient opportunity to describe. But scenes like these, and the rogue-stories which arise from them, were not enough to cover Smollett's generous canvas, and he was led, almost instinctively compelled, into that world of romance which he had rejected in the preface to *Roderick Random*. Important tracts of the novel deal with adventures in a kind of fairyland, where knights-errant attempt to rescue ladies imprisoned in castles; or where desperate deeds of banditry are committed on lonely heaths in midnight thunderstorms; or where an owl may be heard to screech from the ruined battlement of a church, as the door is opened by a sexton

who, by the light of a glimmering taper, conducted the despairing lover to a dreary isle, and stamped upon the ground with his foot, saying, "Here the young lady lies interred." [10]

The first type of episode looks back into the seventeenth century and beyond; the other two look forward into a world of "gothic" adventures which was to be more resolutely and frequently explored in the next few decades.

The flirtation with romance was temporary. In *Sir Launcelot Greaves* we are back in familiar scenes: the reader witnesses a parliamentary election, is shown a country magistrate at work, and is conducted to the King's Bench Prison and a madhouse, where he is allowed an appreciative glimpse (ch. xxiii) of the eminent psychiatrist, Dr. William Battie.[11] Smollett's model was no longer *Gil Blas* but *Don Quixote*, and *Don Quixote* imitated in the most mechanical way. Whereas Parson Adams inherited the characteristics of his Spanish prototype, Sir Launcelot Greaves inherited his armour too. In the second chapter he enters a village house armed cap-a-pie and explains to the assembled company that his intention is "to combat vice in all her forms, redress injuries, chastise op-

10. *Ferdinand Count Fathom,* ch. lxii.
11. See Ida Macalpine and Richard Hunter, "Smollett's Reading in Psychiatry," *Modern Language Review,* LI (1956), 409–11; and G. S. Rousseau, *Doctors and Medicine in the Novels of Tobias Smollett* (Princeton Dissertation, 1966), chap. iii.

pression, protect the helpless and forlorn, relieve the indigent." He does; and the plan may be admitted to lend coherence to another of Smollett's "large, diffused pictures." But it is a mere piece of copying, unworthy of Smollett's powers of invention. The reader is tempted to adopt the words of the morose Ferret as he comments on Sir Launcelot's proposal:

"What! (said Ferret) you set up for a modern Don Quixote?—— The scheme is rather too stale and extravagant. What was an humorous romance, and well-timed satire in Spain, near two hundred years ago, will make but a sorry jest, and appear equally insipid and absurd, when really acted from affectation, at this time a-day, in a country like England." [12]

II

The search for a suitable manner of representing "familiar scenes in an uncommon and amusing point of view" was continued after an interval of ten years in Smollett's last novel, *The Expedition of Humphry Clinker* (1771). As in *Roderick Random*, the principal character (Matthew Bramble, not Humphry Clinker) has come from a remote region where manners are simple to observe the ways of life in a reputedly civilized community. This time the remote region is not Scotland but Wales, for Scottish manners will be needed for further contrast with English manners in the latter part of the book; and the protagonist, though unused to the ways of the world he visits, is neither a raw young man, nor a vain young man, neither a *picaro* nor a Quixote, but an elderly country squire, peevish but benevolent, ailing in body, but still in full possession of his senses, and endowed with an even fuller measure of that nervously irritable sensibility already remarked in *Roderick Random*.

With an elderly valetudinarian—as the eighteenth century dubbed its invalids—at the center of the novel, Smollett's choice of form was restricted. One might claim that it was fortunately restricted. The picaresque of *Fathom* was ruled out by Bramble's character; the quixotry of *Greaves* and the redemptive process in *Pickle* were alike ruled out by his age. So too was the lifetime's

12. *Sir Launcelot Greaves*, ch. ii.

span of *Random*. It would seem as though Smollett were forced back by his protagonist on that fruitful and well-tried form, the journey.

And other considerations seem to have combined to affect his choice. The success of his recent *Travels through France and Italy* (1766) had shown how suitably the record of a journey could take account of the character and customs of a country; and the form of letters to imaginary correspondents, in which the *Travels* were presented, encouraged a familiar manner of writing, in which the jaundiced exasperation of the traveler himself is disclosed. It also permitted an occasional anecdote, now more sparingly used than in *Roderick Random* and *Peregrine Pickle*, and more economically and pointedly related; and it allowed for different subjects to be discussed with different correspondents: thus Letter VII to a lady describes women's fashions in France, and Letter XI to a doctor describes a consultation with a French physician. The point of view of the writer is slightly shifted as he turns from one correspondent to another.

It is not surprising that Smollett should have decided to profit by this experience when he returned once more to his large diffused picture of life. Taking a hint from Anstey's *New Bath Guide* (1766), he increased the number of his letter writers, and thus provided himself with a simpler means of shifting his topic and his point of view. Bramble is the principal letter writer, but we are also allowed to read the letters of his fellow travelers, his nephew and niece, Jery and Lydia Melford, his sister, Tabitha Bramble, and their servant, Winifred Jenkins. Each has a character to sustain and acquaintances to describe. Many of them we have already met in classical comedy. But not only has Smollett a touch of nature at his command to individualize his types—Bramble is something more than the testy old gentleman, Lismahago something more than the soldier of fortune—he has shown that he can "catch the manners living as they rise": the Duke of Newcastle is drawn from life at one of his levees, and (a much greater achievement) in Micklewhimmen he has drawn the first of a type of Scotch lawyer in whom Scott was later to specialize. Better still are his more distant views of humanity in the mass: the caddies' banquet at

Edinburgh; the mixture of social classes in the Pump Room at Bath, where we see

a broken-winded Wapping landlady squeeze through a circle of peers, to salute her brandy merchant, who stood by the window, prop'd upon crutches; and a paralytic attorney of Shoe-Lane, in shuffling up to the bar, kicked the shins of the chancellor of England, while his lordship, in a cut bob, drank a glass of water at the pump; [13]

or the Rowlandsonian vision of the clergy off duty:

Not a soul is seen in this place, but a few broken-winded parsons, waddling like so many crows along the North Parade. There is always a great shew of the clergy at Bath: none of your thin, puny, yellow, hectic figures, exhausted with abstinence and hard study, labouring under the *morbi eruditorum;* but great overgrown dignitaries and rectors, with rubicund noses and gouty ankles, or broad bloated faces, dragging along great swag bellies; the emblems of sloth and indigestion.[14]

Scenes such as these point to a shift of interest, perhaps even to a different intention. Smollett has not yet exhausted his merry tales, and he still retains his enjoyment of the booby-trap; but his principal characters are now deployed to see more often than to act. It is true that his criticism of the Methodists is achieved by showing how the women of the party were affected. Thus Winifred Jenkins recounts to her friend Mary Jones the delights of Sadler's Wells, but remembers in time to add

But, thank God! I'm now vaned from all such vanities; for what are all those rarities and vagaries to the glory that shall be revealed hereafter? O Molly! let not your poor heart be puffed up with vanity.[15]

She then proceeds:

I had almost forgot to tell you, that I have had my hair cut and pippered, and singed, and bolstered, and buckled in the newest fashion,

---

13. *Humphry Clinker,* April 30.
14. *Ibid.* May 17.
15. *Ibid.* June 3.

by a French freezer——*Parley vow Francey*——*Vee madmansell*——I
now carries my head higher than arrow private gentlewoman of Vales.
Last night, coming huom from the meeting, I was taken by lamp-light
for an iminent poulterer's daughter, a great beauty——But as I was
saying, this is all vanity and vexation of spirit——The pleasures of
London are no better than sower whey and stale cyder, when compared to the joys of the new Gerusalem.

It is also true that a plot of sorts is provided: Lydia languishes in
love for a strolling player, who is later discovered to be the son of
an old friend of her uncle, and Tabitha Bramble's search for a husband is at last rewarded by Lismahago; but this scarcely serves to
distract the characters from their principal duty of observing and
recording what are often divergent opinions on what they see. To
Lydia the pleasure gardens of Vauxhall are

part laid out in delightful walks, bounded with high hedges and trees,
and paved with gravel; part exhibiting a wonderful assemblage of the
most picturesque and striking objects, pavilions, lodges, groves, grot-
toes, lawns, temples, and cascades; porticoes, colonades, and rotundos;
adorned with pillars, statues, and painting; the whole illuminated
with an infinite number of lamps, disposed in different figures of suns,
stars, and constellations; the place crowded with the gayest company,
ranging through those blissful shades, or supping in different lodges on
cold collations, enlivened with mirth, freedom, and good-humour, and
animated by an excellent band of musick.[16]

But to Matthew Bramble's jaundiced eye the same scene presents

a composition of baubles, overcharged with paltry ornaments, ill conceived, and poorly executed; without any unity of design, or propriety
of disposition;

and as for the company, the "crowds of noisy people," he sees them

sitting on the covered benches, exposed to the eyes of the mob; and,
which is worse, to the cold, raw, night air, devouring sliced beef, and
swilling port, and punch, and cyder.[17]

16. *Ibid.* May 31.
17. *Ibid.* May 29.

And it is Bramble, of course, with the keen recollection of the Welsh farm he has left behind him, who draws attention to the Londoners' food, their bread "a deleterious paste, mixed up with chalk, alum, and bone-ashes," their sophisticated wine, their adulterated milk, "the tallowy rancid mass called butter, manufactured with candle grease and kitchen stuff"; and as for the fruit,

it was but yesterday that I saw a dirty barrow-bunter in the street, cleaning her dusty fruit with her own spittle; and, who knows but some fine lady of St. James's parish might admit into her delicate mouth those very cherries, which had been rolled and moistened between the filthy, and, perhaps, ulcerated chops of a St. Giles's huckster.[18]

The social historian who might consider using this passage would do well to reflect that it is not pure reporting. It is an account as seen through the eyes of a character of a peculiar disposition, and it is part of a view of society set out to prepare for one more favorable when this party from Wales has reached Scotland. It is a view based on fact, but it is well this side of fiction. The form itself helps to place the reporting on the borderland of fiction and fact. "There have been so many letters upon travels lately published," writes the imaginary bookseller, in the second letter of the novel; "What between Smollett's, Sharp's, Derrick's, Thickness's, Baltimore's, and Baretti's, together with Shandy's Sentimental Travels, the public seems to be cloyed with that kind of entertainment." Here was a pretence of another in the same kind, another "mutation" of form such as the writers of this century delighted to produce; and in this variant Smollett found the happiest answer to the problem, which had engaged him from the first, of representing "familiar scenes in an uncommon and amusing point of view."

18. *Ibid.* June 8.

Smollett the Historian: A Reappraisal

———•———

DONALD GREENE

Once, when Mr. Crawley asked what the young people were reading, the governess replied, "Smollett." "Oh, Smollett," said Mr. Crawley, quite satisfied. "His history is more dull, but by no means so dangerous as that of Mr. Hume. It is history you are reading?" "Yes," said Miss Rose; without, however, adding that it was the history of Mr. Humphrey Clinker.

Thackeray, *Vanity Fair*, Chapter X.

I spent much of the day over Smollett's History. It is exceedingly bad; detestably so. I cannot think what had happened to him. His carelessness, partiality, passion, idle invective, gross ignorance of facts, and crude general theories do not surprise me much. But the style, wherever he tries to be elevated, and wherever he attempts to draw a character, is perfectly nauseous; which I cannot understand.

Macaulay, Diary, December 8, 1838, quoted
in Trevelyan, *Life and Letters of Lord Macaulay*

THERE has been little dissent from Macaulay's verdict on these fifteen (or sixteen) octavo volumes of the *History of England*,[1] written at the height of Smollett's creative powers between 1757 and 1761 (the last possibly in 1765), after an apprenticeship which

1. The eleven volumes of the second edition of the *Complete History of England* (1758–59; first published in four volumes quarto, 1757–58), bringing the history of England down to the Peace of Aix-la-Chapelle, 1748; four volumes of the *Continuation of the Complete History of England* (1760–61), bringing it down to the accession of George III, 1760; and the rare and mysterious Volume V of the *Continuation*, published in 1765 and narrating events

had produced *Roderick Random* and *Peregrine Pickle* among other things. The shorter histories of English literature seldom find space even to mention its existence; in the fifteen-volume *Cambridge History of English Literature*, it achieves a few decisive sentences by William Hunt: "History was written as hackwork by two authors of eminent genius [the other being Goldsmith]. . . . It favours the tory side and is written in a robust and unaffected style. . . . Neither Smollett, though he took his *History* seriously, nor Goldsmith should be considered as a historian." [2] The historians of historiography give it, if possible, even shorter shrift: it is not so much as mentioned (if their indexes are to be believed) in such large works as Harry Elmer Barnes's *History of Historical Writing*, M. A. Fitzsimons, A. G. Pundt, and C. E. Nowell's *The Development of Historiography*, and J. W. Thompson's two-volumed *History of Historical Writing*. The longest account of it I have found in a, to be sure, desultory search through such works is a hot-and-cold one in an obscure mid-nineteenth century *Lives of the British Historians*: "This work, so rapidly and carelessly written, so full of inaccuracies and intentional misrepresentation, is yet printed as the best continuation we have of the earlier narrative of Hume. . . . Whatever other faults it may have, it is certainly interesting; Smollett had the power of fixing the attention of the

---

of the first few years of George III's reign. The history of publication is admirably set out by Lewis M. Knapp in his article "The Publication of Smollett's *Complete History* . . . and *Continuation*," *The Library*, Fourth Series, XVI (Dec. 1935), 295–306.

Knapp makes a convincing case for Smollett's authorship of Volume V; but perhaps the bare possibility of its having been written by William Guthrie should not yet be completely ruled out. Knapp's case is based mainly on internal evidence, that of style and content; but Guthrie, as well as Smollett, could write lively, incisive narrative and, like Smollett, he was a Scot and sometimes stigmatized a "Tory" and "Jacobite"; it is a pity we do not know more than we do about Guthrie. As this note is written, Volume V has been temporarily rescued from oblivion by Mary Dorothy George, who, in a heated correspondence in the *Times Literary Supplement* concerning George III's "madness" (January 29, 1970, p. 110), cites the story current in the 1840's (although it originated at least twenty years earlier) that the volume was suppressed because it hinted that the king had a bout of insanity in 1765. Knapp quotes the passage in question, which, as he says, is "vague and innocuous," and gives no support whatever to the theory of insanity.

2. Vol. X, p. 293.

reader to whatever he produced; and in this respect, at least, he takes a position far above the Cartes, Bradys, and Oldmixons." [3]

The biographers and critics of Smollett themselves, presumably predisposed to admire their subject, are generally at best apologetic. Here is all that the most recent, Robert Donald Spector, finds himself able to say for the work—and Spector, on the evidence of his excellent *English Literary Periodicals and the Climate of Opinion During the Seven Years' War*, is much more knowledgeable about the milieu in which the *History* was written than many Smollettians:

The work has a strong Tory bias. . . . Smollett's history was certainly a vehicle for expressing his personal prejudices. . . . As for the literary merits of the history . . . they appear not considerable but sufficient. . . . At no time was it considered a significant or serious contribution to historical knowledge.[4]

And Spector quotes, as a fair summing up, the judgment of an earlier biographer of Smollett, David Hannay:

Whoever will turn to his history without expecting more than he ought to expect, will find a well-written narrative belonging, for the most part, to the same order of work as the summaries of the year printed by some newspapers, only decidedly better done than such things usually are.

On the whole, the highest estimate of the work has come from Lewis Knapp: after referring to the competent campaign of publicity which most commentators cite as the sufficient cause for the great contemporary popularity of the work (its sales made Smollett, if not rich, at least financially secure for the rest of his life), Knapp justly adds, "But the intrinsic merits of the work itself were also largely responsible for its wide appeal. Smollett wrote a successful history because he had significant purposes which he executed with unusual ability. . . . Smollett's *History* was not only well organized, well grounded, and carefully revised; it was written in prose at

3. Eugene Lawrence, *The Lives of the British Historians* (New York, 1855), Vol. I, pp. 394–95.
4. Robert Donald Spector, *Tobias Smollett* (New York, 1968), p. 29.

once masterly and readable. Furthermore it seems to have been set forth from a relatively disinterested and objective point of view." Such praise comes as a surprise after the chorus of denigration recorded above. Nevertheless, even Knapp feels compelled to undercut a good deal of it by the concession, "Without any pretense of creating philosophical history, found in some degree in Hume, Robertson, and Gibbon, he simply built up a masterly synthesis of historical fact." [5]

An inspection of these comments reveals some contradictions. The future Sir Pitt Crawley—himself the apotheosis of dullness: at Cambridge "he failed somehow, in spite of a mediocrity which ought to have insured any man success"—found it "dull." This presumably means that Thackeray did too—or, more likely, as with many other pieces of casual criticism, it means that Thackeray had not read the work, but merely parroted what he believed the consensus to be. But others, while granting it no other merits, at least agree that it is "interesting" or "well-written." [6] And it is curious that Macaulay, vehement though he is about its thorough detestability, nevertheless "spent much of the day" reading it. Many commentators stress some well-known figures about the extremely short time Smollett is supposed to have spent writing it, and hence, like Hunt, dismiss it as hackwork, on the grounds presumably that hackwork can *a priori* have no merit. Yet Johnson's *Ramblers* and *Rasselas*—and Shakespeare's plays, for that matter—were written in what seems to us a miraculously short time, under pressure, and for money, and hence could equally be classified as "hackwork": hackwork is not necessarily a guarantee of complete absence of merit. Moreover, as Knapp points out, whatever the statistics of the

5. Lewis M. Knapp, *Tobias Smollett: Doctor of Men and Manners* (Princeton: Princeton University Press, 1949), p. 193.
6. Arnold Whitridge dismisses the *History*—and Hume's!—in an equally cavalier way: "The art of history has undergone such changes since the day of Hume and Smollett that it is not easy to understand how the reading public could have plowed through their arid volumes" (*Tobias Smollett: A History of His Miscellaneous Works,* privately printed, [1925], p. 19). This is disappointing from Whitridge, who gives the fullest and most appreciative treatment available of *The History and Adventures of an Atom,* a quasi-historical work which needs to be studied carefully, along with the *History of England,* in any study of Smollett's political career (if indeed Smollett wrote *The Atom*). But clearly Whitridge had not read the *History* with the care he gave to *Adventures of an Atom,* or perhaps not really read it at all.

time Smollett spent writing it, the result displays highly competent craftsmanship. "Partiality," "intentional misrepresentation," flagrant "Tory" partisanship are frequently charged against it; yet Knapp, agreeing with Smollett's own emphatic declaration in his preface, insists that it was written "from a relatively disinterested and objective point of view." But on one point there is unanimous agreement: it is intellectually shallow—merely a "synthesis of fact," Knapp sadly concedes, "without any pretence of creating philosophical history," as did Hume, Robertson, and Gibbon—and, Macaulay and his admirers would certainly have added, Macaulay.

Fashions in historiography change, however; and seldom has there been a more drastic change of fashion than that which took place in the second quarter of the twentieth century and is associated, in British historiography, with the name of Sir Lewis Namier. The historical "philosophizing" of Macaulay, J. R. Green, Lecky, and the Trevelyans, in which every incident in the political history of Great Britain, from King Alfred down, is assessed in terms of its place in the great movement that irresistibly led to Victorian liberal democracy (when, as in *1066 and All That*, history came to an end), has been thoroughly discredited. Such egregious generalizations as Macaulay's "Through the whole of that great movement [from Magna Carta to the Reform Act of 1832] there have been, under some name or other, two sets of men, those who were before their age [Whigs] and those who were behind it [Tories]" and "The History of England is emphatically the history of progress. It is the history of a constant movement of the public mind, of a constant change in the institutions of a great society. . . . Each successive wave rushes forward, breaks, and rolls back; but the great flood is steadily coming on" [7] seem, after the gruesome annals of the twentieth century, too childishly naïve to be borne. A soberer approach, in which the study of the motivation—economic, dynastic, psychological—of the individuals responsible for political action forms the core, has replaced such "philosophizing"; to be sure, much to the discontent of those who find it more comforting to think of history as being created by grandiose "move-

7. From, respectively, the reviews of Lord Mahon's *War of the Spanish Succession* and Sir James Mackintosh's *History of the Revolution in England in 1688*.

ments" and "ideas" than by the fallible and unsatisfactory individual human beings who may or may not hold those "ideas."

It is worth asking how Smollett's *History of England* looks today in the post-Namier and post-World War II era. If the psychology and motivation of the individuals who make history are again the staple of historiography—as, of course, they were for Suetonius and Tacitus, whose example clearly influenced many seventeenth- and eighteenth-century historians, Smollett included—perhaps a brilliant novelist, specializing in the psychology and motivation of individual human beings, is at least as well qualified to write history as men like Macaulay, Lecky, and Sir George Trevelyan, practicing politicians whose "philosophy of history" very often boils down to more or less subtle propaganda to assist the current needs of their party. In particular, it is worth asking whether the usual contemptuous reflections on Smollett's *History* as vastly inferior to Hume's, to which the portion of Smollett's dealing with the years between 1688 and 1760 was so often appended, are justified. The effect of my own recent rereading of Smollett's, at any rate, has been to convince me that it is a greatly underrated work, that it often furnishes quite as much delight and instruction for the intelligent modern reader as its more highly touted rivals, and that it is a composition by no means unworthy of the author of *Roderick Random* and *Peregrine Pickle*. I should like briefly to reconsider the three main charges that have been made against it, poverty of style, intellectual shallowness, and gross partisanship—briefly, since a full-dress defense would have to be carried on by means of quotation too copious to fit into the limited space of this essay. Lewis Knapp, to be sure, has vigorously stated his dissent from all but the second of these accusations; but it may be useful to try to illustrate concretely the grounds for such dissent.

First, style. There is no need to spend much time on this point, since Pitt Crawley's, or Thackeray's, strictures are obviously an aberration from the majority opinion that Smollett's *History*, whatever else it may be, is eminently readable and attention-holding. Indeed, in his "Plan" (preface), Smollett lists this quality as the first aim that he wishes to achieve in it:

His aim is to retrench the superfluities of his predecessors, and to present the public with a succinct, candid, and complete history of our own country, which will be more easy in the purchase, more agreeable in the perusal, and less burthensome to the memory than any work of the same nature produced in these kingdoms.

This seems like a curious anticipation of his critic Macaulay's ambition, to write history that would be as readable as a novel—not too surprising an aim for a successful novelist, of course. How well he succeeded can be judged by juxtaposing a not untypical piece of Smollettian narrative with Hume's narrative of the same incident—part of that highly dramatic event, the arrest and trial of the seven bishops in 1688. First, Hume:

The people were already aware of the danger to which the prelates were exposed; and were raised to the highest pitch of anxiety and attention with regard to the issue of this extraordinary affair. But when they beheld these fathers of the church brought from court under the custody of a guard, when they saw them embark in vessels on the river, and conveyed towards the Tower, all their affection for liberty, all their zeal for religion, blazed up at once; and they flew to behold this affecting spectacle. The whole shore was covered with crowds of prostrate spectators, who at once implored the blessing of those holy pastors, and addressed their petitions towards Heaven for protection during this extreme danger to which their country and their religion stood exposed. Even the soldiers, seized with the contagion of the same spirit, flung themselves on their knees before the distressed prelates, and craved the benediction of those criminals whom they were appointed to guard. Some persons ran into the water, that they might participate more nearly in those blessings, which the prelates were distributing on all around them. The bishops themselves, during this triumphant suffering, augmented the general favour, by the most lowly submissive deportment; and they still exhorted the people to fear God, honour the king, and maintain their loyalty; expressions more animating than the most inflammatory speeches. And no sooner had they entered the precincts of the Tower than they hurried to chapel, in order to return thanks for those afflictions, which Heaven, in defence of its holy cause, had thought them worthy to endure.[8]

8. Hume, James II, sub anno 1688. Hume's History of England, with the Smollett Continuation of it, appears in so many varied formats that it may be most convenient for the reader merely to refer quotations to reign and year, which are usually indicated in the page headlines and margins. I am using a thirteen-volume octavo set published in London in 1807 with the imprint,

Competent prose, certainly; but a little—shall we say—ponderous?
There is a good deal of padding and cliché in it: "the highest pitch
of anxiety"; "those holy pastors" (we are sure that Hume did not
think them so, but it is hard to detect any ironic intention here);
"this affecting spectacle." If Smollett is accused of "journalism," it
must be confessed that Hume's prose here sometimes sounds like
the kind of Victorian journalese parodied by Joyce in *Ulysses*.[9]
    Then Smollett:

The king resolved they should be conveyed to the Tower by water, as
the whole city was in commotion. The people were no sooner informed
of their destination, than they ran to the side of the river, which was
lined with an incredible multitude. As the reverend prisoners passed,
the populace fell upon their knees, and great numbers ran into the
water, craving their blessing, calling upon heaven to protect them, and
exhorting them to suffer nobly for their religion. The deportment of
the bishops was modest, humble, and resigned. They conjured the people to fear God, honour the king, and maintain their loyalty. A vast
crowd was assembled at the Tower, where they were received in the
same manner. The very soldiers by whom they were guarded, affected
by the spectacle, kneeled before them, imploring their benediction and
forgiveness. The prelates went immediately to the Tower-chapel, to
thank heaven for those afflictions, which for the sake of religion, they
were thought worthy to endure.[10]

Much leaner, more economical, more swift-moving prose, surely;
only half the length of Hume's account, and it would be hard to
point to anything omitted from Hume's prolixity whose loss we
regret.

"Printed by J. M'Creery for Cadell and Davies, J. Johnson [and twenty-five
other booksellers]." The pre-1688 quotations from Smollett come from a
mixed set of the *Complete History*, with some volumes from the second edition, 1758, and some from the third edition, 1759.
9. For example, in the "Cyclops" chapter (Modern Library Giant edition,
p. 301): "A torrential rain poured down from the floodgates of the angry
heavens upon the bared heads of the assembled multitude which numbered at
the lowest computation five hundred thousand persons. A posse of Dublin
Metropolitan police superintended by the Chief Commissioner in person
maintained order in the vast throng for whom the York Street brass and reed
band whiled away the intervening time by admirably rendering on their black-
draped instruments the matchless melody," etc., etc.
10. Smollett, James II, 1688.

A wealth of other attractive passages could be quoted from Smollett, if there were space, to prove the same conclusion—that as a historiographical stylist, he is incisive, fresh, and businesslike, a master of rapid narrative. Here is another passage, a little farther on than the one previously quoted:

Meanwhile the seven bishops were admitted to bail, and the twenty-ninth day of June was fixed for their trial. They were attended to Westminster-hall by nine and twenty peers, a great number of gentlemen, and an immense croud of people. This cause was looked upon as a crisis that would produce either national slavery or freedom; and therefore it was heard with the most eager attention. The dispute was learnedly managed by the lawyers on both sides. Halloway and Powel, two of the judges, declared themselves in favour of the bishops. The jury withdrew into a chamber, where they passed the whole night; but next morning they returned to the court, and pronounced the bishops "not guilty." Westminster-hall instantly rung with loud acclamations, which were communicated through the whole extent of Westminster and London. They even reached the camp at Hounslow, while the king was at dinner in lord Feversham's tent. This nobleman went out to learn the noise of those shouts; and, when he returned, he told the king it was nothing but the joy expressed by the soldiers at the acquittal of the bishops. "Call you that nothing!" (said the king) "but so much the worse for them." He forthwith returned to Whitehall, and published a proclamation, forbidding the populace to assemble in the streets: but, notwithstanding this prohibition, the whole city was lighted up by bonfires and illuminations. The same rejoicings were made in all the principal towns of England, to the unspeakable mortification of James, who threatened to deliver up the bishops to the ecclesiastical court, and, as a mark of his indignation, deprived Halloway and Powel of their offices.[11]

By comparison, Hume often seems exasperatingly pompous and bumbling, and when we examine his "superfluities," as Smollett calls them—the term in Smollett's preface is surely consciously directed at his rival Hume at least as much as at other earlier historians—they are seldom found to contain anything very "philosophical," only hackneyed circumlocution.

11. *Ibid.*

In Macaulay, of course, the same incident—the trial of the seven bishops—furnishes him with an opportunity for some of his most brilliant stylistic pyrotechnics; his narrative is one of the classics of English purple prose, and every adolescent is thrilled by it when he first encounters it. Yet after a time the overdramatization, the relentless overstatement, becomes tiresome and even ludicrous: Joyce's amusing burlesque of Macaulayan historical prose in *Ulysses* is not too far from the original:

The debate which ensued was in its scope and progress an epitome of the course of life. Neither place nor council was lacking in dignity. The debaters were the keenest in the land, the theme they were engaged on the loftiest and most vital. The high hall of Horne's house had never beheld an assembly so representative and so varied nor had the old rafters of that establishment ever listened to a language so encyclopaedic. A gallant scene in truth it made. Crotthers was there at the foot of the table in his striking Highland garb, his face glowing from the briny airs of the Mull of Galloway [etc.].[12]

It would be difficult to find anything to burlesque in Smollett's businesslike but attention-holding prose. Macaulay's strictures on Smollett's style were, in fact, confined to places where "he tries to be elevated, and wherever he tries to draw a character." Macaulay goes on to give an example: "He says of old Horace Walpole that he was an ambassador without dignity, and a plenipotentiary without address. I declare I would rather have a hand cut off than publish such a precious antithesis." Macaulay does not quote the passage in full, and hence exaggerates its badness; it actually reads

The first [Walpole] had, in despite of nature, been employed in different negociacions: he was blunt, awkward, and slovenly: an orator without eloquence, an ambassador without dignity, and a plenipotentiary without address.[13]

Even so, one can grant with Macaulay that Smollett here is trying to be "elevated," that it does not come off too effectively, and that

12. The "Oxen of the Sun" chapter (Modern Library Giant edition, p. 410).
13. Smollett, George II, 1728.

Macaulay did this kind of thing better. Still, Smollett's strivings for "elevation" are not very frequent; as for his "characters" in general, the reader can judge from examples given below.

The charge of shallowness—the lack of "philosophical" depth—is not easy to separate from that of partisanship. Strict partisanship, the automatic making of judgments on historical incidents and persons by the application of criteria based on accepted party doctrine, would surely seem to be the most intellectually shallow, the least "philosophic" kind of history possible. No great exercise of deep ratiocination is needed, surely, to write an undeviatingly Marxist history of England, or an undeviatingly ultramontane Roman Catholic history (like Hilaire Belloc's)—or, for that matter, an undeviatingly Whig history, like Macaulay's. On the contrary, to do so would appear to be an abdication of the power of independent rational judgment. Still, it seems that such expression of partisan (Whig) dogma as that embodied in the generalizations quoted from Macaulay on p. 25 above is what has passed for "philosophical" history among Smollett's critics: and, if so, it must be granted that Smollett's *History* is distinctly not philosophical in that sense. Smollett consistently maintains his right to vigorous independent judgment, which he exercises freely—oftener, to be sure, on individual historic personages and actions than on "movements" or "tendencies" (of which one finds few, if any, in the work). Yet it may be argued, since Namier, that emphasis on the role played in shaping history by the individual motivation of political activists, and extreme caution about detecting impersonal "movements," cannot simply be dismissed as "unphilosophical" history and "journalism," but may in fact be the most truly instructive kind of historiography possible.

The drawing of "characters" of its leading actors was, indeed, the principal vehicle whereby generalized judgments on history were transmitted by many earlier historians, from Tacitus, through Clarendon, to Hume and Smollett—as were the "speeches" in Thucydides and some others—and certainly they play an important role in the "philosophical" content of the histories even of Gibbon and Macaulay. It would be hard, I think, to argue that Smollett, in his "characters," displays less talent for original and convincing insight into human motivation than Hume or Macaulay; again, it is well to remember his training as a novelist. Take, for instance, his "character" of that still puzzling phenomenon, Henry VIII. Smollett accurately senses the strong element of what we would now call paranoia in his make-up, and it is surely acute to suggest that, through his education, Henry was a man of the Middle Ages (as the eighteenth century thought of them) rather than the Renaissance:

Henry VIII before he became corpulent, was a prince of a goodly personage, and commanding aspect, rather imperious than dignified. He excelled in all the exercises of youth, and possessed a good understanding which was not much improved by the nature of his education. Instead of learning that philosophy which opens the mind, and extends the qualities of the heart, he was confined to the study of gloomy and scholastic disquisitions which served to cramp the ideas, and pervert the faculties of reason, qualifying him for the disputant of a cloister, rather than the law-giver of a people. In the first years of his reign, his pride and vanity seemed to domineer over all his other passions; though from the beginning he was impetuous, headstrong, impatient of contradiction and advice. He was rash, arrogant, prodigal, vain-glorious, pedantic, and superstitious. He delighted in pomp and pageantry, the baubles of a weak mind. His passions, soothed by adulation, rejected all restraint: and as he was an utter stranger to the finer feelings of the soul, he gratified them at the expence of justice and humanity, without remorse or compunction. He wrested the supremacy from the bishop of Rome, partly on conscientious motives, and partly for reasons of state and convenience. He suppressed the monasteries in order to supply his extravagance with their spoils; but he would not have made those acquisitions so easily, had not they been productive of advantage to his nobility, and agreeable to the nation in general. He was frequently at war; but the greatest conquest he obtained, was over his own parliament and people. Religious disputes had divided them into two factions. As he had it in his power to make either scale preponderate, each courted his favour with the most obsequious submission, and in trimming the ballance, he kept them both in subjection. In accustoming themselves to these abject compliances, they degenerated into slaves; and he from their prostitution acquired the most despotic authority. He became rapacious, arbitrary, froward, fretful, and so cruel, that he seemed to delight in the blood of his subjects. He never betrayed the least symptoms of any tenderness in his disposition; and, as we have already observed, his kindness to Cranmer was an inconsistency in his character. He seemed to live in defiance of censure whether ecclesiastical or secular; he died in apprehension of futurity; and was buried at Windsor with idle processions, and childish pageantry, which in those days passed for real taste and magnificence.[14]

Hume, by comparison, seems perfunctory and superficial:

It is difficult to give a just summary of this prince's qualities: He was so different from himself in different parts of his reign, that, as is well remarked by Lord Herbert, his history is his best character and description. The absolute uncontrolled authority which he maintained at home, and the regard which he acquired among foreign nations, are circumstances which entitle him in some degree to the appellation of a great prince; while his tyranny and barbarity exclude him from the character of a good one. He possessed, indeed, great vigour of mind, which qualified him for exercising dominion over men, courage, intrepidity, vigilance, inflexibility: And though these qualities lay not always under the guidance of a regular and solid judgment, they were accompanied with good parts and an extensive capacity; and every one dreaded a contest with a man who was known never to yield or to forgive, and who, in every controversy was determined either to ruin himself or his antagonist. A catalogue of his vices would comprehend many of the worst qualities incident to human nature: Violence, cruelty, profusion, rapacity, injustice, obstinacy, arrogance, bigotry, presumption, caprice: But neither was he subject to all these vices in the most extreme degree, nor was he at intervals altogether destitute of virtue: He was sincere, open, gallant, liberal, and capable at least of a temporary friendship and attachment. In this respect he was unfortunate, that the incidents of his reign served to display his faults in their full light: The treatment which he met with from the court of Rome provoked him to violence; the danger of a revolt from his superstitious subjects, seemed to require the most extreme severity. But it must at the same time be acknowledged, that his situation tended to throw an additional lustre on what was great and magnanimous in his character: The emulation between the emperor and the French king rendered his alliance, notwithstanding his impolitic conduct, of great importance in Europe: The extensive powers of his prerogative, and the submissive, not to say

14. Smollett, Henry VIII, 1547.

slavish disposition of his parliaments, made it the more easy for him to assume and maintain that entire dominion, by which his reign is so much distinguished in the English history.[15]

How less vivid and concrete a picture of Henry we get from this than from Smollett!

Smollett's account of Oliver Cromwell, though unable to do full justice to the immense complexity of the man, at least makes him more real than Hume's highly abstract summary:

Hume:

If we survey the moral character of Cromwel with that indulgence which is due to the blindness and infirmities of the human species, we shall not be inclined to load his memory with such violent reproaches as those which his enemies usually throw upon it. Amidst the passions and prejudices of that period, that he should prefer the parliamentary to the royal cause, will not appear extraordinary; since, even at present, some men of sense and knowledge are disposed to think that the question, with regard to the justice of the quarrel, may be regarded as doubtful and uncertain. The murder of the king, the most atrocious of all his actions, was to him covered under a mighty cloud of republican and fanatical illusions; and it is not impossible, but he might believe it, as many others did, the most meritorious action that he could perform. His subsequent usurpation was the effect of necessity, as well as of ambitions; nor is it easy to see, how the various factions could at that time have been restrained, without a mixture of military and arbitrary authority. The private deportment of Cromwel, as a son, a husband, a father, a friend, is exposed to no considerable censure, if it does not rather merit praise. And, upon the whole, his character does not appear more extraordinary and unusual by the mixture of so much absurdity with so much penetration, than by his tempering such violent ambition and such enraged fanaticism with so much regard to justice and humanity.[16]

Smollett:

He expired on the third day of September, the anniversary of the victories he had obtained at Dunbar, and Worcester; and his death was

15. Hume, Henry VIII, 1547.
16. Hume, *The Commonwealth*, 1658.

rendered remarkable by one of the most violent tempests which had blown in the memory of man, as if nature had intended to celebrate the fate of such an extraordinary person. Cromwell died in the fifty-ninth year of his age, leaving all Europe in astonishment at the incidents of his fortune. We have already observed that he was descended of a good family in Huntingdonshire. His father died while he was young; but his mother survived his elevation to the protectorship. She was a virtuous woman, of the name of Stuart, and said to be related to the royal family. Oliver was of a robust make and constitution, and his aspect was manly though clownish. His education extended no farther than a superficial knowledge of the Latin tongue: but he inherited great talents from nature; though they were such as he could not have exerted to advantage at any other juncture than that of a civil war inflamed by religious contests. His character was formed from an amazing conjunction of enthusiasm, hypocrisy, and ambition. He was possessed of courage and resolution, that overlooked all danger, and saw no difficulty. He dived into the characters of mankind with wonderful sagacity; while he concealed his own purposes under the impenetrable shield of dissimulation. He reconciled the most atrocious crimes to the most rigid notions of religious obligation. From the severest exercise of devotion he relaxed into the most ludicrous and idle buffoonery. He preserved the dignity and distance of his character in the midst of the coarsest familiarity.[17]

As might be expected, the closer he comes to his own time, the more vivid and independent Smollett's judgments become. Robert Walpole was subjected to many unflattering characterizations in his time, but it is doubtful whether any of them, even those by Pope and Swift, are more effective—because of the acuteness of its analysis—than Smollett's:

The interior government of Great-Britain was chiefly managed by Sir Robert W., a man of extraordinary talents, who had from low beginnings raised himself to the head of the Treasury. Having obtained a seat in the Lower House, he declared himself one of the most forward partisans of the Whig faction. He was endued with a species of eloquence, which, though neither nervous nor eloquent, flowed with great facility, and was so plausible on all subjects, that even when he misrepresented the truth, whether from ignorance or design, he seldom

17. Smollett, *The Commonwealth*, 1658.

failed to persuade that part of his audience for whose hearing his harangue was chiefly intended. He was well acquainted with the nature of the publick funds, and understood the whole mystery of stock-jobbing. This knowledge produced a connexion between him and the money-corporations, which served to enhance his importance. He perceived the bulk of mankind were actuated by a sordid thirst of lucre; he had sagacity enough to convert the degeneracy of the times to his own advantage; and on this, and this alone, he founded the whole superstructure of his subsequent administration. In the late reign he had, by dint of speaking decisively to every question, by boldly impeaching the conduct of the Tory ministers, by his activity in elections, and engaging as a projector in the schemes of the monied interest, become a leading member in the House of Commons. By his sufferings under the Tory Parliament, he attained the rank of martyr to his party: his interest, his reputation, and his presumption daily increased: he opposed Sunderland as his rival in power, and headed a dangerous defection from the ministry, which evinced the greatness of his influence and authority. He had the glory of being principally concerned in effecting a reconciliation between the late King and the Prince of Wales: then he was re-associated in the administration with additional credit; and, from the death of the Earls of Sunderland and Stanhope, he had been making long strides towards the office of prime minister. He knew the maxims he had adopted would subject him to the hatred, the ridicule, and reproach of some individuals, who had not yet resigned all sentiments of patriotism, nor all views of opposition: but the number of these was inconsiderable, when compared to that which constituted the body of the community; and he would not suffer the consideration of such antagonists to come in competition with his schemes of power, affluence and authority. Nevertheless, low as he had humbled anti-ministerial association, it required all his artifice to elude, all his patience and natural phlegm to bear, the powerful arguments that were urged, and the keen satire that was exercised against his measures and management, by a few members in the opposition.[18]

Condemnation of the Non-jurors—those "High" Anglicans who refused to take the oaths of adherence to William and Mary and so were deprived of their livelihoods—was customary, and might have been expected from Smollett; what is unusual is his condem-

18. Smollett, George II, 1727.

nation of those Anglican clergy who *did* take the oaths. The whole
passage on the ecclesiastical situation at this time is worth reading
for its sardonic quality:

While William thus endeavoured to remove the prejudices which
had been conceived against his person, the period arrived which the
Parliament had prescribed for taking the oaths to the new government.
Some individuals of the Clergy sacrificed their benefices to their scruples
of conscience; and absolutely refused to take oaths that were contrary
to those they had already sworn in favour of their late sovereign. These
were distinguished by the epithet of Nonjurors: but their number bore
a very small proportion to that of others, who took them with such
reservations and distinctions as redounded very little to the honour of
their integrity. Many of those who had been the warmest advocates for
non-resistance and passive obedience made no scruple at renouncing
their allegiance to King James, and complying with the present act,
after having declared that they took the oaths in no other sense than
that of a peaceable submission to the powers that were. They even
affirmed that the legislature itself had allowed the distinction between
a King de facto and a King de jure, as they had dropped the word
"rightful," when the form was under debate. They alleged that as
prudence obliged them to conform to the letter of the oath, so conscience required them to give it their own interpretation. Nothing
could be more infamous and of worse tendency, than this practice of
equivocating in the most sacred of all obligations. It introduced a general disregard of oaths, which hath been the source of universal perjury
and corruption. Though this set of temporisers were bitterly upbraided
both by the Nonjurors and the Papists, they all concurred in representing William as an enemy to the church; as a Prince educated in the
doctrines of Calvin, which he plainly espoused, by limiting his favour
and preferment to such as were latitudinarians in religion, and by his
abolishing Episcopacy in Scotland. The Presbyterians of that kingdom
now tyrannised in their turn. They were headed by the Earl of Crawford, a nobleman of a violent temper and strong prejudices. He was
chosen President of the Parliament by the interest of Melvil, and oppressed the Episcopalians in such a manner, that the greater part of
them, from resentment, became well-wishers to King James. Every circumstance of the hardships they underwent was reported in England;
and the Earl of Clarendon, as well as the suspended Bishops, circulated
these particulars with great assiduity. The oaths being rejected by the
Archbishop of Canterbury, the Bishops of Ely, Chichester, Bath and

Wells, Peterborough and Gloucester, they were suspended from their functions, and threatened with deprivation. Lake of Chichester, being seized with a dangerous distemper, signed a solemn declaration, in which he professed his adherence to the doctrine of non-resistance and passive obedience, which he believed to the distinguishing characteristick of the Church of England. After his death this paper was published, industriously circulated, and extolled by the party as an inspired oracle pronounced by a martyr to religious truth and sincerity.[19]

Smollett is bitter in his opposition to the international wars that Britain engaged in during the eighteenth century for the aggrandizement of her trade and empire. Of the War of the Austrian Succession, and the subsidies voted by Parliament to support Britain's Continental allies, he writes (in 1757),

Had these fruitless subsidies been saved; had the national revenue been applied with economy to national purposes; had it been employed in liquidating gradually the publick incumbrances; in augmenting the navy, improving manufactures, encouraging and securing the colonies, and extending trade and navigation; corruption would have become altogether unnecessary, and disaffection would have vanished: the people would have been eased of their burthens, and ceased to complain: commerce would have flourished, and produced such affluence as must have raised Great-Britain to the highest pinnacle of maritime power, above all rivalship or competition. She would have been dreaded by her enemies; revered by her neighbours: oppressed nations would have crept under her wings for protection; contending Potentates would have appealed to her decision; and she would have shone the universal arbitress of Europe. How different is her present situation! her debts are enormous, her taxes intolerable, her people discontented, and the sinews of her government relaxed. Without conduct, confidence, or concert, she engages in blundering negociations: she involves herself rashly in foreign quarrels, and lavishes her substance with the most dangerous precipitation: she is even deserted by her wonted vigour, steadiness, and intrepidity: she grows vain, fantastical, and pusillanimous: her arms are despised by her enemies; and her councils ridiculed through all Christendom.[20]

The history, especially the later volumes, contains a great deal of such incisive and insightful comment, which, whether or not it

19. Smollett, William and Mary, 1689.
20. Smollett, George II, 1746.

is entitled to the term "philosophical," is certainly at least the outcome of serious thought and reflection on what constitutes the
welfare of a nation, and is far from being mere "synthesis" or
"journalism." Smollett's acid little "characters" and asides on men
and events become even more frequent and effective as he nears
the contemporary scene: for instance,

[On Burnet's "proof" that James II's son was supposititious] Doctor
Burnet, who seems to have been at uncommon pains to establish this
belief, and to have consulted all the whig nurses in England upon the
subject, first pretends to demonstrate that the queen was not with
child; secondly, that she was with child, but miscarried; thirdly, that a
child was brought into the queen's apartment in a warming-pan;
fourthly, that there was no child at all in the room; fifthly, that the
queen actually bore a child, but it died that same day; sixthly, that the
supposititious child had not the fits; seventhly, that it had the fits, of
which it died at Richmond: therefore the chevalier de St. George must
be the fruit of four different impostures.[21]

The last partisan of the ministry was Sir William Yonge, one of the
Lords Commissioners of the treasury; a man who rendered himself
serviceable and necessary, by stooping to all compliances, running upon
every scent and haranguing on every subject with an even, uninter-
rupted, tedious flow of dull declamation, composed of assertions without veracity, conclusions from false premises, words without meaning,
and language without propriety.[22]

Lord Bolingbroke is said to have been the chief spring which, in secret,
actuated the deliberations of the Prince's court. That nobleman, seem-
ingly sequestered from the tumults of a publick life, resided at Batter-
sea, where he was visited like a sainted shrine by all the distinguished
votaries of wit, eloquence, and political ambition. There he was cultivated and admired for the elegance of his manners, and the charms of
his conversation. The Prince's curiosity was first captivated by his character, and his esteem was afterwards secured by the irresistible address
of that extraordinary personage, who continued in a regular progres-
sion to insinuate himself still farther and farther into the good graces
of his Royal Patron. How far the conduct of his Royal Highness was

21. Smollett, James II, 1688 (footnote).
22. Smollett, George II, 1731.

influenced by the private advice of this nobleman we shall not pretend
to determine: but, certain it is, the friends of the ministry propagated a
report, that he was the dictator of those measures which the Prince
adopted; and that, under the specious pretext of attachment to the
Heir Apparent of the Crown, he concealed his real aim, which was to
perpetuate the breach in the Royal family. Whatever his sentiments
and motives might have been, this was no other than a revival of the
old ministerial clamour, that a man cannot be well affected to the King,
if he pretends to censure any measure of the administration.[23]

[On the coalition that took office after Walpole's fall] But this harmony
was of short duration. It soon appeared, that those who had declaimed
the loudest for the liberties of their country had been actuated solely
by the most sordid, and even the most ridiculous motives of self-interest.
Jealousy and mutual distrust ensued between them and their former
confederates. The nation complained, that, instead of a total change of
men and measures, they saw the old ministry strengthened by this coalition; and the same interest in Parliament predominating with re-
doubled influence. They branded the new converts as apostates and
betrayers of their country; and in the transports of their indignation,
they entirely overlooked the old object of their resentment. That a
nobleman [Carteret? Gower?] of pliant principles, narrow fortune, and
unbounded ambition, should forsake his party for the blandishments
of affluence, power, and authority, will not appear strange to any person acquainted with the human heart; but the sensible part of mankind will always reflect with amazement upon the conduct of a man
[Pulteney], who seeing himself idolized by his fellow-citizens, as the
first and firmest patriot in the kingdom, as one of the most shining ornaments of his country, could give up all his popularity, and incur the
contempt or detestation of mankind, for the wretched consideration of
an empty title, without office, influence, or the least substantial ap-
pendage. One cannot, without an emotion of grief, contemplate such
an instance of infatuation—One cannot but lament, that such glory
should have been so weakly forfeited: that such talents should have
been lost to the cause of liberty and virtue. Doubtless he flattered himself with the hope of one day directing the councils of his Sovereign;
but this was never accomplished, and he remained a solitary monument
of blasted ambition.[24]

23. Smollett, George II, 1748.
24. Smollett, George II, 1741.

In all these, as in much of Smollett's *History*, there is a dry, sometimes almost cynical skepticism about politicians and political activities in general that gives the idiom of the whole work a very different flavor from that of the Victorian histories, where, though the bad guys remain very bad indeed, there is a fervid devotion to the good guys, whose strength is as the strength of ten because their hearts are pure, a whole-hearted commitment by the historian to their noble causes, and a more than Tennysonian conviction that somehow good will be the final goal of ill. Smollett, by contrast, sounds, as one of my students remarked, like Benjamin the donkey in Orwell's *Animal Farm*: "Windmill or no windmill, he said, life would go on as it had always gone on—badly." [25] No doubt it is this skeptical tone which so annoyed Macaulay, as the same tone in *Travels Through France and Italy* so annoyed Sterne. But Benjamin's attitude can hardly be called absence of philosophy; it is a very definite philosophy, and if not the perfect one, at least preferable to the more energetic philosophies of Snowball and Napoleon, to judge from the results. There is a realism about it, as in Johnson's "Life is a state in which little is to be enjoyed and much is to be endured," which may seem to the mature reader of the later twentieth century closer to the truth and hence, in the end, more useful than Macaulayan optimism; perhaps the philosophy of Smollett's *History* can be best summed up, as a commentator on *Animal Farm* summed up that work, by a line from Edna St. Vincent Millay: "I know. But I do not approve. And I am not resigned." Moreover, Smollett often clearly gets a wry amusement out of the absurdities of political history that he narrates, an amusement that, despite his constant dead-pan, is communicated by the sheer exuberance of his style. Smollett's claim to greatness, after all, is as a comic novelist, and perhaps a comic novelist is not the least qualified person to write a *Complete History of England*.

If what has just been said about the skeptical idiom of Smollett's *History* has any validity, the charge of "partisanship" will be a hard one to maintain—skeptics are, by definition, not partisans. The point was made emphatically by E. C. Mossner many years ago

---

25. Another suggestion was that he sounds like Mr. A. J. P. Taylor.

when combatting the same charge against Hume's *History of England*;[26] Smollett's skepticism as a historian, it can be confidently maintained, on the basis of a comparative sampling of the two works, is certainly no less than Hume's. Mossner's argument, however, has not prevented authors of manuals of literary history from continuing to parrot the old phrase, Hume's "Tory history." Smollett has suffered even more, since even fewer modern commentators on his work have bothered to read it before setting down this judgment on it. "Smollett was a Jacobite, and, of course, a Tory," one early writer sums it up with convenient patness,[27] and something of the kind has been repeated by the majority of later commentators—even Mr. Spector, who is in a position to know better.

It is too much to hope that so firmly established a myth will be at once banished by calling attention to the evidence. But at least the evidence can be put on record. Smollett himself, of course, vigorously denied the charge of Jacobitism—"Even Mr. Secretary Conway himself will never be able to persuade me that I am a Jacobite, or that I ever exhibited the outward signs and symptoms of that Infection"[28]—and a glance at the relevant parts of the *History* reveals its absurdity. A Jacobite is one who believes that James II should not have been forced from the British throne, or that his heirs should be restored to it. The treatment of James by Smollett is quite as harsh as in Macaulay's or any other thoroughgoing Whig history:

This flagrant invasion of the laws and religion of the kingdom proved one of the most unpopular acts of the king's whole reign: but, indeed, by this time he had made considerable progress towards absolute dominion, and had some reason to think the nation in general

---

26. "Was Hume a Tory Historian? Facts and Reconsiderations," *Journal of the History of Ideas*, II (1941), 225–36.
27. Lawrence, *British Historians* (New York, 1855), p. 394.
28. *Letters of Tobias Smollett, M.D.*, ed. E. S. Noyes (Cambridge, Mass.: Harvard University Press, 1926), p. 102; to John Hunter, February 24, 1767. "Mr. Secretary Conway" is the Rt. Hon. Henry Seymour Conway, brother of the Marquess of Hertford and friend and cousin of Horace Walpole, Secretary of State for the Northern Department—to whom, oddly enough, the other great "Tory and Jacobite" historian, Hume, was at this time acting as Under-Secretary.

acquiesced in its slavery; for he was flattered even in his highest pretensions by the clergy, the laity, and all sorts of communities; among these
the society of the Temple distinguished themselves by a fulsome address, in which they declared, that the prerogative being the gift of
God, no earthly power could diminish it; and that it necessarily remained entire and inseparably attached to his royal person. Yet the
tory parliament, submissive as they were in the beginning, and attached to the king by the ties of affection, could never be brought to a
compliance with his ultimate designs upon the religion and constitution of their country . . .[29]

—the condemnation of "fulsome" addresses, presumably "Tory,"
assuring James of the divine and absolute nature of his royal prerogative, is noteworthy.

Their opinion was supported by very clear and convincing reasons,
which, while they irritated the king against his son-in-law, served to
confirm great part of the nation in the resolution which they had
lately taken to oppose the arbitrary designs of the ministry. They began
to perceive that the kingdom would infallibly be reduced to slavery,
and the protestant religion extinguished, unless they should engage in
some speedy and effectual measures for their own preservation.[30]

Every individual, whether whig or tory, who knew the value of
liberty, and was attached to the established religion, now plainly saw,
that without an immediate and vigorous opposition to the measures of
the king, the nation would be reduced to the most abject state of spiritual and temporal subjection.[31]

It is true that Smollett's picture of James at the end of his life,
dying a broken exile, is sympathetic, and that Smollett disap-
proved of the severity of the punitive measures that were taken
against the rebels of 1715 and 1745. But one need be neither a
Tory nor a Jacobite to hold such common humanitarian sentiments—though there were undoubtedly high-flying Whigs who
disagreed.

One of the classic characteristics of "Toryism"—and, histori-

29. Smollett, James II, 1687.
30. *Ibid.*
31. Smollett, James II, 1688.

cally, probably the most valid one—is staunch support of the Church of England as against the claims of other denominations. Whatever religion Smollett nominally adhered to—and this seems to be something of a mystery—his *History* is full of sarcasms against churchmen of all kinds, certainly including Anglicans (as are his novels). His unexpected attack on the "Jurors" as well as the "Non-Jurors" has already been quoted. He is (like Hume) vigorously anti-Roman Catholic and makes much of the monastic scandals revealed at the time of Henry VIII's dissolution of the monasteries and of the intrigues of the Jesuits who surrounded James II. But (also like Hume) the Presbyterians of his native Scotland often come off no better. One of the most delightfully written passages in the *History* is his account of the famous Sacheverel affair, which pitted Tory "High Churchmen" against Whig "Low Churchmen": Smollett narrates it in a way which casts the utmost ridicule on the Tories:

Sacheverel was a clergyman of narrow intellects, and an over-heated imagination. He had acquired some popularity among those who distinguished themselves by the name of High-churchmen; and took all occasions to vent his animosity against the Dissenters. At the summer assizes at Derby, he held forth in that strain before the Judges; on the fifth day of November in St. Paul's church, he, in a violent declamation, defended the doctrine of non-resistance: inveighed against the toleration and Dissenters; declared the Church was dangerously attacked by her enemies; and slightly defended by her false friends: he sounded the trumpet for the church, and exhorted the people to put on the whole armour of God. Sir Samuel Garrard, the Lord-Mayor, countenanced this harangue, which was published under his protection, extolled by the Tories, and circulated all over the nation. The Complaint of Mr. Dolben against Sacheverel was seconded in the House of Commons by Sir Peter King, and other members. The most violent paragraphs were read: the sermons were voted scandalous and seditious libels. Sacheverel, being brought to the bar of the House, acknowledged himself the author of both, and mentioned the encouragement he had received from the Lord-Mayor to print that which was intitled, "The Perils of False Brethren." Sir Samuel, who was a member, denied he had ever given him such encouragement. The Doctor being ordered to withdraw, the House resolved he should be impeached of high crimes and misdemeanors; and Mr. Dolben was ordered to impeach him at the bar of the House of Lords, in the name of all the commons of England. A committee was appointed to draw up articles, and Sacheverel was taken into custody. At the same time, in order to demonstrate their own principles, they resolved, That the Reverend Mr. Benjamin Hoadley, rector of St. Peter-le-Poor, for having often justified the principles on which her Majesty and the nation proceeded in the late happy Revolution, had justly merited the favour and recommendation of the House; and they presented an address to the Queen, beseeching her to bestow some dignity in the church on Mr. Hoadley, for his eminent services both to the church and state. The Queen returned a civil answer, though she paid no regard to their recommendation.[32]

The hero who emerges from Smollett's account—modern students will be surprised, for much "High Church" propaganda against him has been innocently accepted by them as gospel in recent years—is the "latitudinarian" Benjamin Hoadly:

Hoadley was a clergyman of sound understanding, unblemished character, and uncommon moderation, who, in a sermon preached before the Lord-Mayor of London, had demonstrated the lawfulness of resisting wicked and cruel governors; and vindicated the late Revolution. By avowing such doctrines, he incurred the resentment of the High-churchmen, who accused him of having preached up rebellion. Many books were written against the maxims he professed. These he answered; and in the course of the controversy, acquitted himself with superior temper, judgment, and solidity of argument.[33]

Smollett is no admirer of Swift, "whose muse seems to have been mere misanthropy; he was a cynick rather than a poet, and his natural dryness and severity would have been unpleasing, had he not qualified them by adopting the extravagant humour of Lucian and Rabelais."[34] All this seems to add up to a kind of "liberal" or latitudinarian Low-Churchmanship, with perhaps more than a touch of general anti-clericalism. This is a strange sort of "Toryism."

A third example. Anyone who has been told that Smollett is a

32. Smollett, Anne, 1709.
33. *Ibid.*
34. Smollett, George I, 1727 (concluding footnote).

bigoted Tory—and a mere synthesizer—must be astonished when he begins to read the *History* at the point where most modern readers would naturally begin to read it, in its most accessible form—the section printed as the "Continuation" of Hume, beginning in 1688.[35] For the first thing he will encounter there is an extensive piece of reflection on the significance of the Revolution of that year, the great touchstone of eighteenth- and nineteenth-century Whiggism. To Macaulay, as to his mentors Burke, Fox, and Mackintosh, it was the glorious culmination of the long first stage—four and half centuries—of that "great movement," the triumphant vindication of Whig principles, which began with Magna Carta and was to go on to its apotheosis in the coming to power of Lord Grey's administration in 1832 (and the appointment of the young Whig M.P., Macaulay, to ministerial office). Macaulay's continuous and unreserved extolling of the Revolution is too well known to need quotation. Hume, likewise, though he very properly suggests that there is more to be said for the earlier

35. Consisting of the *Complete History* from 1689 to 1748 and the *Continuation* from 1748 to 1760. The *Continuation* of Hume's *History* must not, of course, be confused with the *Continuation of the Complete History*. It needs to be emphasized that neither Hume nor Smollett contemplated this splicing of their work: it was a booksellers' project, devised after both their deaths. The usual formula on the title page of the Smollettian part of the combined work is misleading, "The History of England from the Revolution to the Death of George the Second (Designed as a Continuation of Mr. Hume's History)." It was not so designed by Smollett. One is curious about the following statement in the "Advertisement" to the Smollettian section: "In the latter part only of this work has the present Editor found it necessary to make any alterations. The war before the last had its source in America, and thereby drew forth our settlements there into consequence. This, with the loss of most of those settlements since to Great-Britain, had brought with it so many changes, that what was found politicks and good sense then, is now totally deranged: even facts themselves are become changed, and the very state of the two countries has undergone a metamorphosis which was impossible to be foreseen by the shrewdest politician. To assist the views of so eminent a writer as Smollett, as well as to gratify the expectations of the judicious reader, a few, very few, alterations have been made on those heads. To have proceeded farther would have been a kind of sacrilege, and no less a fraud upon the original author, than upon the publick." A fair amount of spot-checking has not yet revealed to me any differences between the text published in Smollett's lifetime and that of the combined Hume-Smollett text; but of course a full collation should be made.

Stuart monarchs than the Whig publicists are willing to say, and that Whig partisanship and political power in the eighteenth century "has proved destructive to the truth of history and has established many gross falsehoods," and sturdily maintains that "a regard to liberty, though a laudable passion, ought commonly to be subordinate to a reverence for established government," nevertheless has no criticism to make of the Revolution itself: as a result of it, "the powers of royal prerogative were more narrowly circumscribed and more exactly defined than in any former period of the English government," and

The revolution forms a new epoch in the constitution; and was probably attended with consequences more advantageous to the people, than barely freeing them from an exceptionable administration. By deciding many important questions in favour of liberty, and still more by that great precedent of deposing one king, and establishing a new family, it gave such an ascendant to popular principles, as has put the nature of the English constitution beyond all controversy. And it may justly be affirmed, without any danger of exaggeration, that we, in this island, have ever since enjoyed, if not the best system of government, at least the most entire system of liberty, that ever was known amongst mankind.[36]

This is Whiggish, surely, almost Whiggish enough to satisfy Macaulay. For all the stereotype of Hume as a "Tory," it is worth remembering that his not inconsiderable involvement in public affairs—after his *History* had been published—as Secretary to the British embassy in Paris and as Under-Secretary of State, was under the aegis of the powerful Whig connection of the Seymour Conways,[37] well known to readers of their cousin, Horace Walpole, as one of the few Whig groups which met his exacting standards as upholders of the pure, unadulterated Whiggism of his father, the great Sir Robert.

Smollett, to our bewilderment, begins the post-1688 part of his work with a stringent critique of the Revolution settlement—but not, as one might have expected from the "Toryism" attributed to

36. Hume, James II, 1688, *ad fin.*
37. See note 28 above.

him, on the grounds that it reduced the royal prerogative too
much: instead, on the grounds that it reduced it too little!

On this occasion, the zeal of the Parliament towards their deliverer
seems to have overshot their attachment to their own liberty and privi-
leges: or at least they neglected the fairest opportunity that ever occ-
ured, to retrench those prerogatives of the crown to which they im-
puted all the late and former calamities of the kingdom. Their new
monarch retained the old regal power over parliaments in its full
extent. He was left at liberty to convoke, adjourn, prorogue, and dis-
solve them at his pleasure. He was enabled to influence elections, and
oppress corporations. He possessed the right of choosing his own council; of nominating all the great officers of the state, and of the household, of the army, the navy, and the church. He reserved the absolute
command of the militia: so that he remained master of all the instruments and engines of corruption and violence, without any other restraint than his own moderation, and prudent regard to the claim of
rights, and principle of resistance, on which the Revolution was
founded. In a word, the settlement was finished with some precipitation, before the plan had been properly digested and matured; and
this will be the case in every establishment formed upon a sudden
emergency in the face of opposition. It was observed, that the King,
who was made by the people, had it in his power to rule without them;
to govern jure divino, though he was created jure humano; and that,
though the change proceeded from a republican spirit, the settlement
was built upon Tory maxims; for the execution of his government continued still independent of his commission, while his own person remained sacred and inviolable.[38]

This emphatic declaration, in a highly prominent place in the
History, that the Revolution was not revolutionary enough seems
to present a considerable puzzle. Only three years later, according
to Professor Spector, Smollett in *The Briton* was offering "additional evidence of his conservative temperament. Like the earlier
Tory satirists, he expresses fear of the Whigs' inclination toward
innovation and lack of respect for tradition. He opposes the principles of the Glorious Revolution that had dethroned the majestic
symbolism of monarchy. He argues for the king's prerogative as a

38. Smollett, William and Mary, 1689.

right that parliament was trying to usurp." [39] Is the passage in the *History* then an elaborate hoax—a piece of extended irony of a subtlety not usually associated with Smollett? Or did Smollett, at the time his fellow Scot, Bute, took office, really undergo a sudden and complete reversal of his former principles? Or is it possible that Spector has, to some extent at least, misread *The Briton*, finding in it the things which he expected to find in it, but which, when it is carefully scrutinized, are not there at all—something that has been done, as we have seen, with the *History*?

Fully to explain this passage (and several others in the *History*) would require extensive research in two areas which this study does not afford space to consider fully: first, a careful analysis of Smollett's political position (or positions) throughout his lifetime; and, second, continued investigation of just what the words "Tory" and "Whig," as used in the eighteenth century, meant. Both deserve such inquiry, perhaps not so much for what they might contribute to the biography and criticism of Smollett as for the light they might throw on still highly obscure matters concerning the terms of political life in eighteenth-century Britain. A reading of Smollett's *History* should at least convince us that "Tory," as applied to that work, indicated nothing more than a refusal to be bound by the strict Whig party line of interpretation of the events of British history and an insistence on exercising some independence of judgment concerning them, and surely suggests that it is high time for scholars to give up the naïve practice of using the term as though it always guaranteed certain political beliefs—that royal prerogative should be increased rather than diminished, that the Revolution was a deplorable "innovation," that the dignity of the Church of England ought always to be supported. It seems very plausible, indeed, that as good a synonym for "Tory" as any, in modern American political terminology, is "independent." [40]

It also becomes clear that Smollett's "Toryism" in particular is difficult to fit into any neat predetermined pattern. Even if a clear-

---

39. Spector, *Tobias Smollett* (New York, 1968), p. 34.
40. I have argued this thesis at greater length in my study of the *Politics of Samuel Johnson* (New Haven: Yale University Press, 1960), Chapters I and VIII.

cut definition of "Tory" as it applied to the English political scene
were available—and it is not—the question is at once confused by
the fact that Smollett was a Scot. An acute observation by Richard
Pares is worth keeping in mind when considering not only Smollett, but the host of other enterprising Scots for whom the noblest
prospect was the high road to England—Thomson, Hume, Boswell, Mallet, even Lord Bute.

Thinking the English factions made a lot of fuss about little or nothing,
they [Scots politicians] could have no scruples about selling their votes
to the Government of the day, in return for personal advantages for
themselves or sectional advantages for Scotland. Exactly the same things
would happen today if Great Britain were to join the U.S.A.: knowing
and caring nothing about the differences between Democrats and Re-
publicans, the British members of Congress would be, for a time, a
disturbing and demoralizing force, since they would feel free to bargain with either party for their own advantage or that of Great Britain.[41]

Or, as Samuel Johnson put it, "A Scotchman must be a very sturdy
moralist who does not love Scotland better than the truth"—in
this case, political truth as understood by Englishmen.

Most of the intellectual Scottish immigrants attached themselves
to Leicester House—the residence of Frederick, Prince of Wales,
where Bute was the dominant influence—and hence were oppositionists until the accession of George III in 1760. As oppositionists, they vociferously proclaimed the "principles"—or at least
slogans—which, A. S. Foord has pointed out,[42] all oppositionists,
whatever party label they wore, adhered to in the eighteenth century: limitation of the power of the executive ("royal prerogative"), more frequent election of parliaments, greater "civil liberty"—freedom of the individual from interference by agents of
the administration—suspicion of "entangling alliances" on the
Continent (particularly with Hanover), reduction of the regular
"standing" military forces (controlled by the Crown) and strength-

41. *King George III and the Politicians* (Oxford: Clarendon Press, 1953),
p. 73, n. 1.
42. *His Majesty's Opposition, 1714–1830* (Oxford: Clarendon Press, 1964).

ening of the part-time, non-professional militia (controlled by Parliament); in short, anything that tended to limit the effective power of the current administration. (When Bute and his supporters themselves became the administration in 1761, there was, needless to say, a radical alteration in these attitudes.) Hence such a passage as that quoted above about the insufficiency of the Revolution in reducing the prerogative is not so surprising from Smollett, in the 1750's, as it might seem. Nor is the occurrence in the *History* of both the fervent dedication to Pitt, "not to the minister, but to the patriot," "an undaunted assertor of British liberty . . . a steady legislator intimately acquainted with the constitution of your country, which you have so nobly defended from encroachment"—by the Crown, that is—and a fervent denunciation of the same Pitt as the leader of a House of Commons "in which opposition lay strangled at the foot of the minister; in which those demagogues, who had raised themselves to reputation and renown by declaiming against continental measures, were become so perfectly reconciled to the object of their former reprobation, as to cultivate it even with a degree of enthusiasm unknown to any former administration," with resulting oppressive taxation for military purposes and a war in which there were a million casualties. (The explanation is that the dedication was written in March or early April 1757, when Pitt, temporarily in office but on the point of being dismissed, was in uneasy alliance with Leicester House against Newcastle and the old-line Whigs, and the second passage in 1759 or 1760, when the alliance had utterly broken down, and Bute was planning to oust Pitt, as he eventually did.)

The most eventful part of Smollett's political career was to come in the hectic decade of the 1760's, after the completion of the main body of *History*—Bute's accession to power in 1761, Smollett's editorship of *The Briton*, an organ of propaganda for the Bute administration, Smollett's unsuccessful application to Bute for a consulship in 1762, Bute's resignation, the compilation of the mysterious 1765 volume of the *History* and the extremely puzzling *History and Adventures of an Atom*. To sort out all these confused events and put them in the perspective of Smollett's own political attitudes will have to be the task of some later student. Meanwhile, however, it can be safely asserted that very little illumination will be shed either on this part of Smollett's political career, or on the *History*, by the term "Tory."

To sum up, contrary to what Pitt Crawley thought, Smollett's *History of England* is considerably less dull, and potentially a good deal more dangerous, than Hume's.

The Pilgrimage and the Family:
Structures in the Novels of Fielding and Smollett

IT is common supposition that Smollett accused Fielding of stealing Strap and Miss Williams from *Roderick Random* and transplanting them in, respectively, *Tom Jones* (Partridge) and *Amelia* (Miss Matthews).[1] The resemblance between Partridge and Strap was probably coincidental, cowardice being a characteristic of the stock fictional servant which either writer might have obtained independently from Sancho Panza. Miss Matthews, however, is surprisingly like Miss Williams in character and utterance, and *Amelia* as a whole is a departure for Fielding that might draw our

1. We know surprisingly little, in fact, about the famous Fielding-Smollett feud. In *Habbakkuk Hilding* (1752) the author allegorically accused Fielding of having stolen Partridge from Strap and Miss Matthews from Miss Williams. This was attributed to Smollett on the strength of a *Gentleman's Magazine* statement that it was "supposed to be written by the author of *Peregrine Pickle*" (see H. S. Buck, *A Study in Smollett* [New Haven, 1925], pp. 109–21; Lewis M. Knapp, *Tobias Smollett* [Princeton, 1949], p. 131). Stylistically, *Habbakkuk Hilding* could be Smollett's, but it is by no means so certainly his as, say, *The Adventures of an Atom*, and any statements regarding its attribution must be made with extreme caution. As Knapp says, it could as easily have been written by Dr. John Hill or William Kenrick. G. S. Rousseau, in his forthcoming biography, *The Literary Quack: A Life of Sir John Hill*, lists various reasons that make Hill a more likely author than Smollett and notes that William Kenrick, a known attacker of Fielding, is also as likely a candidate as Smollett. If Smollett was the anonymous author of this lampoon, his signed account of Fielding was more respectful and tolerant: "The genius of Cervantes was transfused into the novels of Fielding, who painted the characters and ridiculed the follies of the age with equal strength, humor, and propriety" (*Continuation of the Complete History of England* [1766], II, p. 160).

attention to similarities in *Peregrine Pickle*. It is perhaps safe to say that once the two novelists became aware of each other as the chief practitioners of the comic novel, strange parallels began to occur. In the long run, Smollett may owe more obvious debts to Fielding than the other way around: there are suggestive echoes of *Joseph Andrews* in *Roderick Random,* the opening of *Ferdinand Count Fathom* appears to derive from *Jonathan Wild,* and the idea of *Sir Launcelot Greaves* is perhaps related to *Don Quixote in England* and Fielding's other mediating versions of the Cervantean hero. But a much more interesting and, it seems to me, profound parallel occurs in *Peregrine Pickle,* which followed *Tom Jones* by two years. We could begin by pointing to Smollett's abrupt adoption of the third-person narrator, after the peculiarly Smollettian effects achieved with the first-person in *Roderick Random*—effects which he did not completely recapture until his *Travels through France and Italy* and *Humphry Clinker.* Assessment, distancing, and a more discursive effect were among the qualities he achieved in his second novel, and in these he may have emulated Fielding's successful example.

More suggestive, however, is the fact that *Peregrine Pickle* follows *Tom Jones* by beginning with the period before the hero actually makes his appearance and by presenting at great length the relatives and neighbors who are influences on the hero's character. Both novels open at a time before the birth of their heroes, at least, of their sentience. In *Tom Jones* it takes two books or twenty-three chapters for Tom to make his appearance, during which time we get to know the Allworthys, the Blifils, the Partridges, and the gossipy Somersetshire community in general. In *Peregrine Pickle* it takes eleven chapters to bring Peregrine on stage (whereas Roderick Random was in charge by chapter ii). I can think of no earlier English novel in which the appearance of the hero is so long delayed. It does not happen again until *Tristram Shandy,* where the idea of late entry is pursued with a vengeance, and Tristram does not emerge as an actor until the seventh volume.

Fielding's evident aim is to set in motion and develop a theme through antinomies of simplicity and prudence, feeling and form. The baby Tom is himself present at the outset, not as a character, but as a touchstone. The first half of Book I is centered on the poor bastard child, the second half on the rich spinster Bridget Allworthy, with the contrasted reactions one might expect from two such different touchstones. Tom brings out the good nature in Allworthy and the calculation in Bridget, Deborah Wilkins, and the other formalists; Bridget reveals calculation in fortune-hunters like the Blifils, brotherly love in Allworthy, and (since, unlike the baby Tom, she is an actor as well as a passive object) something of herself. Book II then ("containing scenes of Matrimonial Felicity in Different Degrees of Life") employs a similar structure to parallel the Partridge and the Blifil families—examples of marriages in low life and high life begun from the same motive, the woman's "fortune" (in Partridge's case "twenty pounds," in Blifil's a fortune), and with exactly the same consequences in domestic horror. Book III introduces young Tom into this world, and is structured on the contrast of Tom and Blifil, the offspring of Bridget and Captain Blifil, who extend, respectively the examples of simplicity and formalist calculation.

Fielding has also, however, been setting up a variety of families and heritages for Tom. Allworthy, despite a few half-hearted rumors as to Tom's paternity, is, in fact as well as in practice, his uncle. Under his benevolent gaze move Tom's real mother, Bridget (his real father, the scholar Summer, is dead), and his stepfather Captain Blifil, who also soon dies; Benjamin Partridge, his putative father, and Mrs. Partridge, who suspects Partridge of the paternity, gets him expelled from the region, and herself dies; Jenny Jones, his putative mother, who is also expelled as a result of Mrs. Partridge's jealous accusations; and Tom's half-brother Blifil. So we have a real mother but only a very shadowy father, and a putative mother and father with whom Tom will have complex relations later in his history. In fact Tom's history consists largely of his discovery of his true relationship to everyone else— to all those people in the first two books.

Read chronologically, the first books leave Tom the "natural" child a blank among all these hypothetical genealogies, the point being that he is *without* the name, relatives, and fortune that would place him socially. One of the remarkable features of *Tom Jones,* however, is that Fielding deposits ambiguities along the way which have to be reconsidered by the reader when he finally sees the whole narrative in a true light. Scene after scene means one thing on first reading, and something different on second reading; the "sagacious reader" who is Fielding's ultimate audience knows and does not know that Bridget is Tom's real mother and that Mrs. Waters is Jenny Jones, who is supposed to be Tom's mother but in fact is not. Knowing and not knowing, he experiences some very curious ironic effects in the scenes between Tom and his "mothers." [2] In Book III, Chapter 6, the narrator tells us of the stories being circulated about Bridget's "degree of intimacy" with Square, to which "we will give no credit, and therefore shall not blot our paper with them," which is usually Fielding's signal that where there is smoke we may expect fire.[3] When the narrator then explains that upon Tom's growing up to be a handsome and gallant youth,

at last she so evidently demonstrated her affection to him to be much stronger than what she bore her own son, that it was impossible to mistake her any longer. She was so desirous of often seeing him, and discovered such satisfaction and delight in his company, that before he was eighteen years old he was become a rival to both Square and Thwackum; and what is worse, the whole county began to talk as loudly of her inclination to Tom as they had before done of that which she had shown to Square . . . (p. 96).

Fielding gives this inclination as another motive for Square's dislike of Tom (as later in the parallel case of Square's and Tom's rivalry for Molly Seagrim). Yet it is hard to imagine why Fielding lumps together in just this conjunction what we suspect of Bridget's inclinations (and of Square's) with her affection for Tom. At the moment, we read this as sexual attraction; in retrospect, it refers to Bridget's motherly love; but does the former to some extent remain in the retrospect?

What such passages may mean is perhaps suggested by another

2. The critical problem of how to read *Tom Jones* is treated in an interesting way by John Preston in "Plot as Irony: The Reader's Role in *Tom Jones*," *ELH*, XXXV (1968), 365–80.
3. *Tom Jones*, ed. George Sherburn (New York, Modern Library Edition, 1943), p. 95. My citations, for ease of reference, are to this edition.

irony, implicit in Mrs. Wilkins's remark that it would be better
for such creatures as Tom "to die in a state of innocence, than to
grow up and imitate their mothers; for nothing better can be expected of them" (p. 8). Tom may be thought to have inherited his
propensity for the other sex, or at least his acquiescence, from his
mother, as Blifil presumably inherited his mother's *and* father's
worst qualities of hypocrisy and ill nature. The mother-son relationship haunts Tom through the climactic books, in the figures
of both true and false mothers, until the final revelation that his
real mother had acknowledged him on her deathbed. Clamoring
against the disasters at Upton and London is the less directly inherited blood of Squire Allworthy. The search into origins is a
characteristic of *Tom Jones* in general, with its extraordinary emphasis on motives, causes, and explanations, especially as Tom approaches his crises with Molly in the bushes, with Mrs. Waters at
Upton, and with Lady Bellaston in London. The family becomes
one significant context which helps to explain Tom's character
and conduct.

The relationships and hereditary pressures that are only hinted
at obliquely and ambiguously in *Tom Jones* are made explicit, indeed materialized, in *Peregrine Pickle*. At the outset of his history,
Peregrine is not even in sight. Rather his uncle and father, representatives of the previous generation, appear. Commodore Trunnion's quirk of seeing everything in nautical terms is an indication
of his utter innocence of life on shore, and Gamaliel Pickle, who
sees everything in business terms, is in his way equally innocent,
though his peculiarity may be less endearing. Pickle's letter proposing to Miss Appleby, which begins, "Understanding you have a
parcel of heart, warranted sound, to be disposed of," could easily
be transposed into Trunnionese.[4] Pickle does indeed become part
of a business transaction from which he cannot free himself. The
soul of passivity, he is already dominated by his sister Grizzle, and
when he marries Miss Appleby he merely exchanges one master
for another, though a much harder one.

Once Mrs. Pickle is in charge of the Pickle household, and pregnant with Peregrine, she sets about persecuting Grizzle until she

4. *Peregrine Pickle,* I, p. 21.

drives her out. Grizzle then, naturally looking around for a new
kingdom to rule, hits upon the other household in the neighborhood, Trunnion's "garrison," a parody family which consists of
himself, his first mate Hatchway, and Pipes, and has the advantage
of lacking a female presence. She conquers poor Trunnion, who
like Pickle is innocent of the wiles of women and their desire for
domination. Grizzle's urge to dominate is traced back to "the may-
oralty of her papa" who had arrived at this position of honor in
London after "small beginnings," and with her in charge of the
garrison, "in less than two hours, the whole economy . . . was
turned topsy-turvy"; "in less than three months [Trunnion] became a thorough-paced husband" (pp. 3, 64, 67). To consolidate
her position she uses the same device Mrs. Pickle had used on her,
though Grizzle's pregnancy proves a false one.

The heading of chapter xi tells us that she "Erects a Tyranny
in the Garrison, while her Husband conceives an Affection for his
Nephew Perry, who manifests a Peculiarity of Disposition even in
his Tender Years." The chapter-heading connects the two facts,
intimating that the child is the new hope, the reaction against subjection and the affirmation of personal liberty. From his first appearance Perry moves from victory to victory, demonstrating his
independence and moral vigor; he is a chastiser of folly and evil,
a stripper-off of false appearances, in sharp contrast to the obsequious and dim Mr. Pickle and the subjugated Commodore.
Unlike his younger brother Gam (significantly his father's name-
sake), he will not be curbed by his mother. But the danger in his
self-expression and refusal to be curbed is evident in the fact that
if he does not resemble his father he does, in a remarkable way, resemble his mother.

The satiric yet painful jokes she plays during her pregnancy on
poor Grizzle remain in the reader's memory when he encounters
Perry's, which amount to his most pronounced characteristic, and
suggest a similarity in disposition. Mrs. Pickle's pranks are calculated as part of her plan for driving out Grizzle and subjugating
the household, and yet, like Peregrine's, each practical joke reveals
something true about a foible of the victim as well as the perpe-
trator. To get Grizzle out of the house, she exploits that woman's
folly concerning her family pride, sending Grizzle all over the

neighborhood to satisfy Mrs. Pickle's pregnant cravings and ensure a good birth.[5] She satirizes not only Grizzle's fixation on a family heir but also Trunnion's pose as "Hannibal Tough" (she exposes his cowardice by craving three black hairs from his beard). But always the larger folly, Mrs. Pickle's apparent madness, is itself sinister: she is not merely demonstrating folly but tampering with other people's lives, using their follies for her own ends, producing painful effects, and revealing her basic desire for dominance. Practical jokes, like those of Mrs. Pickle and Peregrine, were always ambiguous symbolic acts to Smollett, both the satirist's devices for exposing and punishing affectation, and a cruel imposition of oneself on others. The ambiguity is made clear at once in Mrs. Pickle, and later in Perry. We are reminded of her when our attention is first drawn to Perry and his "Peculiarity of Disposition"—to "a certain oddity of disposition," to "the caprice of his disposition" (ch. xi pp. 74–75). The equally apparent caprice of her disowning Perry is the logical conclusion of their incompatibility. They are so alike that neither will allow himself to be subdued by the other. She is appalled to discover that having found a perfectly subservient husband she has produced a son who is a chip off her own block. She needs another son who resembles the father, and so she banishes Perry and sets about producing other children who will be more to her liking.

Her dismissal of and refusal to acknowledge Peregrine as her son also point up the difference between mother and son: he is proud and arrogant, but generous and somehow lovable—loved by the Trunnion clan, and in particular by Hatchway, who can hardly tear himself away from Perry when the latter goes off to school. He never loses his generosity and kindness, and his evil tendency is merely the reverse side of his good characteristics, which are his moral independence and his indignation at the folly of others. He demonstrates that his indocility—a corrective to the subservience of his father and uncle—can lead to what appears to be a greater freedom and autonomy, the role of the godlike satirist. Actually such indocility is servility to social status, to sophistication and luxury, very like that of Grizzle and Mrs. Pickle. The

5. See G. S. Rousseau's account of the wit in this chapter, "Pineapples, Pregnancy, Pica, and *Peregrine Pickle*," below pp. 79–109.

point is underlined when Perry, at his lowest ebb, ends as a dependent not unlike Mr. Pickle and Trunnion. This dependency, while cancelling his generosity and moral purpose, only gives greater weight to his pride (now false pride).

But these are the consequences that fill out the novel up to his final redemption. We are concerned with his relationship to his parents. Like Tom Jones he had a bad real mother who repudiates him and a shadowy cipher of a father. All that he inherits from his parents comes from his mother; he has none of his father's mercantile obsession, let alone his stolidity—his brother Gam inherits these. When he sins, it is for love of dominance or pride or satiric compulsion, not for money. Dispossessed by his mother, Perry goes to live with his uncle and aunt, the Trunnions. The account of Grizzle's false pregnancy and Trunnion's chagrin at not having a child had been immediately followed by the introduction of the baby Perry; and the "affection" Trunnion conceives for him, we are told, "did not end but with his life" (p. 74). Although Grizzle, for hatred of Perry's mother, had once been known to stick him with pins, now her "regard for him was perceived to increase in the same proportion as his own mother's diminished" (p. 143); also, we gather, as he becomes increasingly "the very image of her papa" (p. 88). To her he is a projection of her inordinate pride in family and desire to have another generation to carry it on; if he inherits anything from her it must be more pride.

Tom's protector, once his mother has denied him, is his Uncle Allworthy; the pranks of both Tom and Perry affect their uncles. Both boys also have younger brothers who are as cold and unfeeling as the heroes are outgoing and generous. (The difference, of course, is that while in Tom Jones they have different fathers and the mother secretly likes Tom better, in Peregrine Pickle they have the same father, and the mother, consciously at least, prefers the docile Gam, who is physically and morally deformed.) There are also wicked schoolmasters who side for prudential reasons with the worse brother, and a girl-friend who is brought into conjunction with the families; in Tom Jones by being part of a neighboring family, in Peregrine Pickle by being introduced to Perry while he is away, though still living with the Trunnions. Gam, having served his purpose, is dropped and is no rival to Emilia's affections as Blifil is to Sophia's. Throughout, we shall see that compared with Fielding's, Smollett's structure is very *ad hoc*.

Although specific borrowings may not be out of the question, I wish to stress only the parallel emphases on the relationships within a family as dominant, replacing the shifting relationships of chance encounters on a road. The effect is perhaps more striking in Smollett, for this is the part of *Peregrine Pickle* that coheres, that has a kind of unity and imaginative interest lacking except in isolated scenes in the rest of the novel; nor would Smollett write as well again until he undertook *Humphry Clinker* and developed the idea further with the Bramble family group. Though his reputation is first and foremost as a writer of the episodic picaresque narrative, Smollett always becomes a tighter, more intense, and more interesting writer when he gets to a small hierarchical group. The best part of *Roderick Random* is the naval episode where Roderick is placed under the control of a captain and a ship's doctor, both oppressive and evil, and turns to a good first mate for help. The family-like structure of a ship's crew remains in Trunnion's garrison, which is converted by his marriage into a real family.

There had always been coincidental re-encounters in the picaresque with figures like Ginès de Pasamonte, and Don Quixote had his Sancho for most of his journey. Joseph Andrews soon picked up with his Adams, and he had not seen the last of Lady Booby; Roderick had his Strap and continued to meet Squire Gawky and other unsavory characters. In England, picaresque structures of satiric exposition, as they grew increasingly more complex, tended to become intense knots of these chance relationships. But there is no real precedent in the picaresque tradition for Fielding's opening of *Tom Jones*. It reminds us that the relationship that interested most was that between Don Quixote and Sancho, but Fielding goes much further in the direction of replacing coincidence of recurrence with causality by choosing as his locus the family.

It is possible that Richardson's example may have suggested the virtue of using the family as a center of relationships. By replacing the servant-master relationship in *Pamela* with the family in

Clarissa, Richardson was able to correct some of the misunderstandings that arose from Mr. B's being both Pamela's master and the man she wanted to marry. In the patriarchal Harlowe family the father *does* exact complete obedience, and there are also grandfathers, uncles, and siblings who exert their various pressures on the daughter-heroine; the lover, a tempting symbol of freedom, is therefore outside looking in.[6] A family is Richardson's meaningful unit of relationship; and the effect of this patriarchal structure is almost wholly prescriptive, opposed implicitly to the conjugal family that would result from the daughter's choosing her own husband and leaving the family stronghold. One parallel to the pattern of *Tom Jones* might be detected in Clarissa's flight from the safety of her family to the great world where she is at the mercy of Lovelaces and Mrs. Sinclairs. Fielding's awareness of *Clarissa* is not only explicit in his letter to Richardson but perhaps implicit in the "middle" of *Tom Jones* where Sophia does *not* run off with her "Lovelace" Jones, does *not* disobey her father, and insists that she will never marry without his consent, and yet marries the man she loves.[7] *Clarissa* cannot, however, explain Fielding's crucial need to get back behind the protagonist to prior causes, and also, perhaps, to place the blame on the mother and absolve the father.[8]

The standard structure for a novelist of this time was still the picaresque series of encounters, which could be used satirically or sentimentally. Another structure, which tends to inform this random series in English fiction, is the spiritual pilgrimage.[9] In a

6. See William M. Sale, Jr., "From *Pamela* to *Clarissa,*" in *The Age of Johnson,* ed. F. W. Hilles (New Haven, 1949); reprinted in *Samuel Richardson: A Collection of Critical Essays,* ed. John Carroll (Englewood Cliffs, N.J., 1969), pp. 39–48.
7. See Aurélien Digeon, *Les Romans de Fielding* (Paris, 1923), pp. 181–85.
8. Although I do not take it for a source, an interesting analogue to the cipher father and the unnatural mother who disowns her son can be found in Johnson's *Life of Mr. Richard Savage,* first published in 1744. Another curious mother-son relationship which bears a resemblance to that of Perry and his mother appears in Mrs. Mary Davies's *The Accomplish'd Rake* (1727).
9. I use the word "pilgrimage" in its sense of "the course of mortal life figured as a journey, or a 'sojourn in the flesh,' esp. as a journey to a future state of rest or blessedness" (*OED*), as it was used by many Protestant writers in the seventeenth and eighteenth centuries and lingered on, remaining an

general way many works of fiction in the eighteenth century, ranging in time from *Robinson Crusoe* to *Rasselas*, and including *Clarissa*, send the hero out on his journey following a withdrawal from Eden: he may go of his own volition, as Crusoe and Clarissa and Rasselas do, denying their fathers or wanting to escape paradisal boredom; or he may be expelled as Tom Jones is. His journey then becomes an attempt to re-create—with Crusoe, literally to reconstruct—out of available materials that lost Eden; and as it turns out this was a fortunate fall in that it gives him an opportunity to make choices of his own, become a moral agent, prove and educate himself, and win for himself a "heaven" that would have been out of the question if he had remained in Eden.

Robinson Crusoe starts with the family unit, though the father, mother, and brothers are very sketchily indicated. What is clear is that Robinson disobeys his father, who is equated with God-the-Father as Robinson himself is with Adam and the Progidal Son, and leaves his family to wander among the dangers and temptations of the world; thereafter, as if this were the essence of the fallen world, relationships are chance and fleeting. Defoe's allusions end with God and Adam; Richardson's and Fielding's extend to Milton's Satan. Richardson had attached associations of Satan to Lovelace, who lures Clarissa out of her garden through lies and promises; and the Augustan satirists, of whose tradition Fielding's own early work formed a part, evoked Milton's version of the Temptation as a paradigm of evil. Fielding is explicit after Tom is expelled from Paradise Hall: "The world, as Milton phrases it, lay all before him; and Jones, no more than Adam, had any man to whom he might resort for comfort or assistance" (p. 270). Blifil's name rhymes with the eighteenth-century pronunciation of Devil and his lies help to bring about Tom's expulsion; both Tom and the narrator later equate him with the source of evil, and at the end, after his own expulsion, he goes off, like the Devil, to live in the north (pp. 572, 783, 884). Molly Seagrim, like Eve, seduces her Adam: "she soon triumphed over all the virtuous

---

important literary structure, after the process of secularization had set in. It has a more local, eighteenth-century currency than other words I might have used such as "quest" with its myth-ritual overtones.

resolutions of Jones; for though she behaved at last with all decent reluctance, yet I rather choose to attribute the triumph to her, since, in fact, it was her design which succeeded" (p. 126).

With his particular social and literary assumptions, Fielding was naturally more concerned than Defoe with the centrality of the society from which the individual is wrongly or rightly expelled. Looking therefore for an expansion of the "beginning" of the expulsion story, as well as for explanations of its protagonist's actions, he might well have wished to push back his enquiry, like Milton's, from the Fall of Man to its antecedents and causes such as the fall of Satan. Bridget Allworthy and Mr. Summer, among other characters, have to fall before Tom can do so. The mythic structure, moreover, is by no means exclusively normative in *Tom Jones*. There is an irony at work when the narrator adds after the passage about Tom's setting out in the world like a Miltonic Adam: "Men of great and good characters should indeed be very cautious how they discard their dependents; for the consequence to the unhappy sufferer is being discarded by all others" (p. 270). Allworthy, though the master of Paradise Hall, head of the family, and analogue to God, is nevertheless merely a human being. Like a more sympathetic version of Clarissa's father, he finds that he has driven out an angel and must himself seek forgiveness of Tom at the end. When the name "Paradise Hall" is first revealed, Allworthy is about to take his place on the "chair of justice" and wrongfully condemn and expel Partridge as he later does Tom (p. 59); and before this, Allworthy's house has been characterized as open "to all men of merit," "men of genius and learning," who, however, turn out to be exclusively represented by Dr. and Captain Blifil, Thwackum, and Square. Allworthy is the man whose most significant actions, besides adopting Tom in the first place (a simple act of benevolence, which Bridget had prudently foreseen), are to condemn the wrong persons (Partridge, Jenny) and then the right person for the wrong reasons (Tom). Allworthy is the all-powerful patriarch, good but human and therefore fallible enough to make misjudgments. One of the many examples in *Tom Jones* of absolute authority placed in a human being, he is the absolute head of a family. When Tom is in the family circle the problems are family problems, but when he is expelled into the world, the problems become larger—the threat of the Pretender, Jacobite "Divine Right," summed up in the gypsy episode, and the narrator's speaking out on the dangers of absolute monarchy. The novel is concerned with contrasts between the theoretical paragon and the "mixed character," absolute monarchy and limited (constitutional) monarchy, and law (or justice) and mercy. In this context the matter of the true, false, putative, and surrogate father, as well as the heavy weight of the past, become important.

The significant facts would appear to be, first, that the Fall in *Tom Jones*—perhaps as a further testing of Richardson's limited definition of virtue as chastity—is sexual, though the evil is not in the sexual act so much as in the betrayal of Sophia; and secondly, that the true sin is thus contrasted with the sin Allworthy *thinks* Tom perpetrates, which is disobedience of the Father. Tom is not guilty of Adam's and Crusoe's sin, nor can he, under the circumstances, be guilty of Clarissa's (it is Sophia who successfully weathers that storm). In a larger sense, of course, his betrayal of Sophia may be a disobedience of his true, heavenly Father. The allusions to Genesis and *Paradise Lost*, though sometimes ironic, are not playful; Fielding himself, as he pursues and explores the metaphor, is the human parallel to the true Father-as-Creator—his creation, the novel *Tom Jones*. As Blifil attempts to corrupt God's creation by drawing attention to Tom's so-called lapses of conduct by concealing the reality of his true character, so the "reptiles," as Fielding calls the critics, attempt to undermine "this great creation of our own" by drawing attention to local defects while ignoring the great plan of the whole (pp. 446, 490–91).

Smollett, so far as I can see, makes no meaningful allusions to the Christian myth that lies behind Perry's "expulsion," but his treatment of it is an adumbration of Fielding's. He shows much concern with the relationship between the part devoted to the family, which takes up between a fourth and a fifth of the novel (ch. i–xxxvii), and the pilgrimage or quest that makes up the rest. Perry leaves the garrison (and his Emilia) to tour the continent, and this segment (ch. xxxviii–lxxi) ends again at the garrison, having carried much further the story of his dehumanization. Presumably being away from the family is a contributory factor, because as long as he was near people like Trunnion, Hatchway, and Pipes, or Jennings the schoolmaster, his egoism was directed into a desire to excel at laudatory pursuits. Off on his own, with only fools like Hornbeck, Pallet, and the Doctor around, he rises toward the eminence of hubris from which he is eventually able to contemplate raping Emilia. Chapter for chapter and scene for scene, however, this long section is dull and chaotic; the few bright spots, like the dinner in the manner of the ancients, could as easily have been in another novel.

The third part of *Peregrine Pickle*, to which this interval has all too slowly led us, made up of chapters lxxi to lxxxv, ends in the garrison once again and is followed by the excruciating "Memoirs of a Lady of Quality." In chapter lix, Trunnion dies, and in chapter lxxxii Perry makes his attempt on Emilia. Though clumsily handled, the attempted rape dominates this part of the novel and represents Perry's fall and expulsion from Eden. This fall might be compared with Tom's, a similarly sexual encounter in which, however, he was seduced and by a second girl, with whom he was *not* in love. Moreover, Perry's fall does not involve alleged disobedience of a father. He could not be expelled by the father-uncle, Trunnion; but as if Smollett considered this possibility and discarded it, in chapter xxviii Trunnion comes close to breaking with Perry over the latter's disobedience in his single-minded pursuit of Emilia, but the Commodore capitulates and apologizes. He is not an Allworthy. However, as if he were unable to abandon the idea completely, Smollett has Trunnion die in the proximity of the attempt to rape Emilia, and Perry's expulsion from his loved one coincides with his being cut off from his uncle and the Garrison. Perry returns there momentarily at the end of this part (ch. lxxxv), but all Smollett gives us is the epitaph on Trunnion's monument; the dismissive letter from Emilia's mother and Trunnion's epitaph, both in this chapter, close off the past for Perry, and he sets out into the world, a Crusoe. It is as if both Smollett and Fielding felt that the expulsion had to involve loss of the father as well as loss of the loved one.

Peregrine Pickle has run over half its course, and the next large piece is not Perry's own story at all but the Lady of Quality's.

Only then does Perry set out with Cadwallader Crabtree, and chapters lxxxix to the end are interrupted only by a return to the Garrison in chapter xciv to "perform the last Offices to his Aunt." This part, corresponding to a pilgrimage, documents his decline in fortune but rise in awareness, and ends with his return to his real father's deathbed and his reconciliation with Emilia. On his return, we are told, "Peregrine, instead of alighting at the garrison, rode straightway to his father's house" (p. 262). His father, all passivity, has been able to use his passivity to one active end: by failing to write a will, he assures Perry of succession and thwarts his wife. Thus Perry does in fact resume his real father's estate at the end, something that Tom cannot do.

Looking back, we are reminded that Perry's life was in fact a series of expulsions. As Tom's first expulsion was his mother's renunciation of him to save her reputation, Perry's was also from the house of his real father and mother, for sinisterly obscure reasons. He had done nothing, his mother irrationally expelled him (though, as with Bridget, we divine her motives), and the uxorious Mr. Pickle acquiesced. There is not even a feigned disobedience of the parents, only a basic discontinuity between the generations. But the precise Adam and Eve situation has been transformed into one in which their sin leads not to their expulsion (Eve has deceived the patriarchal figure of Paradise Hall) but to the expulsion of their offspring. After his expulsion, Perry goes to his second father and mother, his uncle and aunt, and builds himself a more satisfactory life. When he leaves to tour the Continent it is his own doing, as conscious an act as Crusoe's and as disastrous, but without the explicit disobedience. The second explicit fall is his own but parallel to his mother's; his rape attempt as effectually drives away Emilia as her fury did him. It is the complication of this pattern, perhaps inherited from *Tom Jones*, that makes the first half of *Peregrine Pickle*, even when it is not admirable, interesting. Adam and Eve betray us and send us out naked into the world, but we betray God ourselves every time, recreating our parents' sin. "In Adam's fall/We sinned all."

In *Tom Jones* and *Peregrine Pickle* the myth appears in its clearest, least concealed form, and this is a story distinct from Richardson's in which the father is a strong and cruel tyrant, the mother weak and acquiescent. The son has a real mother and father who are wicked and shadowy respectively; the one repudiates or expels the son, the other is dead or so uxorious as to offer no opposition. The blame was clearly placed by Defoe on the son, but here the father as God-the-Father is replaced by an Adam and Eve couple who quite literally visit the sins of the fathers on the son. The son, having inherited his original sin (unlike Crusoe, who created it himself), re-enacts the parents' fall; Tom does so quite literally, but in both cases the fall comes through a sexual lapse followed by repudiation by the girl they love. Their pilgrimages are directed toward salvaging this love and building a new life, not toward reconciliation with the parent.

An earlier novel, *Roderick Random*, may be informative here. The actual mother dies as a result of the grandfather's cruelty and the actual father disappears; the grandfather then replaces the dispossessed parents, and the good uncle, Bowling, is required to save Roderick. Smollett conceals his myth here by displacing the guilt from the parents to a grandfather, pushing it back one generation, and then dropping the parents completely (the father reappears only at the end). Even here, however, it is the mother who is in some sense suspect; she was the outsider the grandfather refused to accept. The ship's crew offers another example of transference: the captain is bad but a relatively passive figure, like Smollett's uxorious fathers, while the ship's doctor, who Eve-like influences the captain, is Roderick's implacable enemy. The mate (who reminds one of Uncle Bowling, another mate) is Roderick's protector on the ship.

In *Tom Jones* and *Peregrine Pickle* the uncle has come to the center and adopted the repudiated son, but as soon as he becomes a substitute father, and not merely a rescuer, he takes on some of the father's authoritarian aura, and the second fall is away from him. The re-enactment of the parents' sin causes Tom to be expelled from Paradise Hall by his uncle, and we have seen that Smollett almost did the same with Perry and Trunnion, but that the Commodore simply lacked the authority for such a role. Trunnion is, after all, a comic parent, reminding us that in *Tom Jones* the structure is further complicated by a set of putative parents, Jenny Jones and Partridge, who do give Tom love of a sort denied him by his mother and dead father, although that love happens to be the love of a mistress and of a scheming servant.[10] As a pair of parents, Perry's second set, the Trunnions, are as comically and as obviously surrogates.

If we look at Fielding's other novels now, we will see that in *Joseph Andrews* there is also a good uncle (or father substitute) figure, Parson Adams, as well as a bad sibling, Joseph's putative sister Pamela. Here, where the family situation is most concealed and conventional, there are the putative mother and father who exist only so that Fielding can use their daughter Pamela as Joseph's bad adviser and later repudiate her by revealing that she is not really his sister. The putative parents as well as the true father Wilson are minor figures in the background. Adams is in his way as human a paragon as Tom's uncle: as Allworthy is associated with God, Adams carries echoes of the Biblical Abraham, at least partly to suggest the loose fit that results when placed on a human being. Adams sets up the test equation himself when he says, "Had Abraham so loved his son Isaac as to refuse the sacrifice required, is there any of us who would not condemn him?" [11] Immediately following are the news that his young son has drowned and his very human reaction. Adams's assumption that "Knowledge of Men is only to be learnt from Books" (p. 176), his reliance on the authority of the Church Fathers, the Stoic philosophers, and his own sermons (such as the one on vanity) lead to folly and misjudgments not unlike Allworthy's, though on the level of unpaid inn-bills; and Joseph's problem is to learn to act without hindrance from the two authorities that have formerly guided his life, Adams's "excellent Sermons and Advice, together with [his sister Pamela's] letters" (p. 46). Adams, in short, is both a good parental figure as uncle and a representative of the folly of following authority for authority's sake.[12]

10. Partridge is, in fact, named after a bird noted for hatching other birds' eggs; when they are hatched, the young birds fly away to find their true parents (see, for example, *The Bestiary*, ed. T. H. White [New York, 1960], p. 136).
11. *Joseph Andrews*, ed. Martin C. Battestin (Oxford, 1967), p. 308.
12. If Adams is an uncle figure in *Joseph Andrews*, the bad mother-Eve may be Lady Booby, to whom Joseph feels as a son and a servant, while she regards him as a potential lover. This is perhaps a concealed version of what emerges in *Tom Jones*, where Lady Booby, in her hypocrisy and lechery and am-

On the other side of *Tom Jones*, Amelia Booth has a domineering widowed mother, a wicked sister, a good (but still ambiguous) uncle-type in Dr. Harrison, and a weak but basically good husband in Billy Booth. As a result of the husband's failure, Amelia is thrown out into the dangers of the state of nature. The guilt has been so thoroughly shifted from the heroine to the others—to her mother and sister and husband and to society as a whole—that Fielding skirts sentimentality. But the excesses of *Amelia* can be traced back to the gradual shifting of responsibility from son to parents and environment in *Joseph Andrews* and *Tom Jones*, as well as in Smollett's *Peregrine Pickle*.

By both novelists the immediate family is presented as a perversion of a norm, with the wife, Eve, in control. But Fielding, at least, while not wishing to repudiate the father and mother as such (and so making them only particular fallen persons), does attempt to question the whole matter of the father's absolute authority. And so he includes an uncle who is the patriarch, the effective father, and proves that the whole patriarchal structure is, because embodied in humans, oppressive. Beneath both the structure of pilgrimage and of the family we have seen gradually emerge a yet more basic structure related to the category of experience Fielding called the "ridiculous," or affectation, the imitation of fashion or some other external authority, which at its worst, as hypocrisy, may serve as a mask for conscious ill-doing.

This emphasis on imitation, which in England derives, I believe, from structures of exposition Fielding inherited from the Augustan satirists, is related to what René Girard, speaking of the great novelists of the Continental tradition, has called "triangular desire." [13] In *Joseph Andrews* the structure is clear in Joseph's

---

biguous attitude toward Joseph, becomes Bridget Allworthy, Tom's real mother (Lady Bellaston, of course, is another somewhat refined version of Lady Booby). Although the threat of incest only enters momentarily when Joseph and Fanny appear to be siblings, the taboo hovers over the Lady Booby–Joseph as well as the Bridget–Jenny–Tom relationship, as perhaps it does around all relationships between older women and boys.

13. See my *Satire and the Novel in Eighteenth-Century England* (New Haven, 1967), esp. pp. 80–85; René Girard, *Desire, Deceit, and the Novel*, tr. Yvonne Freccero (Baltimore, 1965), *passim*. In a modified form, which I suspect did not directly influence Fielding or Smollett, this structure may be detected in Defoe's *Moll Flanders* and *Colonel Jacque*.

imitation of Adams's precepts, Pamela's letters, London fashion, and romantic love clichés. It is best dramatized in his re-enactment of the role of the Biblical Joseph vis-à-vis Potiphar's wife (Lady Booby), when he adds, "But I am glad she turned me out of the Chamber as she did: for I had once almost forgotten every word Parson Adams had ever said to me" (pp. 46–47), and in his adherence to Pamelian precept when he

absolutely refused, miserable as he was, to enter [the coach], unless he was furnished with sufficient covering, to prevent giving the least Offence to Decency. So perfectly modest was this young Man: such mighty Effects had the spotless Example of the amiable Pamela, and the excellent Sermons of Mr. Adams wrought upon him. (p. 53)

Simple-minded chastity and nearly self-destructive modesty are the consequences of following Pamela's, Adams's, and the Biblical injunctions literally. And these are the mediators Joseph learns to do without, aided, of course, by his *unmediated* love for Fanny Goodwill. The characters surrounding him, from Lady Booby, whose talk reminds Joseph of its source, the rant of a stage heroine, to Adams with his *Aeschylus*, from Mrs. Tow-wouse to Parson Trulliber and Peter Pounce, behave by imitating (or exploiting) externally prescribed manners.

Such characters still abound on the periphery of *Tom Jones*, but Tom himself is explained as imitating only to the extent that he is conditioned by his background, by heredity, and in crucial cases by circumstances of climate, season, alcohol, and a sense of personal joy or loss. Tom's basically unmediated response is shown to be influenced by complex causal patterns; opposing it is that ambiguous concept "prudence," both a worldly calculation and a prime virtue, which is the basic mediation needed for anyone to get safely through the world in his search for his particular Sophia.

In the prominence they give to the family, *Tom Jones, Peregrine Pickle,* and *Amelia* are the harbingers. The last is almost wholly concerned with the family, focused on the husband and wife, though the parent figures remain. From these we can look ahead to *Tristram Shandy*, where time is pushed back until the

family, heredity, and environment of the hero rather than the
hero himself make the novel's subject; the emphasis has been
shifted completely from the pilgrimage back to the cause of expulsion (the Fall being another way of describing what Tristram
is trying so desperately to explain with his typography and marbled
pages). The journey is never undertaken, and we never move
beyond the family; only an epitome is vouchsafed in Tristram's
tour of France in Volume VII.

Tristram Shandy makes clear much that is obscure in the eighteenth-century novel. The tight, close interrelations of the family,
which of course are nothing of the sort, become, in *Tristram
Shandy*, a symbol of unrelatedness, the more unrelated because
among people who should be close. While in one sense this is turning the family structure on its head, in another it is merely detecting the broken relations inherent in Fielding's, Smollett's, and
Richardson's families as well. Once again Tristram follows his
uncle rather than his father and mother; and the uncle, though
lovable, is hardly an ideal to set before him. While the mother is,
compared to the rest of the family, characterless, she is also the
wife who at a crucial moment reminds her husband to wind the
clock and stops his ardor with a cold, cold eye. The relations between the father and mother and uncle tend to define Tristram,
who himself appears only fleetingly.[14] Now *Tristram Shandy* may
owe something of its emphasis to a satiric progenitor, *The Memoirs of Martinus Scriblerus*, which devotes the first half to the
father's adventures before turning to the son; its unfinished state

14. I should mention the theory, which I owe to Richard A. Macksey's paper
delivered to the Tudor and Stuart Club at the Johns Hopkins University in
May 1968, that Walter may not be Tristram's father. Conceived on the first
Sunday in March (Walter's sciatica kept him chaste from December to February), Tristram was born 5 November, "which," he says, "to the aera fixed
on, was as near nine kalendar months as any husband could in reason have
expected"; when our attention is drawn to the matter in this way, we notice
that the period was only eight months. For other hints, as to the discrepancy
in Walter's and Tristram's size, etc., see *Tristram Shandy*, ed. James A. Work
(New York, 1940), pp. 331 (IV, 30) and 437 (VI, 18). I accept this as yet
another hint of unrelatedness in Tristram's world, not necessarily as proof
that Tristram was a bastard. But we should also note that if Walter may be
only a putative father, Yorick is the character who most resembles Tristram
in temperament as well as stature.

leaves by far the larger part concerning the father. But whatever
Sterne's direct inspiration, he was carrying on a trend of the
English novel that had begun with Fielding and Smollett, and
would continue with even greater modifications in *Humphry
Clinker*.

In his last novel Smollett brought the family and the pilgrimage
together by taking the family group on a tour of Great Britain.
By placing the father and his family with the grown (but unknown) son he could have both the environment and the hero at
once. Indeed, except that Humphry himself writes no letters, it is
a situation rather like that of Tristram grown and writing about
his father, mother, and uncle before and at his birth. Here the
good uncle figure for Humphry turns out after all to have been
his father, and the problem of the earlier novels is resolved.
Bramble is Humphry's protector, fulfilling the uncle's function,
including his comically ambiguous wielding of authority; but at
the end Bramble, the good uncle, turns out also to be the true
father, who abandoned Humphry long ago, and the comically unrelated letter-writers have become, as Win Jenkins says, a "family
of love" (WJ—Oct. 14).

To distinguish from this line the possible influence of *Clarissa*
on the trend toward family-as-structure, we can display Goldsmith's *Vicar of Wakefield*, in which the family is the social unit,
the father is the protagonist, the problem that of disposing of sons
and daughters, and the "pilgrimage" the father's setting out to
retrieve a lost daughter. He is still a weak husband with a wife who
dominates him and has her unfortunate way with the children.
Such families and pilgrimages (or flights) sit uneasily together in
the gothic romance; in the novel of manners the family is the
nexus of the action, the expulsion shrinking to an occasional
elopement, like Lydia's in *Pride and Prejudice*. In the novels of
Jane Austen the protagonist has become one of the daughters, a
strong and sensible daughter who inherits the strength of the
mother (but something of her waywardness too), the sense of the
father, and who only leaves home at the end when she satisfactorily
marries.[15]

15. The equation of the wife with Eve may have remained somewhere in the
background of these eighteenth-century families, but a general strengthening

In *Clarissa* and the novels we have been examining, the family acts as fetters around a strong intelligent offspring, and perhaps something of this still remains in Jane Austen. In *Tom Jones* and *Peregrine Pickle* the family is, as well as a restrictive force, a context of explanation and serves as mitigation for the protagonist's sins; even in Jane Austen's novels the heroine and her sisters can usually be explained by the traits of the mother and father. What Fielding and Smollett, and of course Richardson too, show us is the emergence of this as the dominant structure of the English novel as it moves toward the nineteenth century.

---

of the female fibre in literary creation was taking place. The strong figures for good are also female: the Sophias and Emilias may be subordinate characters, but not the Clarissas and Amelias, who draw on the heroines of "she tragedy" and the increasingly resourceful heroines of stage comedy. If Sophy Primrose is the best daughter that can be found in *The Vicar of Wakefield* (she alone recognizes Burchell's worth), in *She Stoops To Conquer* Goldsmith adds to the weak father and the strong, unpleasant mother a strong, intelligent daughter, who is a striking contrast to the hero-lover, Marlow, the last person in the play to be let in on the intrigue. But the succession of female protagonists from Pamela to Elizabeth Bennet is another subject.

Pineapples, Pregnancy, Pica,
and *Peregrine Pickle*

——•——

G. S. ROUSSEAU

"THIS young lady, who wanted neither slyness nor penetration
. . . replied with seeming unconcern, that for her own part
she should never repine, if there was not a pine-apple in the universe, provided she could indulge herself with the fruits of her own
country." [1] Mrs. Pickle's remark is calculated and represents the
basis of a plan to rid herself of the "teizing and disagreeable Mrs.
Grizzle." In fact, Smollett tells us that if a certain "gentleman happening to dine with Mr. Pickle" had not mentioned pineapples,
Peregrine might not have seen the light of day: the ridiculous Mrs.
Grizzle would have remained at the side of her sister-in-law
throughout gestation, teasing and torturing her with obsequious-
ness, dementing her imagination, which at this period seemed to
be strangely diseased, and "marking" her still unborn child. [2] A
"diseased imagination" in the mother, Mrs. Grizzle would have
argued, produced inferior progeny (Peregrine born with the image
of a pineapple clearly defined on his body!), but a "dish of pineapples" could produce no progeny at all. Mrs. Grizzle's search for
pineapples for "three whole days and nights" is thus futile: Peregrine, our hero, must be born. But then, a pregnant woman's
desires must not be balked—Mrs. Grizzle would have continued—
and Mrs. Pickle had told her that "she had eaten a most delicious
pine-apple in her sleep." Unaware of the consequences of these

1. *Peregrine Pickle,* I. p. 32.
2. *Peregrine Pickle,* I. p. 31. Passages quoted in this paragraph are from *Peregrine Pickle,* I. pp. 32–36.

alternatives, Mrs. Grizzle makes the wrong choice, furnishing her sister-in-law with two ripe pineapples, "as fine as ever were seen in England." Propitiously, however, Mrs. Pickle did not partake of the fruit—at least, Smollett never tells us that she did. Her swooning at the dinner table, the ensuing hysteria, the nocturnal dream—all are devices to encourage Mrs. Grizzle to leave the Pickle household.

It is curious that these chapters (v–vi) describing the incubation and birth of Peregrine have never received any attention. This fact is further puzzling when one recalls that they are among the most amusing in the novel. Smollett's eighteenth-century readers would have been amused by Mrs. Grizzle's obstetric handbooks and pious medical beliefs, and perhaps entertained by Mrs. Pickle's intense dislike of her "sister." But they must have been doubly amused by the elder's "researches within the country" (Smollett's hyperbole) for pineapples: such peregrinations for fruits "which were altogether unnatural productions, extorted by the force of artificial fire, out of filthy manure!" [3] For her distaste for pineapples and her pretentious medical learning—Aristotle and Nicholas Culpepper [4]—eighteenth-century audiences could have forgiven Mrs. Grizzle; they could not forgive her for an inability to put learning into practice. Her immense concern for pineapples, however, must have struck them as particularly topical, for readers of *Peregrine Pickle* would have understood Mrs. Grizzle's new-fangled theories of the effects of this fruit on pregnant women in the context of eighteenth-century medicine. We, as modern readers, view her actions and statements as part of Smollett's use of learning for the purposes of wit. A clue to the extensiveness of Smollett's knowledge of the subject can be observed in the first full-length book on pineapples in English, John Giles's *Ananas, a Treatise on the Pine*

3. *Peregrine Pickle,* I. p. 32. Grown in elephantine stoves in specially-built hothouses, pineapples were considered an exotic and artificial fruit in the eighteenth century. I discuss the fruit more fully below.

4. *Peregrine Pickle,* I. p. 31: "She purchased Culpepper's midwifery, which, with that sagacious performance dignified with Aristotle's name, she studied with indefatigable care, and diligently perused the Compleat House-wife, together with Quincy's dispensatory, culling every jelly, marmalade and conserve which these authors recommend as either salutory or toothsome, for the benefit and comfort of her sister-in-law, during her gestation."

Apple (London, 1767), a book which Smollett may or may not have read. This technical handbook for scientists and expert gardeners confirmed Mrs. Grizzle's belief that pineapples were an unlucky sign for pregnant mothers. Much of Smollett's comic irony in these chapters derives from the audience's familiarity with contemporary ideas about pineapples. It is not surprising, however, to discover medical learning used for comic purposes in the novels of an author who was a physician by profession and whose works abound with a variety of scientific references.

For our purposes chapters v and vi of *Peregrine Pickle* contain the key passages in which Mrs. Pickle describes her unexplainable desires: for a fricassee of frogs, for a porcelain chamber-pot, for three black hairs from Mr. Trunnion's beard—and for pineapples. Then we are told that only in the case of exotic foods did Mrs. Grizzle interfere:

She restricted her [Mrs. Pickle] from eating roots, pot-herbs, fruit, and all sort of vegetables; and one day when Mrs. Pickle had plucked a peach with her own hand, and was in the very act of putting it between her teeth, Mrs. Grizzle perceived the rash attempt, and running up to her, fell upon her knees in the garden, intreating her, with tears in her eyes, to resist such a pernicious appetite. Her request was no sooner complied with, than recollecting that if her sister's longing was baulked, the child might be affected with some disagreeable mark, or deplorable disease, she begged as earnestly that she would swallow the fruit, and in the mean time ran for some cordial water of her own composing, which she forced upon her sister, as an antidote to the poison she had received.[5]

The witty context of this description and the ridiculous actions of the women it involves should not lead us to conclude that Smollett was distorting or ridiculing contemporary theories of embryology. Actually Smollett's accounts of the treatment of pregnant women (such as Mrs. Pickle) were based upon experiments with foetuses performed in the third and fourth decades of the eighteenth century and speculations of respected scientists of the Royal College of Physicians such as James Augustus Blondel, Daniel

5. *Peregrine Pickle*, I. p. 31.

Turner, and William Smellie, a leading obstetrician to whom
Smollett was apprenticed and in whose medical library he educated
himself. It is essential to note biographically that at the very same
time—1750—Smollett was composing *Peregrine Pickle,* he was
also editing, annotating, and preparing for the press Smellie's
Treatise on the Theory and Practice of Midwifery, which was published the same year as Smollett's novel. In 1750, then, Smollett
was deep in the study of obstetric medicine and, particularly, in
abnormal pregnancy, for that subject occupies the largest portion
of Smellie's book. Smollett's novel was the first in English (a
decade before *Tristram Shandy*) [6] to refer to heated controversies
about the role of imagination in abnormal pregnancy, a subject
Smellie treated at length and which abundantly stimulated Smollett's own imagination. The humorous episode built upon Mrs.
Grizzle's extreme distrust and dislike of pineapples also reflects the
popularity of this exotic fruit in England and in Scotland in the
1740's and 1750's, its alleged medicinal qualities, and its being a
forbidden fruit to pregnant women. Although Smollett did not
live long enough to see the appearance of Edward Topham's
widely read *Letters from Edinburgh written in the years 1774, and
1775,* he would have taken Scottish pride in Topham's observation
that in the 1740's and 1750's Scotland, no less than England, was
the garden of Europe—at least as far as exotic *ananas* were concerned:

. . . if the Scotch are deprived, by the nature of their situation, of enjoyment of natural fruit, they have the opportunity of furnishing
themselves with hot-houses . . . and, in this respect, have the advantage
of the rest of Great Britain. There are few gentlemen of any consequence that are not supplied with fruit by this means; and indeed,
melons, pineapples, grapes . . . are produced here with great success.[7]

6. Some attention to embryological theory of the eighteenth century and
Tristram Shandy is given in Louis A. Landa, "The Shandean Homunculus:
The Background of Sterne's 'Little Gentleman,' " *Restoration and Eighteenth
Century Literature,* ed. Carroll Camden (Chicago, 1963), pp. 49–68. I have
discussed Smollett's novels and medicine in *Doctors and Medicine in the
Novels of Tobias Smollett* (Princeton University dissertation, 1966).
7. *Letters from Edinburgh* (Edinburgh, 1776), "On . . . Gardening," p. 229.

I

"Mrs. Pickle's longings," Smollett tells us, "were not restricted to the demands of the palate and stomach, but also affected all the other organs of sense, and even invaded her imagination, which at this period seemed to be strangely diseased." The notion that a mother's "imagination" influenced her foetus and subsequently, her child, was as old as Aristotle. In his treatise *De Generatione et Corruptione*, the Greek philosopher had discussed the matter at length in "Rules for the First Two Months of Pregnancy." "Let none present any strange, or unwholesome thing to her, not so much as name it, lest she should desire it, and not be able to get it, and so either cause her to miscarry, or the child have some deformity on that account." [8] The sections in Aristotle's book dealing with gestation and pregnancy were extracted in the seventeenth century and bound together, under the title *The Experienced Midwife*. Galenic medicine of the seventeenth century had little to add to Aristotle's precepts. Occasionally an author such as Shakespeare capitalized upon Aristotle's admonishment: thus Pompey, the jester in *Measure for Measure*, comes on stage bellowing that his Mistress Elbow "came in, great with child, and longing for stewed prunes; Sir, we had but two in the house, which at that very distant time stood in a fruit dish, a dish of some threepence." Distinguished physicians like Thomas Sydenham and Thomas Willis adhered to the ideas stated in *The Experienced Midwife*, and less illustrious doctors were equally obeisant.

Throughout the seventeenth and early eighteenth centuries this work was a standard textbook for physicians and midwives, and was the major source for Nicholas Culpepper's *Directory for Midwives* (first published in 1651), a book which Smollett must have read at least by the time he prepared Smellie's *Treatise on Midwifery* for the press. Culpepper's *Directory* had become so popular

---

8. *Aristotle's Compleat Master-Piece. Displaying the Secrets of Nature in the Generation of Man* (32nd ed.: London, 1782), pp. 33–4. See Fielding H. Garrison, *An Introduction to the History of Medicine* (4th ed. rev.: London, 1929), pp. 101 ff.

by the 1730's—years during which Smollett was in medical
school—that it evoked in 1735 this enthusiastic rhapsody from an
anonymous commentator:

And if he [any young doctor] applies himself to the Obstetrical Art, let
him turn over Culpepper's *Midwife enlarg'd* night and day. That little Book is worth a whole Library. All that is possible to be known in
the Art is there treasur'd up in a small *Duodecimo.* Blessed, yea for
ever blessed, be the memory of the inimitable Author, who, and who
alone, had the *curious happiness* to mix the profound learning of Aristotle with the facetious Humour of Plautus.[9]

A physician himself, Culpepper repeated Aristotle's advice to pregnant women who, like Mrs. Trunnion, wished to give birth to un-
scarred infants. "Sometimes there is an extraordinary cause, as
imagination, when the Mother is frighted, or imagineth strange
things, or longeth vehemently for some meat which if she have not,
the child hath a mark of the colour or shape of what she desired,
of which there are many examples." [10]

It was not the pregnant mother's "strange longings"—a condition known as "pica" [11]—that disconcerted physicians and midwives so much as the ill effects of these yearnings on the foetus.
According to Culpepper even a single instance of bizarre desire
would produce "Hermaphrodites, Dwarfs or Gyants," and this idea
was repeated again and again in medical works of the period. John
Maubray discussed it at length in *The Female Physician, Containing all the Diseases Incident to that Sex, in Virgins, Wives and
Widows* (1724). In a chapter entitled "Of Monsters" he complained that too few authors were "ready to discuss the proper
Causes of *Monstrous* BIRTHS," and continued to give his explanation for the occurrences: [12]

9. *An Essay for Abridging the Study of Physick* (London, 1735), p. 17.
10. *A Directory for Midwives* (London, 1684), p. 145.
11. The name given to the condition by Ancient Greek physicians, and also
called "citta" or "malatia." See Hermann Heinrich Ploss, Max and Paul
Bartel, "The Longings of Pregnancy" in *Woman: An Historical and Anthropological Compendium* (London, 1935), II, pp. 455–60. A recent study of the
medical aspects of *pica* is by M. Cooper, *Pica* (Springfield, Ill., 1957).
12. *The Female Physician,* p. 368. See also Part II, Chapter 7, which discusses
numerous cases of foetuses that had been marked. Maubray was one of the

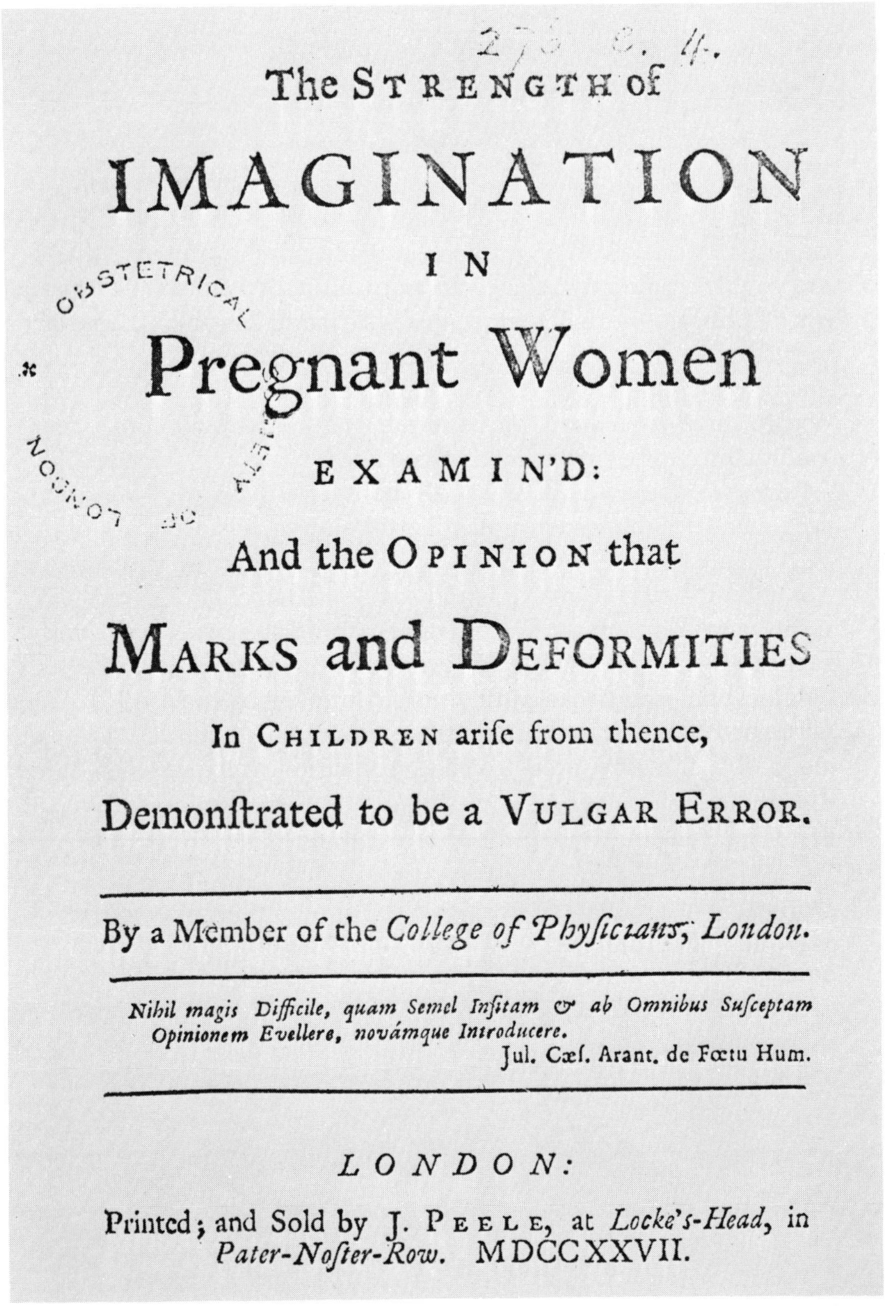

The STRENGTH of

IMAGINATION

IN

Pregnant Women

EXAMIN'D:

And the OPINION that

MARKS and DEFORMITIES

In CHILDREN arife from thence,

Demonftrated to be a VULGAR ERROR.

By a Member of the *College of Phyficians*, *London*.

Nihil magis Difficile, quam Semel Infitam & ab Omnibus Sufceptam Opinionem Evellere, novámque Introducere.
Jul. Cæf. Arant. de Fœtu Hum.

LONDON:

Printed; and Sold by J. PEELE, at *Locke's-Head*, in *Pater-Nofter-Row.* MDCCXXVII.

PLATE II—Title page of James Augustus Blondel's *The Strength of Imagination in Pregnant Women Examin'd . . . By a Member of the College of Physicians, London.* London, 1727.

PLATE III—Plate illustrating the abnormal cravings of pregnant women. From George Alexander Stevens, *The Dramatic History of Master Edward*, London, 1763.

PLATE IV—Plate illustrating the abnormal cravings of a pregnant woman.
From George Alexander Stevens, *The Dramatic History of Master Edward*,
London, 1763.

PLATE V—The Pineapple Picture, by Henry Danckerts (c. 1625–1679?), showing Charles II presented with the allegedly first pineapple grown in England.
(By kind permission of the Marchioness Cholmondeley.)

First then, I take the Imagination to have the most prevalent *Power* in Conception; which I hope may be readily granted, considering how common a Thing it is, for the *Mother* to mark her child with *Pears, Plums, Milk, Wine,* or any *thing else,* upon the least trifling *Accident* happening to her from thence; and *that* even in the latter ripening *Months,* after the Infant is entirely formed, by the *Strength of her Imagination* only, as has been already manifestly set forth at large.

Maubray extended his case to the male as well, noting that "a Foetus with a *Calf's, Lamb's, Dog's, Cat's-Head,* or the Effigy of any other thing whatsoever," might be the result of "a *copulating* Man, if he should imprudently set his Mind on such Objects, or employ his perverted *Imagination* that way." The powerful and lasting effects of the imagination, Maubray contended, were not limited to humankind, but extended also to lower species. "This absurd *Imagination* takes place even among the very *Brutes,* as Lemnius relates of a Sheep with a Seal's, or *Sea* Calf's-Head, having no doubt seen that Animal in the critical Time of *Conjunction* or *Conception.*" Like many doctors in the previous century, Maubray enjoined would-be mothers to suppress their "absurd Imaginations," lest they bring into the world no children but "Monsters formed in the Womb."

An incident late in 1726 which Smollett probably had heard about, contributed much to the popular fear that women with "absurd Imaginations" during pregnancy would bring forth monsters: this was the extraordinary case of the pregnant Mary Tofts of Godalming who insisted that she had eventually given birth to at least seventeen rabbits and other curious progeny. Unable to afford rabbits, she nevertheless craved them throughout her pregnancy, and one day, while working in the fields, she actually saw one who may or may not have frightened her. The case itself has recently been discussed in such detail that I do not pretend to add

---

first physicians in London to offer private instruction for midwives. See F. H. Garrison, *History of Medicine,* p. 399. A great believer in monsters, he earned notoriety in 1723 by assisting in the delivery of a Dutch woman, who produced a monstrous manikin called *de Suyger,* with "a hooked snout, fiery sparkling eyes, a long neck, and an acuminated, sharp tail." Maubray called it a moldy-warp (mole) or sooterkin.

new discoveries or theories,[13] but will suggest that its widespread fame and the satires it provoked—for example, Hogarth's "Credulity, Superstition, and Fanaticism"—added further fuel to existing fears. On 5 December 1726, Pope wrote to John Caryll who lived not far from Godalming and might be expected to have heard more details than Londoners: "I want to know what faith you have in the miracle at Guildford; not doubting but as you past thro' that town, you went as a philosopher to investigate, if not as a curious anatomist to inspect, that wonderful phenomenon. All London is now upon this occasion, as it generally is upon all others divided into factions about it." [14] If Caryll replied to Pope's inquiry, as he may well have, the letter is not extant, but numerous Scriblerian satires are. One of these was a series of verses by Pope, "The Discovery: Or, *The* Squire turn'd Ferret. An Excellent New Ballad. To the Tune of *High Boys! up go we; Chevy Chase;* Or what you please," published in December 1726, again in January, and several times thereafter. Here Pope turned his light artillery particularly upon two scientists, Nathaniel St André, a Swiss anatomist and medical attendant on the King, and Samuel Molyneux. Mary Tofts had first been attended by John Howard, a Guildford surgeon and male midwife who had not known her until he was called in on her case. After having devoted most of his time to her for several days, delivering nine rabbits, he moved her to Guildford, to which he invited anyone who doubted the veracity of the reports he had been giving. St André, unfortunately for himself, accepted the invitation and made the trip to Guildford, taking with him Samuel Molyneux, secretary to the Prince of Wales, a scientist of great distinction, particularly important for his work in developing the reflecting telescope. Molyneux was not a medical man and made no pretense to knowledge of midwifery; St André, on the other hand, although he had taken no degree, had been apprenticed to a surgeon and had held the post of local

13. The most complete account is by S. A. Seligman, "Mary Tofts: the Rabbit Breeder," *Medical History,* V (1961), 349–60, which is based upon extant contemporary accounts. Another less extensive treatment is by K. Bryn Thomas, *James Douglas of the Pouch and his pupil William Hunter* (London, 1964), pp. 60–68.

14. *Correspondence of Alexander Pope,* ed. George Sherburn (Oxford, 1956), II, pp. 418–19.

surgeon to the Westminster Hospital Dispensary. It was the un-offending Molyneux, however, who bore the brunt of Pope's satire—perhaps because Pope knew more about telescopes (he had grown interested in the optical effects of the reflecting telescope) than about midwifery: [15]

> But hold! says Molly, first let's try
>   Now that her legs are ope,
> If ought within we may descry
>   By help of Telescope.
> The Instrument himself did make,
>   He rais'd and level'd right.
> But all about was so opake,
>   It could not aid his Sight . . .
>
> Why has the Proverb falsely said,
>   *Better two Heads than one;*
> Could *Molly* hide this *Rabbit's* Head,
>   He still might show his own.

Pope's satire on the "Rabbit Breeder" was one among many. He himself may or may not have contributed another "ballad" on the Tofts case to the *Flying Post*, published on 19 December 1726. In the *Flying Post* it was "Said to be Written by Mr. Pope to Dr. Arbuthnot"; the published title is simply "Mr. P—— to Dr. A——t." Here the satire is chiefly directed at Sir Richard Man-ningham, son of the Bishop of Chester and godson of Sir Hans Sloane, "society's most distinguished man-midwife," whose atten-tion to Mary Tofts had been ordered by King George himself. Many others may be found in the Library of the Royal Society of Medicine in an apparently unique scrapbook, "A Collection of 10 Tracts" on "Mary Tofts, the celebrated pretended Breeder of Rab-bits." Among these is a one-page set of verses, "The Rabbit-Man-

---

15. I follow the text given by Norman Ault in *Minor Poems of Alexander Pope, The Twickenham Pope: Vol. VI* (London, 1964). pp. 259–64. St André was a Fellow of the Royal Society and contributed papers to the *Philosophical Transactions*. His appointment as Surgeon and Anatomist to the Court seems to have been made rather for his linguistic ability than his medical ability. Mary Tofts's confession put an end to his Court position, and he was never again to attain medical recognition.

Midwife," inscribed in an eighteenth-century pencilled hand, "by
John Arbuthnot." Another is a tract of ten pages, *The Opinion of
the Rev'd Mr. William Whiston concerning the Affair of Mary
Tofts, ascribing it to the Completion of a Prophecy of Esdras*, written by William Whiston, formerly Lucasian Professor of Astron-
omy at Cambridge, Isaac Newton's successor. In the apocryphal
book of Esdras, said Whiston, "Tis here foretold that there should
be 'Signs in the Women' or more particularly that "Menstrous
[sic] Women should bring forth Monsters." [16] Presumably writing
years after the Mary Tofts affair, when the story had been "long
laughed out of Countenance," Whiston insisted that he believed it
to be true "as the fulfilling of this Ancient Prophecy before us."
Still another satire in the Royal Society of Medicine scrapbook is
a pamphlet of 1727, purportedly written by "Lemuel Gulliver,
Surgeon and Anatomist to the Kings of Lilliput and Blefuscu, and
Fellow of the Academy of Sciences in Balnibarbi": *The Anatomist
Dissected: or the Man-Midwife finely brought to Bed*, London,
1727.[17] If one of the Scriblerians was responsible for this thirty-
five-page pamphlet, it was Dr. Arbuthnot, who need not have
concealed authorship since *The Anatomist Dissected* was far above
the average tract on the rabbit-woman. It professes to be chiefly
"An Examination of the Conduct of Mr. St André, Touching the
late pretended Rabbit-bearer," based on St André's defense of
himself, *A Short Narrative of an Extraordinary Delivery of Rabbits*. But scrutiny reveals that it is the work of a physician with extensive knowledge of anatomy and experience in childbirth. He

16. According to the title page of the tract, these pages were copied from the
second edition of Whiston's *Memoirs*, published in London in 1753. The
interpretation of the Tofts case does not appear in the first edition of 1749,
and, so far as I can determine, was not published separately. See K. Bryn
Thomas, *James Douglas* (London, 1964), p. 65.
17. See Marjorie Nicolson and G. S. Rousseau, *This Long Disease, My Life:
Alexander Pope and the Sciences* (Princeton, Princeton University Press,
1968), p. 114:

"Early in 1727 when the small talk of London seems to have been divided between
Mary Tofts and Lemuel Gulliver—*Gulliver's Travels* had appeared the preceding
autumn and provoked almost universal applause—it was inevitable that at least
one pamphlet on the rabbit woman should be attributed to Jonathan Swift. Those
who have done him that dubious honor have failed to notice that Swift had returned
to Ireland a month before the Tofts affair, and while he probably heard of it in
letters, he had no such background for parody as Scriblerians in London."

points out inconsistencies in St André's account, pausing over matters of the temperature and pulse of a woman in labor, and the influence of her demented imagination on the foetus.

I have strayed afield and treated the Tofts case at length because it stirred a controversy among physicians and other scientists that was to last in England more than forty years. Less than a month after the episode of the "rabbit breeder," James Augustus Blondel, a distinguished member of the College of Physicians of London, brought out a treatise denying the possibility of such an occurrence: this work was later advertised by Dr. Blondel as "My first Dissertation, *The Strength of Imagination in pregnant Women examin'd*, published upon the Occasion of the Cheat of *Godalming*, hastily, and without Name, as coming from one, who neither designed to be known nor to meddle any more in this Controversy." Trained in Leyden by Boerhaave, Blondel maintained that deformities in birth were caused by other factors— such as actual delivery—than the mother's imagination. He was challenged by Daniel Turner, another physician and Fellow of the Royal College of Surgeons, who dogmatically asserted the opposite.[18] The two physicians, both distinguished and both fellows of the same society, stirred considerable debate within the College

18. The chronology of works in the controversy was as follows: Turner, *De Morbis Cutaneis* (London, 1726; first published in 1714); Blondel, *The Strength of Imagination in Pregnant Women Examin'd* (London, 1727); Turner, *A Discourse concerning Gleets . . . to which is added A Defence of . . . the 12th Chapter of . . . De Morbis Cutaneis, in respect of the Spots and Marks impress'd upon the Skin of the Foetus* (London, 1729); Blondel, *The Power of the Mother's Imagination Over the Foetus Examin'd* (London, 1729); Turner, *The Force of the Mother's Imagination upon her Foetus in Utero . . . in the Way of A Reply to Dr. Blondel's Last Book* (London, 1730). Turner's first work, *De Morbis Cutaneis*, was written in part as a defense of Malebranche's theory that the mother marks her child. See *Father Malebranche's Treatise concerning the Search after Truth*, trans. T. Taylor (Oxford, 1694), "Book the Second Concerning the Imagination." As a conclusion to this book, Malebranche wrote: "When the Imagination of the Mother is disordered and some tempestuous passion changes the Disposition of her Brain . . . then . . . this Communication alters the natural Formation of the Infant's Body, and the Mother proves Abortive sometimes of her foetus" (p. 60). When the Tofts case revived the issue among medical men, Turner turned from Malebranche to a then real-life example. In this and other footnotes, I have dealt at length with these medical tracts because they were clearly read by the masses in their time and now are so little known.

of Physicians. Since Blondel felt he had been attacked personally by Turner, he responded with a one-hundred-and-fifty-page defense of himself: *The Power of the Mother's Imagination Over the Foetus Examin'd. In Answer to Dr. Daniel Turner's Book, Intitled a Defence of the XIIth Chapter of the First Part of a Treatise, De Morbis Cutaneis* (1729). In his preface Blondel stated his purpose: "My Design is to attack a vulgar Error, which has been prevailing for many Years, in Opposition to Experience, sound Reason, and Anatomy: I mean the common Opinion, that Marks and Deformities, which Children are born with, are the sad Effect of the Mother's irregular Fancy and Imagination." Without providing any historical survey of the controversy Blondel noted "that the Doctrine of Imagination, relating to the Foetus, had gone through several Revolutions," and continued to indict the "Imaginationists." [19]

'Tis silly and absurd; for what can be more ridiculous, than to make of Imagination a Knife, a Hammer, a Pastry-Cook, a Thief, a Painter, a Jack of all Trades, a Juggler, Doctor Faustus, the Devil, and all?

'Tis saucy and scandalous, in supposing that those, whom God Almighty has endowed, not only with so many charms, but also, with an extraordinary Love and Tenderness for their children, instead of answering the End they are made for, do breed Monsters by the Wantonness of their Imagination.

'Tis mischievous and cruel; it disturbs whole Families, distracts the Brains of credulous People, and puts them in continual Fears, and in Danger of their Lives: In short 'tis such a publick Nuisance, that 'tis the Interest of every Body to join together against such a Monster, and to root it entirely out of the World.

19. *The Power of the Mother's Imagination*, p. xi. Blondel singled out from medical literature the six most common causes of spotted children: "1. A strong Longing for something particular, in which Desire the Mother is either gratified, or disappointed. 2. A sudden Surprise. 3. The Sight and Abhorrence of an ugly and frightful Object. 4. The Pleasure of Looking on, and Contemplating, even for a long Time, a Picture or Whatever is delightful to the Fancy. 5. Fear, and Consternation, and great Apprehension of Dangers. 6. And lastly, an Excess of Anger, of Grief, or of Joy" (p. 2). Later (p. 4) Blondel notes that item (1) of the list above was the most common of the six, especially in the case of certain fruits, "the strong Desire of *Peaches,* or *Cherries.*" Presumably he would have included in this list pineapples!

In less than six months the "Imaginationists" led by Turner retorted with a reassertion of the influence of the mother on her foetus. Parodying Blondel's title, Turner called his treatise *The Force of the Mother's Imagination upon her Foetus* (1730). This work was over two hundred pages and was a definitive defense of the majority view of the time. One of Turner's arguments was "the authority of Antiquity": he had culled hundreds of ancient and medieval medical writings and prepared a list of monstrous births in which the mother's demented imagination was the apparent cause. Most common among these, Turner affirmed, was her craving for exotic fruits—plums, cherries, grapes, prunes, and now pineapples. Unlike Blondel, Turner was not concerned with the physiological processes by which the foetus was actually "marked." He abstained from proving the truth of his argument by appealing to "sensation, the nerves, and the circulation of the foetus." Instead, he cited numerous ancient and modern authorities, known and obscure—Hesiod, Heliodorus, Jacobus Horstius, Ambroise Paré, Johann Schenkius, Thomas Bartholin, Charles Cyprianus, Robert Boyle, Sir Kenelm Digby—who had reported instances of deformed children; moreover, Mary Tofts herself, although "a cheat," had been frightened by rabbits while sowing in the fields, and in Turner's estimation there was a definite connection between the imagination and the foetus. Learned though his argument seemed, Turner was scurrilously satirized by his opponents in several pamphlets and poems, perhaps the most witty and scrofulous among them a burlesque set of verses written in Butlerian octosyllables entitled "The Porter Turn'd Physician," and published in 1731.

Although Blondel and Turner after 1730 did not publish works concerning the mother's imagination, the controversy over which they differed continued to be a topic of concern in medical and lay circles for at least three decades. Fellows of the Royal Society, many of whom were Smollett's personal friends, and other scientifically inclined gentlemen, hesitated to drop so controversial an issue. Doctors Hunter and Monro spent considerable time on the topic in their anatomical lectures, and we know that Smollett not only heard these but was in 1748–50 in medical dialogues with these men. As late as 1747, John Henry Mauclerc, an M.D. of no great distinction, published a lengthy treatise entitled *Dr. Blondel confuted: or, the Ladies Vindicated, with Regard to the Power of Imagination in Pregnant Women: Together with a Circular and General Address to the Ladies on this Occasion* (London).[20] Odd as it may appear, Mauclerc's book approved rather than confuted—his own term—Blondel's theory that imagination alone was unable to harm the foetus. "The Design of the Dissertation," he wrote in the preface of his book intended especially for women, "is to prove that the Opinion, which has long prevail'd, that the Marks and Deformities, Children bring into the World, are the sad Effect of the Mother's irregular Fancy and Imagination, is nothing else but a vulgar Error, contrary to sound Reason and Anatomy." Later in his preface Mauclerc writes as if the controversy were still inflaming the hearts of medical men, twenty years after the fact: "I don't despair of Success: Interest alone should prevail, upon the Party, which is chiefly concerned in this Controversy." Dr. Mauclerc disbelieving in old wives' tales and other odd superstitions, presents—to quote his own words—"a Sketch of the true Cause of Monsters—I hope, 'tis sufficient for the present, to give a general, and yet a clear Solution of those strange Phenomena [monsters]." If Blondel had his supporters, so did Turner, although both men had been dead for many years. In 1765, Isaac Bellet, a French physician residing in London, wrote *Letters on the Force of the Imagination in Pregnant Women*, in which he denied the possibility that pregnant women could mark their children, but was compelled to agree rather with Turner's explanations than Blondel's. The result was a second-rate medical work fraught with contradiction, but nevertheless one showing how very much alive the matter still was. Dr. Smollett, probably the author of the review in the *Critical Review*,[21] found the book

20. An earlier version of this work appeared in 1740 with the title page, *The Power of Imagination in Pregnant Women Discussed: with an Address to the Ladies in Reply to J. A. Blondel*. So far as I can learn Mauclerc published no other works.

21. *Critical Review*, XX (July 1765), 63–65. On pages 125–33, Bellet provides a fair estimate—in his opinion—and a history of the controversy from the time of Malebranche. There is reason to believe that Smollett and Bellet had met and that Smollett was impressed by his knowledge of medical history.

very appealing: "We declare upon the whole," he wrote, "that he [Bellet] has fulfilled his scope, and executed his undertaking with great precision, and that he has clearly demonstrated the impossibility of a pregnant woman's marking her child with the figure of any object for which she has longed, or which may have made a deep impression upon the imagination." It is difficult, if at all possible, to state accurately what Smollett's views on the subject were almost twenty years earlier, when he was writing the early chapters of *Peregrine Pickle*, but there is every reason to believe that even then the probability of a mother marking her child seemed remote to him. Hunter, Monro, and Smellie doubted the possibility, and medically speaking, they exerted much influence on his thought.

Throughout the 1740's cases of extraordinary childbirth of every sort continued to interest the English public, especially physicians and scientists. One could compile with ease a long list of works written in the decade about strange childbirths. Nor was the subject treated in books and tracts only. Popular periodicals that enjoyed large amateur audiences devoted much space in their issues to these freaks of nature. *The Gentleman's Magazine*, for example, contained no fewer than ninety-two articles (essays, reviews, and letters) on the question of extraordinary childbirth.[22] Curiosity was especially aroused by a woman who never became pregnant until she drank Bishop Berkeley's tar water in 1745. More specialized in its reading audience, the *Philosophical Transactions* of the Royal Society (to which Smollett never was elected but many of whose Fellows he knew) was flooded with communications about bizarre births attesting to the interests of its fellow members in the subject. Professor Knapp's biography makes it clear that Smollett was familiar with some of these publications. An idea of the range and diversity of such cases may be gained by

---

I treat this in my forthcoming book, *Doctors and Medicine in the Novels of Smollett*.

22. A list of references is too long to be given here. The two cases that attracted the most attention were "A Foetus of Thirteen Years," *The Gentleman's Magazine*, XIX (1749), 415, and in the same publication, "Fatal Accident: Woman carry'd a child sixteen years," XIX (1749), 211.

listing a few of the titles of these articles: [23] "Account of a monstrous boy"; "Account of a monstrous child born of a woman under sentence of transportation"; "An Account of a monstrous foetus resembling an hooded monkey"; "Case of a child turned upside down"; "A remarkable conformation, or lusus naturae in a child"; "Part of a letter concerning a child of monstrous size"; "Account of a child's being taken out of the abdomen after having lain there upwards of 16 years"; "a letter concerning a child born with an extraordinary tumor near the anus, containing some rudiments of an embryo in it"; "An account of a praeternatural conjunction of two female children"; "Part of a letter concerning a child born with the jaundice upon it, received from its father's imagination, and of the mother taking the same distemper from her husband the next time of being with child"; "An account of a monstrous foetus without any mark of sex"; "An account of a double child born at Hebus, near Middletown in Lancashire." So interesting to laymen and amateur scientists were many of these cases that they were abstracted from the *Philosophical Transactions* and reported in abbreviated form as news items in *The Gentleman's Magazine*.

The controversy originally stirred by Blondel and Turner, and about which Smollett must have heard, also provoked considerable commentary in the 1740's in books (essays, novels, and poems). Fielding Ould, among the most famous male-midwives of his age and best known for *A Treatise of Midwifery* (1742) [24]—frequently called by historians of medicine the first important text on midwifery in English—considered the mother's imagination important in the health of the foetus, although he seems to have doubted the validity of Turner's views. Not infrequently the subject ap-

23. Respectively *Philosophical Transactions*, XLI (1740), 137; XLI (1741), 341; XLI (1741), 764; XLI (1741), 776; XLII (1742), 152; XLII (1743), 627; XLIV (1747), 617; XLV (1748), 325; XLV (1748), 526; XLVI (1749), 205; XLVII (1750), 360. Some of these cases were abridged and printed in popular monthlies such as *The Gentleman's Magazine* and *The Monthly Review*.

24. First published in Dublin and numerous times thereafter in London. For Ould's contributions to midwifery see John R. Brown, "A Chronology of Major Events in Obstetrics and Gynaecology," *The Journal of Obstetrics and Gynaecology*, LXXI (1964), 303; and Fielding H. Garrison, *An Introduction to the History of Medicine* (4th ed. rev.; London, 1929), pp. 338–40.

peared in novels. Sir John Hill, an arch-enemy of Smollett in 1751, created a marvelous female character in *The Adventures of George Edwards, A Creole,*[25] who touched a robin-red-breast during pregnancy (her fancy having led her to this curious action!) and, thereafter, bore a child with a red breast—or red chest. In the same year that *Peregrine Pickle* was published, 1751, he also wrote a satire on the subject of curious births entitled *Lucina sine concubitu.* Here the reader finds the theories of preformation (according to which organisms are already fully formed in their seeds) and panspermism (minute organisms developed in fluids owing to the presence of germs) satirically treated, as well as those of the influence of the mother's imagination on her child. Although Hill was unable to attain membership in the Royal Society because of his disagreeable personality, his hoax *Lucina* was nevertheless widely read by such professional medical men as Dr. Smollett, who had good reason to take note of Hill in 1751.[26] The famous case,[27] two years earlier, of a woman "who carried with child 16 years," also helped to create the background for Smollett's witty treatment of the state of the mother's imagination.

Peregrine Pickle was published twelve years too early to bear any traces of awareness of George Alexander Stevens's *Dramatic History of Master Edward* (London, 1763). But this collection of extraordinary occurrences in 1730–1760—written, as the title page indicates, by the "Author of the celebrated Lecture upon Heads"— demonstrates how fully formed a type of writing (most accurately described as a *leit motif*) about abnormal births had emerged by the 1760's. In the opening pages (7–13), Stevens has Thomas recount to David a series of histories, all dealing with ab-

25. First published in 1751 and reprinted in *The Novelists' Magazine,* XXIII (1788). The complicated history of Smollett's interaction with John Hill is narrated in my forthcoming biography, *The Literary Quack: A Life of Sir John Hill of London.* One episode is discussed by William Scott, "Smollett, John Hill, and *Peregrine Pickle,*" *Notes and Queries,* CC (1955), 389–92.
26. Two weeks before the publication of *Peregrine Pickle,* Dr. Hill anticipated Smollett's novel by bringing out *The History of a Woman of Quality: or the Adventures of Lady Frail.* While Smollett believed the presence in his novel of Lady Vane's "Memoirs" would enhance sales, Hill's earlier publication greatly diminished sales.
27. *The Gentleman's Magazine,* XIX (1749), 211.

normalities during pregnancy and shortly after birth. The stories, culled from authors in different countries in Europe, are as bizarre and grotesque as scenes from gothic romances (then coming into vogue). Two histories in particular appeal to David, so much so that Stevens included illustrations of them in his revised edition of 1785. In the first (see plate III), *"Aldrovandus* [a seventeenth-century naturalist] relates, that a woman in Sicily observing a lobster taken by a fisherman, and being moved by an ernest longing for it, brought forth a lobster, altogether like what she had seen and longed for." Stevens's "lobster woman" is not very different from Mary Tofts, the "rabbit woman." The second history (see plate IV), richer in complexity and more touching, relates, as Stevens writes, "something singular beyond all these:"

. . . [it] is the tale of *Languis,* of a woman longing to bite the naked shoulder of a baker passing by her; which, rather than she should lose her longing, the good-natured husband hired the baker at a certain price. Accordingly, when the big-bellied woman had bit twice, the baker's wife broke away from the people who held her, would not suffer her to bite her husband again; for want of which, she bore one dead child, with two living ones.

Smollett himself had shown interest in cases of extraordinary childbirth five years before the composition of *Peregrine Pickle.* In *Advice: A Satire* (1746), the character Poet refers to the strange conception, or near-conception, of a hermaphrodite: [28]

> But one thing more—how loud must I repeat,
> To rouse th' engag'd attention of the great,
> Amus'd, perhaps, with C————'s prolific bum,
> Or rapt amidst the transports of a drum."

Here Smollett's own note reads: "This alludes to a phenomenon not more strange than true; the person here meant, having actually laid upwards of forty eggs, as several physicians and fellows of the Royal Society can attest, one of whom, we hear, has under-

28. *The Works of Tobias Smollett, M.D.,* ed. by James P. Browne (London, 1872) I, p. 294.

taken the incubation, and will, no doubt, favour the world with an account of his success. Some virtuosi affirm, that such productions must be the effect of a certain intercourse of organs not fit to be named." Smollett's source for "C——" [29] remains a mystery, although his satiric habit of mind was unlikely to fabricate a source. London newspapers in 1745–46 were filled with reports of such odd occurrences and the populace seemed to be diverted, if not instructed, by these accounts. In 1750, Smollett, while preparing for publication Dr. William Smellie's *Midwifery*, probably read about cases of unnatural birth in the hours he spent annotating. During that year he may have seen "Michael Anne Drouvert," the much talked about Parisian hermaphrodite who was displayed in London and written up as a case history in the *Philosophical Transactions*; may have read James Parsons's *Inquiry into the Nature of Hermaphrodites* (1741) or George Arnaud's new book entitled *Dissertation on Hermaphrodites* (1750); or may even have heard that John Hill's forthcoming book, *A History of Animals* (1750), contained a modern epitome of the subject. At any rate, Smollett's extensive reading in obstetrics in the library of Smellie, and earlier in Dr. James Douglas's library, would have revealed a wealth of real cases from which to create fictional characters and episodes relating to pregnancy. Smollett's own observations, printed in Smellie's *Treatise* (II, 4–5), "On the Separation of the Pubic Joint in Pregnancy," give ample testimony to and palpable evidence of his interest in cases of abnormal birth.

In fact, Smollett never lost interest in the subject and continued from 1750 to 1764 to edit and revise all Smellie's obstetrical works. Smollett's extensive medical reading coupled with his knowledge

29. There is no mention of this case in the *Philosophical Transactions* or other scientific literature I have examined. Perhaps "C——" was the famous "Charing Cross hermaphrodite," about whom Dr. William Cheselden had written in the *Anatomy of the Humane Body* (London, 1713) and about whom Dr. James Douglas wrote many medical fragments in the 1720's. Smollett was too young to have seen that curious organism. By 1751 this hermaphrodite may have become too stale a subject for satire, although K. Bryn Thomas, *James Douglas and his pupil William Hunter* (London, 1964), p. 190, does not think so. I am inclined to believe it was a more recent occurrence, about which Smollett was informed, as the tone of his note indicates.

of the extraordinary case of Sarah Last,[30] who in 1748 underwent normal pregnancy without ever giving birth to her foetus, must have inspired him to draw a parallel case in Mrs. Trunnion in *Peregrine Pickle*. Readers will recall the bizarrely constructed chapters in which the pregnant lady is found to have been swelled with air! Smollett was reflecting contemporary fears about strange childbirth when he described the ultimate chagrin of the Trunnions:

At length she and her husband became the standing joke of the parish; and this infatuated couple could scarce be prevailed upon to part with their hopes, even when she appeared as lank as a greyhound, and they were furnished with other unquestionable proofs of their having been deceived. But they could not forever remain under the influence of this sweet delusion, which at last faded away, and was succeeded by a paroxism of shame and confusion, that kept the husband within doors for the space of a whole fortnight, and confined his lady to her bed for a series of weeks, during which she suffered all the anguish of the most intense mortification.[31]

II

The first pineapple grown in a hothouse in England may well have been planted during the Restoration. A well-known extant painting (see plate V), bearing the inscription *Rose, The Royal*

30. Among numerous accounts of her case the most interesting I have found is in the *The Gentleman's Magazine*, XXI (1751), 214–15: "About the beginning of August 1748, Sarah Last, a poor woman in Suffolk, had the usual Symptoms of pregnancy, which succeeded each other pretty regularly thro' the usual period, at times she was seiz'd with pains . . . the child did not advance in birth . . . after the pains were gone off, the woman grew better . . . her menses return'd at proper seasons as if she had been deliver'd of a child, and continued so to do for several months . . . the poor woman recover'd, and is now perfectly well." The editor commented that "the foregoing case is not singular; we see two of the same kind recorded in the Memoirs of the Royal Academy of Surgery at Paris for the last year . . . and [one] communicated to the French academy."

31. *Peregrine Pickle*, I. p. 72. Smollett's description of Mrs. Trunnion's expectant state tallies well with observations made in John Pechey's *Complete Midwife's Practice Enlarged* (5th ed.; London, 1698), especially the section "Of False Conception" (pp. 57–62). According to a manuscript in the Hunterian Museum, Pechey was included among required authors to be read by students at the Glasgow Medical School, which Smollett attended 1736–39.

Gardener, presenting to Charles II the first pine-apple grown in England, is ascribed to the Dutch artist Danckerts and the gardener is John Rose.[32] Just how long before Monsieur Le Cour, a Frenchman residing in Leyden, Holland, "hit upon a proper Degree of Heat and Management so as to produce pine-apples equally as good as those which are produced in the West Indies," [33] is not known. Even in Leyden, where winters were less brutal than in England, Le Cour used stoves to grow the tropical fruit. Chambers's compendious *Cyclopaedia* (1728) reports that the gardens of England were supplied with pineapples by Le Cour himself, and John Evelyn wrote in his *Diary* on 9 August 1661: "I first saw the famous Queene-pine brought from Barbados presented to his *Majestie,* but the first that were ever seene here in England, were those sent to Cromwell, foure-yeares since" [1658].[34] Evelyn continued several days later with a description of the "rare fruite

32. Without pretending to summarize the vast literature dealing with the date and author of this painting, I mention the following: George W. Johnson, *A History of English Gardening* (London, 1829), pp. 72–81; Alicia Amherst, *A History of Gardening in England* (London, 1910), p. 238 ff.; Miles Hadfield, *Gardening in Britain* (London, 1960), p. 126; J. L. Collins, *The Pineapple* (Honolulu, 1960), pp. 70–86; William Gardener, "Botany and the Americas," *History Today,* XVI (Dec. 1966), pp. 849–55, where the picture was most recently reprinted. In his *DNB* life of John Tradescant the younger, gardener to Charles I, G. S. Boulger writes: "There is a tradition that the younger Tradescant first planted the pineapple in England in the garden of Sir James Palmer at Dorney House, Windsor, where a large stone cut in the shape of a pineapple by way of commemoration early in the seventeeth century is still extant . . . The pineapple pits were therefore pre-Charles II. Surely then John Tradescant the younger grew pineapples here for Charles I. The fact that there is no painting of John the elder or John the younger presenting a home-grown pineapple to Charles I does not disprove the possibility. The Tradescants would have had ready access to pineapples thanks to Sir William Courteen who was one of their principal benefactors. Sir William took out the first settlers to Barbadoes in 1625. The West Indies were one of his regular trade routes." This theory is supported by M. Allan in *The Tradescants: Their Plants, Gardens and Museum 1570–1662* (London, 1964), pp. 143–45. Tradescant was known for his exotic fruits, as is seen in Tom Brown's *Amusements Serious and Comical,* particularly the section entitled "The Philosophical or Virtuosi Country."

33. Robert James, M.D., *A Medicinal Dictionary* (London, 1743–45), article entitled "Ananas."

34. *The Diary of John Evelyn,* ed. E. S. de Beer (Oxford, 1955), Vol. III, pp. 293, 513.

called the King-Pine," the first he had seen: he tasted it and found it not to his liking.

Whether or not those described by Evelyn were the first grown—it is at least plausible that an occasional fruit had been grown earlier—a more likely possibility is that pineapples were first artificially produced in quantity at any rate, in the hothouses of Sir Matthew Decker's famous garden in Richmond. He was a well-known London merchant (president of the East India Company) of Dutch origin who apparently enjoyed a "truly Dutch passion for gardening." [35] Richard Bradley, an authority on gardening in the early decades of the eighteenth century and Professor of Botany at the University of Cambridge, wrote that Sir Matthew's gardener, Henry Tellende, grew the first pineapples for his master "circa 1723." [36] Seven years before this, Lady Mary Wortley Montagu had eaten pineapples at the table of the Elector of Hanover. She wrote to Lady Mar about "2 ripe Ananas's, which to my taste are a fruit perfectly delicious," and continued to note surprise that pineapples had not as yet been cultivated in her native land. "You know they are naturally the Growth of Brasil, and I could not imagine how they could come there but by Enchantment. Upon Enquiry I learnt that they have brought their Stoves to such perfection, they lengthen the Summer as long as they please, giveing to every plant the degree of heat it would receive from the Sun in its native Soil. The Effect is very near the same. I am surpriz'd we do not practise in England so usefull an Invention." [37] From the

---

35. Hadfield, *Gardening in Britain,* p. 126.
36. *Dictionarium Botanicum* . . . (London, 1728), article entitled "Ananas," and "A Particular Easy Method of Managing Pine-Apples" in *New Improvements of Planting and Gardening* (London, 1726), p. 605. Bradley's assertion was challenged in 1780 by Horace Walpole, who wrote to the Reverend William Cole: "There is another assertion in Gough [*British Topography,* 1768], which I can authentically contradict. He says Sir Matthew Decker first introduced ananas. My curious picture of Rose, the royal gardener, presenting the first ananas to Charles II proves the culture here earlier by several years" (*Letters to the Reverend William Cole,* ed. W. S. Lewis [New Haven, Yale University Press, 1937] II, p. 239). Walpole had acquired the painting from William Pennicott in 1780. In his popular handbook, *The Gardener's Dictionary* (London, 1724), Philip Miller attributed the first pineapple to Tellende. See also E. S. Rohde, *The Story of the Garden* (London, 1932), p. 178.
37. *The Complete Letters of Lady Mary Wortley Montagu,* ed. by R. Halsband (Oxford, 1965–67), Vol. I, p. 290.

lengthy discussion about pineapples that Horatio and Cleomenes have in Mandeville's *Fable of the Bees* (1714),[38] it may be assumed that Tellende and his lord, Decker, had raised the delicious and exotic fruit approximately in 1720–23. Mandeville's characters— not dissimilar to several enthusiasts in *Peregrine Pickle*—comment upon a new and "fine Invention" as well as on the intrinsic attributes of pineapples: Horatio says, "I was thinking of the Man, to whom we are in a great measure obliged for the Production and Culture of the *Exotick*, we were speaking of in this Kingdom; Sir Matthew Decker: the first *Ananas*, or Pineapple, that was brought to Perfection in *England*, grew in his Garden at Richmond." That garden was still viewed in the 1730's and Smollett, who had come to London in 1739, may have visited it.

As Richard Bradley had explained in his essay "A particular easy Method of managing Pine-Apples" (1726),[39] the difficulty of cultivation was due to poor hothouses and stoves. Pineapples required a full three years for growth, an exact temperature, ideal moisture conditions, and correctly constructed stoves. As soon as this was achieved, the fruit could be grown in domestic gardens, even if at great financial expenditure. Such was the case and it applied not only to pineapples but to other exotic fruits, limes, papayas, guavas, bananas, and even grapes. The cultivation of pineapples in the third and particularly the fourth decades of the eighteenth century became a hobby—not quite a popular sport— among expert gardeners and aristocrats. Prominent families who could afford the expense sent their head gardeners to Decker's hothouses to observe the new method and educate themselves. Among the first to display home-grown pineapples on their tables were the opulent Earls of Bathurst, Portland, and Gainsborough. The Duke of Chandos, long incorrectly identified as "Timon" in Pope's *Epistle to Burlington*, not only grew pineapples on his estate at Shaw Hall in Berkshire, but he also sold them "at a half a guinea a time," [40] a price even Mrs. Grizzle would have been willing to pay for her sister-in-law!

38. Edited by F. B. Kaye (Oxford, 1924), Vol. II, pp. 193–95.
39. Pages 605–6. Bradley, among other authors, notes that a forty-foot stove was necessary to ripen one hundred pineapples. An average pineapple took three years to ripen and *c.* 1726 its total cost from the time of purchasing seeds was £80.
40. Hadfield, *Gardening*, p. 166, and C. H. Collins Baker and M. I. Baker,

Smollett may not have known first-hand the early history of pineapples in England, but he was old enough to be familiar with its more recent peregrinations. Few people were more excited about the new art of growing pineapples than Alexander Pope. Together with his gardener John Serle, whom the poet employed in 1724, Pope was growing "ananas" by 1734. He had, however, tasted the fruit long before this. On 8 October 1731, Pope wrote Martha Blount, "I'm going in haste to plant Jamaica Strawberries, which are to be almost as good as Pineapples." [41] In the spring of 1735, he wrote to William Fortescue that he was improving and expanding his garden, "making two new ovens and stoves, and a hot-house for anana's, of which I hope you will taste this year." Two or three pineapples grown in the Twickenham hothouse and sent to an intimate friend was perhaps the greatest honor Pope could confer. During this period he was continually experimenting for cheaper and better ways to raise the fruit. In August 1738, Pope and Serle "borrowed" Henry Scott, Lord Burlington's gardener who was an expert in growing pineapples, to consult with him "about a Stove I am building." It is possible that Pope was also reading modern handbooks on the subject. Whatever the case, by 1741 Pope thought he had discovered with the aid of Scott the long-sought method, and attempted to make it known to his friends. How well-circulated among the London *literati* Pope's "discovery" was, it is now impossible to tell; but by 1741, the magisterial poet was too conspicuous among men to veil any of his activities, even his pastimes and hobbies. Smollett, then young and still an *ingénu* among the "wits" in London, kept his ears and eyes open and possibly may have heard about the new pineapple method of Mr. Pope, his favorite author among all authors and a poet whose influence was to rub off considerably on his own writings. In any case, Pope soon wrote to Ralph Allen (to whom he occasionally sent a pineapple or two): "In a Week or two, Mr. Scot will make you a Visit, he is going to Set up for himself in the Art of Gardening, in which he has great Experience, & particularly

---

The Life of James Brydges First Duke of Chandos (London, 1949), p. 103. See also George Sherburn, " 'Timon's Villa' and Cannons," *Huntington Library Bulletin,* VIII (1935), p. 143.
41. *Correspondence of Alexander Pope,* Vol. III, pp. 233 and 453.

has a design which I think a very good one, to make Pineapples cheaper in a year or two." [42] Scott and Allen's gardener, Isaac Dodsley, were apparently successful in building the new type of hothouse with new stoves, for Pope wrote next year to Allen: "I would fain have it succeed, for two particular reasons; one because I saw it was Mrs. Allen's desire to have that fruit, & the other because it is the only piece of Service I have been able to do you, or to help you in." [43]

Poets and prose writers varied in their response to the fashionable king of fruits, some equating it with luxury and viewing it as a symbol of evil, others seeing in its beautiful colors and exotic shape an expression of the beauty of Nature and God. Pineapples were, as James Thomson wrote in "Summer" (a poem which Smollett singled out for praise in the preface of *Ferdinand Count Fathom*), the fruits of the Gods in the Primitive Ages of the world: [44]

> ... thou best Anana, thou the pride
> of vegetable life, beyond whate'er
> The poets imaged in the golden age:
> Quick let me strip thee of thy tufty coat,
> Spread thy ambrosial stores, and feast with Jove."

Still other authors wrote about the medical properties of pineapples. In his didactic poem *The Art of Preserving Health* (1744),

42. *Ibid.*, Vol. IV, p. 360. See also Vol. IV, pp. 405, 420; and Benjamin Boyce, *The Benevolent Man: A Life of Ralph Allen* (Cambridge, Mass., Harvard University Press, 1967), p. 114. On March 25, 1736, Pope wrote to Swift about the new fruits in his garden: "I have good Melons and Pine-apples of my own growth. I am as much a better Gardiner, as I'm a worse Poet, than when you saw me: But gardening is near a-kin to Philosophy, for Tully says *Agricultura proxima sapientiae*" (*Correspondence*, IV, 6). Without documentation Hadfield, *History of Gardening*, p. 187, states that "a year later [1742] Allen was advised not to take Scott's advice." But Pope could not have been the unmentioned person since he fully approved of Scott's method. For Pope's activities as a gardener and ideas about gardening during Smollett's mature years, see Edward Malins, *English Landscaping and Literature 1660–1840* (London, 1966), pp. 26–51.

43. *Correspondence*, IV, p. 429.

44. *The Poetical Works of James Thomson*, ed. by J. L. Robertson (Oxford, 1908), "Summer," lines 685–89.

John Armstrong, with whom Smollett was on intimate terms throughout his life, chose the fruit as an example of a product raised that exhibited the differences and the extremes of cold and heat in diet: [45]

> ... in horrid mail
> The crisp ananas wraps its poignant sweets.
> Earth's vaunted progeny: in ruder air
> Too coy to flourish, even too proud to live;
> Or hardly rais'd by artificial fire
> To vapid life. Here with a mother's smile
> Glad Amalthea pours her copious horn.

Smollett knew his friend's poem very well, had read it numerous times, and called it in *The Present State of All Nations* (London, 1768, II. 227), "an excellent didactic poem."

Long before the prose encyclopaedists (Ephraim Chambers, John Harris, Robert James) discussed the fruit, medical authors had commented upon it. From the time of Nicholas Culpepper's popular handbook, *A Directory for Midwives*, which Mrs. Grizzle had studied so assiduously, pineapples were strictly forbidden to expectant mothers as one of the "Summer Fruits nought for her and all her Pulse." In *The English Physitian* (1674) Culpepper had devoted an entire section to the benefits and ill effects of the fruit: "It marvelously helpeth all the Diseases of the Mother used inwardly, or applied outwardly, procuring Womens Courses, and expelling the dead Child and After-birth, yea, it is so powerful upon those Feminine parts that it is utterly forbidden for Women

45. *The Art of Preserving Health* (London, 1796), including a *Critical Essay* by Dr. John Aikin, lines 334–40. Aikin commented on foods like pineapples as an example of a "too luxurious diet" (p. 14). The medical aspects of pineapples were also discussed in scientific publications. For example, see William Bastard, "On the Cultivation of Pine-Apples," *Philosophical Transactions*, LXVII (1777), pp. 649–52, in which the author describes his hothouse in Devonshire and the effects of the fruit on the body. Armstrong, a Scotsman who practiced medicine in London, probably did not taste pineapples in Scotland. Dr. John Hope, the Regius Professor of Botany at Edinburgh University and a popularizer of Linnaeus in Scotland, allegedly grew in 1762 the first pineapples in Scotland, although I can discover no certain means of verifying this allegation.

with Child, and that it will cause abortment or delivery before the time . . . Let Women forbear it if they be with Child, for it works violently upon the Feminine Part." [46] Seventeenth-century herbalists like Thomas Parkinson also warned their readers not to eat the artificial food. But it was not until pineapples were actually grown in English gardens that physicians and obstetricians became alarmed and abandoned superstition for medical science. Observation had revealed that pregnant women who ate this food miscarried again and again. Dr. Robert James, inventor of the famed "fever powders," writing in the London *Pharmacopaeia Universalis* (1742), commented: "This Fruit is esteemed cordial, and analeptic; and is said to raise and exhilarate the Spirits, to cure a Nausea, and provoke Urine. But 'tis subject to cause a Miscarriage, for which Reason Women with Child should abstain from it." [47] One year later James (whose *Medicinal Dictionary* Smollett knew well) was even more precautionary, stating that pineapples definitely caused miscarriage. Similarly, dietitians and other authors on nutrition warned the pregnant woman to refrain from the pineapple. M. L. Lemery, a prolific author on diet whose works were translated into English because of their popularity, wrote in *A Treatise of All Sorts of Foods*: [48] "Ananas is a delicious fruit,

46. *The English Physitian* (London, 1684), pp. 189–90. Pineapples were not mentioned in the edition of 1651, presumably because they were then unknown in England. Smollett referred to Culpepper's medical handbooks in several novels, and Joseph Addison listed the *Directory for Midwives* among essential books in an eighteenth-century "Lady's Library." See *The Spectator*, ed. Donald Bond (Oxford, 1965), Vol. I, p. 155.

47. *Pharmacopaeia Universalis* (London, 1742), p. 118. John Quincy made the same point in his *Complete English Dispensatory* (rev. ed.; London, 1742), p. 194.

48. *A Treatise of All Sorts of Foods, Both Animal and Vegetable,* trans. by D. Hay, M.D. (London, 1745), p. 350 and pp. 75–76. The signatures of several distinguished physicians of the Royal College of Physicians appear on the frontispage as approving the medical aspects of the book: among them are Edward Brown, Walter Charleton, and John Woodward, whom the Scriblerians satirized. For other comments by dietitians about the medicinal aspect of pineapples, see A. Cocchi, *The Pythagorean Diet, of Vegetables Only, Conducive to the Preservation of Health* . . . , trans. from Italian (London, 1745), pp. 74–76; and Sir Jack Drummond and Anne Wilbraham, *The Englishman's Food* (London, 1939), pp. 228–29. Numerous comments about the danger of pineapples for pregnant women may also be found in Ephraim Cham-

that grows in the West Indies, whose juice the *Indians* extract, and make excellent Wine of it, which will intoxicate. Women with Child dare not drink of it, because they say, it will make them miscarry." Francis Spilsbury, the author of *Free Thoughts on Quacks* (London, 1777), a treatise explaining the circumstances of Oliver Goldsmith's death, compared pineapples to gout (a strange comparison even for an eighteenth-century apothecary!) since he found a "universal comprehensiveness" in both. In his words, just as "the Ananas (vulgarly known under the name of *Pine-Apple*) is considered as containing the taste and flavour of many different fruits, so a great many disorders of the body are, under different appellations to be found in the Gout." [49]

Philosophers as well as medical thinkers pointed to the pineapple as a rare fruit with strange qualities and an exotic taste. Less concerned than physicians with the medicinal aspects of pineapples, they frequently referred to the fruit when discussing the sense of taste. As early as 1690, John Locke singled out pineapples as the best obtainable example of a food whose taste could not be comprehended without actually partaking of it. In a well-known passage in *An Essay Concerning Human Understanding* on "the Blind Man," to which Fielding referred several times in *Tom Jones*, Locke wrote of the impossibility of words replacing direct sensory experience: [50]

He that thinks otherwise, let him try if any words can give him a taste of a pine apple, and make him have the true idea of the relish of that celebrated delicious fruit. So far as he is told it has a resemblance with any tastes whereof he has the ideas already in his memory, imprinted

---

bers's *Cyclopaedia: Or, An Universal Dictionary of Arts and Sciences* (London, 1728), article entitled "Ananas," and in George Cheyne's *An Essay on Regimen* (2nd ed.; London, 1740), pp. 76–77. Chapter XIX of *Roderick Random*, in which the hero meets the French apothecary Lavement, makes it clear that Smollett was thoroughly familiar with the medical effects of different diets.
49. *Free Thoughts on Quacks* (London, 1749), pp. 164–65.
50. *An Essay Concerning Human Understanding*, ed. by Alexander Campbell Fraser (Oxford, 1894), Vol. II, pp. 37–38. Although Locke was an expert botanist and did a great deal of plant research in the Oxford Botanical Garden in 1650–60, there is no evidence that he himself ever grew pineapples. See Kenneth Dewhurst, *John Locke (1632–1704) Physician and Philosopher: A Medical Biography* (London: The Wellcome Historical Medical Library, 1963), pp. 8–9.

there by sensible objects, not strangers to his palate, so far may he approach that resemblance in his mind. But this is not giving us that idea by a definition, but exciting in us other simple ideas by their known names; which will be still very different from the true taste of that fruit itself.

Also speaking of the origin of ideas and the fact that they are grounded in sensory experience (i.e. direct sense experience), Smollett's countryman David Hume noted in the opening paragraph of his *Treatise of Human Nature* (1739) that "we cannot form to ourselves a just idea of the taste of a pineapple, without actually having tasted it." [51] That is, the rare and uncommon pineapple affords the student of philosophy a splendid opportunity to observe that "all our simple ideas in their first appearance are derived from simple impressions, which are correspondent to them, and which they exactly represent." And David Hartley, writing two years before the publication of *Peregrine Pickle,* may not have commented upon pineapples but he increased speculative interest in abnormal pregnancy by the inclusion in his *Observations on Man* of a chapter entitled, "To Examine How Far the Longings of Pregnant Women are agreeable to the Doctrines of Vibrations and Associations." Hartley, a physician by profession, underplayed the variety of longings found in pregnant women—an impressive range, as Smollett's female figures in the novels show—and demonstrated instead that abnormal cravings are caused in the first place by means of "nervous Communications between the Uterus and the Stomach." Both, Hartley maintained, are in "a State of great Sensibility and Irritability" during pregnancy, a view Smollett himself had taken in writing about the pubic joint. Smollett may not have read Locke, Hume, and Hartley—although that is highly unlikely—but he was certainly aware of popular references to pineapples and pregnancies in their works, ideas then so common that they probably required little documentation to a literate eighteenth-century man.

Thus, a decade before the publication of *Peregrine Pickle,* physicians, scientists, gardeners, philosophers, and literary men had all reacted in various ways to the new "King Fruit" which by 1751

51. *A Treatise of Human Nature,* ed. L. A. Selby-Bigge (2nd ed. rev.; Oxford, 1928), p. 5.

had become much more popular than in John Evelyn's day; all had seen in the body of beliefs and superstitions embracing the fruit something different. If gardeners found it their delight and joy, philosophers were not far behind in using it as an emblem of singular sensory experience. If physicians, especially obstetricians, called it the bane of their pregnant women patients, other scientists (biologists, botanists, physiologists) were equally ominous in their belief that pineapples contained strange and unknown chemical properties.

It was therefore left to a literary man, who was a physician as well as a novelist, to see the comic possibilities in all these prevailing theories. It may also be that Smollett, himself editing the obstetric volumes of William Smellie at the time he was composing his novel, saw that the fantastic (indeed absurd) theories of the mother's imagination together with the many muddles and mysteries that had grown up about pineapples could be wedded into one episode. The early chapters of *Peregrine Pickle* illustrate once again how adeptly Smollett used science, particularly medical learning, for the purposes of wit.[52] His satiric portraitures of characters such as Mrs. Pickle, Mrs. Grizzle, and Mrs. Trunnion place great demands on the modern reader who wishes to comprehend the author's powerful wit. But his contemporary readers would have felt much more at home than we do in viewing his comic spectacle: they would have realized that he was using medical and scientific learning for pure levity and genial farce, and in this sense would have read his works as they were reading those of his great contemporary, Laurence Sterne.

We should not be surprised to observe a process of carry-over in Smollett's novels: from his medical writings to the novels and vice-versa. Although he was never a successful physician, if daily practice is a yardstick of measurement, his entire life demonstrates a continuing interest in medical theory. It is, therefore, to be expected that Smollett's medical works—short essays, unsigned medical tracts written pseudonymously for financial purposes,[53] and

52. I have borrowed this phrase from the excellent article of D. W. Jefferson, *"Tristram Shandy* and the Tradition of Learned Wit," *Essays in Criticism,* Vol. I (1951), pp. 225–48.
53. Some of these have recently been studied and attributed to Smollett by

virtually all the reviews of medical books in the *Critical Review* 1756–60 and possibly later—would have rubbed off on his fiction. Indeed, the sensibility pervading both worlds, medical and fictive, was one, and Smollett was at their center. Such interaction serves to remind us, that the place occupied by medicine and by the social aspects of that science which daily seemed to take on ever greater consequence in the eighteenth century, is something of which we have yet to take account in our criticism and biography of Smollett.

G. S. Rousseau, "Matt Bramble and the Sulphur Controversy in the XVIIIth Century: Medical Background of *Humphry Clinker,*" *Journal of the History of Ideas,* XXVIII (1967), 577–90.

Smollett's Picaresque Games

PHILIP STEVICK

I

THE critical apparatus used to examine picaresque fiction tends to carry us away from a consideration of the picaresque event. The word "episodic," for example, focuses critical attention upon structure; and it is ironically true that when one pays particular attention to episodic structure, one is apt to pay rather little attention to the episodes themselves; or the critic who analyzes the philosophical area indicated by such words as "determinism," "necessity," "choice," "chance," "fortune," "contingency," "luck" may illuminate the world view of picaresque fiction while running the risk of taking for granted the precise structure of those characteristic events upon which that world view is predicated. By using the word "picaresque" at all, we are naming a class of works by pointing to an agent; implicitly we are pointing to the acts the agent does, which we assume to show a remarkable consistency from work to work. We are handicapped by the difficulty of rendering "picaro" into English. If we call him a "rogue," then what he does is indulge in "roguery," a word so effete that it is incredible that it has survived as long as it has in discussions of picaresque fiction. If we speak of the picaresque event as a "trick" or "prank," we both narrow and trivialize it. One word which avoids a number of semantic pitfalls while opening certain fresh ways of looking at the picaresque event is the word "game." The word is neutral of value and allows for any degree of frivolity or intensity, any degree of structural simplicity or complexity, and it allows us to hold together in our minds the ideas both of play and of the urgent relation to matters of survival which most picaresque events contain. It is, in fact, the special condition of picaresque fiction to have invested the game with all of the human tension which it can bear. Lazarillo de Tormes's indigent master, starving, picks his teeth. The picking of his teeth, in its social context, is a game. But there is no mistaking the fact that, as he is playing, he is really starving.

From our point of view in the twentieth century, Smollett appears to link the end of one tradition, the great tradition of classic picaresque, with the beginning of another tradition of related and derivative works, such as, in our century, *Felix Krull* and *Invisible Man*; and the common element of both groups, the one that leads up to Smollett and the one that leads away from him, is the interaction between a hero who is bright, quick, often naïve, and clever, and a society which is both powerful and cloddish, that interaction being a series of what we can loosely call games.[1] Those interactions are at once endlessly various, inventive, surprising *and* limited, constricted, and predictable. Such is the nature of games in or out of books, that they be open to chance or excitement yet constrained by rules and "fields." We do homage to the variety of game in any picaresque work not only by speaking as easily as we do of its inventiveness but also by continuing to read a series of events so basically similar and so potentially monotonous. What we need to do, the variety being apprehensible, is to describe, on the other hand, the continuities of picaresque game, its basic paradigms, for in works so loosely organized it is in the repetitive nature of the game that we perceive the unity of the compositions. Smollett's pivotal position, at the end of the classic picaresque tradition, as translator of Le Sage and assimilator of a

1. Every book on picaresque fiction I have seen defines its canon in somewhat different ways. But no one, to my knowledge, has ever excluded Smollett. By speaking of Smollett's place in relation to the tradition that precedes him and the one that follows him, I do not wish to imply that the precise shapes of these two traditions are not highly problematical. They are, of course. Robert Giddings's *The Tradition of Smollett* (London, 1967) attempts to connect Smollett with these two traditions, with uneven success. It is enough for my purposes that the readers share my assumption that Smollett's early work contains sufficient qualities in common with earlier indisputable exemplars of the genre, *Guzmán de Alfarache* say, so that it is legitimate to speak of Smollett's fiction as picaresque.

wide range of earlier works, and as a precursor of the abrasive absurdities of the neo-picaresque that follows him, guarantees his
ability to provide us with patterns of game not only peculiar to
himself but suggestive of the nature of the genre.

Midway through *Roderick Random*, an epidemic of fever
sweeps Roderick's ship. The climate is wretched, provisions are inadequate, and morale is low. The fever rages "with such violence,
that three-fourths of those whom it invaded died in a deplorable
manner; the colour of their skin being, by the extreme putrefaction of the juices, changed into that of soot." [2] Roderick soon contracts the fever, suffers deeply yet manages to survive, largely because he has been able to take a berth apart from the ship's hospital, in which the absence of ventilation would virtually have ensured his death. During Roderick's illness he is visited by a friend,
not by the ship's surgeon, who has no interest in him, and by the
ship's parson, with whom he disputes doctrinal matters with such
heat that his fever breaks and he is cured. Not knowing that he is
suddenly much better, his friend Morgan returns to his side and,
assuming him to be dead, groans, whines, and weeps, while Roderick, feigning death, stifles his own temptation to giggle. Morgan
finally closes Roderick's eyes and mouth, "upon which I suddenly
snapped at his fingers, and discomposed him so much, that he
started back, turned pale as ashes, and stared like the picture of
Horror. Although I could not help laughing at his appearance, I
was concerned for his situation, and stretched out my hand, telling him I hoped to live and eat some salmagundy of his making in
England." Recovered, Roderick uses his recovery as a reproach to
Morgan, whose remedies did not cure him, to the ship's doctor,
who in his indifference did not attend him, and to his rival, who
had wished him dead. Implicitly, his recovery mocks the parson,
who, in attempting to ease him into death, had cured him, and
the captain, whose mindless neglect of the ship's hospital would
have killed Roderick if he had not been able to subvert the captain's discipline.

The gulf that separates Roderick's game from such classic games
as chess or such literary games as Holmes's outwitting of Moriarty
is enormous. Take the question of choice, for example. Roderick

2. *Roderick Random*, I, p. 265.

does not self-consciously choose to dispute with the parson or to pretend, with Morgan, that he is dead in the way in which one "makes moves" in chess. There are no alternatives to anything he does, either in his own mind or in ours. There is no particular play of consequences, nor are there any rewards. Tricking Morgan is not, in any sense, winning, and had Morgan seen through his game, Roderick would not have lost. Roderick's game would be of no interest to the fashioners of those chaste mathematical formulae called game theory, which might not surprise us, but there is a basic sense in which Roderick's game would be incompatible also with the classic socio-cultural theories of game, namely, those of Huizinga and Caillois,[3] which should surprise us. For to Huizinga and Caillois, game, however central to culture, is defined nonetheless by its discrete separability from the useful and the serious, play being, by definition, gratuitous and non-serious; in Huizinga's word, "fun." In Roderick's game, the snapping at Morgan's fingers is inseparable from the almost dying, the exposure of the fraudulence of the ship's parson, the reality of the fever, the callousness of the captain, and so on. Unlike those moments in experience when we stop being productive and lay out the chess board, Roderick plays at the grimmest business life affords, staying alive in the face of substantial odds, and for him there is no separation between play and seriousness, no dialectic between them, but they are, in fact, identical.

Still, Caillois's categories of game can carry us toward a defini-

---

3. Other theories of game, such as the mathematical and the psychological, have their own histories; but the serious socio-cultural treatment of game and play begins with J. Huizinga's *Homo Ludens: A Study of the Play-Element in Culture* (Boston, 1955). Roger Caillois's *Man, Play, and Games,* trans. Meyer Barash (New York, 1961), acknowledges its indebtedness to Huizinga at every point; but Caillois seeks to amend the historical orientation of Huizinga by working from a background rather more anthropological than historical and he further seeks to formulate a set of definitions and categories more rigorous than Huizinga's. *Yale French Studies,* XLI (Fall 1968), begins with the sentence "The time has come to treat play seriously." How seriously, the articles of that issue of *Yale French Studies* demonstrate: they provide the only really substantial reference for those who would wish to see what recent criticism has been able to do with the classic concepts of game and play. It is largely from the example of the editor of that issue, Jacques Ehrmann, in his own article entitled "Homo Ludens Revisited," that I have presumed both to build upon and to differ from Huizinga and Caillois.

tion of the precise nature of Roderick's game, a game, or complex of games, representative of large areas of Smollett's fiction and central to Smollett's purposes. Caillois divides game into four types: [4] *agon*, the contest (such as fencing or chess) in which the outcome depends upon superior strength, or tactic, or skill; *alea*, the game (such as dice or roulette) in which the decision is the result of chance; *mimicry*, the free improvisatory expression of the impulse to imitate; and *ilinx*, the pursuit of vertigo (as in skiing or auto racing), a deliberate attempt to confuse momentarily the stability of perception. We are accustomed, of course, to thinking of *agon* as the predominant form of picaresque game, in Smollett the perpetual result of humiliation and revenge, provocation and response, challenge and defense; the act of revenge or defense being a contest decided by superior cleverness. In the game I have cited, the *agon* is diffuse, with several antagonists, no clear conflict, and with a group of minor triumphs rather than a decision. Also elements of the other three games appear: Roderick's recovery depends heavily on chance, Caillois's *alea*, for example; and the entire action is performed under the disorientation of fever, suggesting Caillois's *ilinx*, a quality that can remind us of all the rolling eyes, the near swoons, and the drunken reeling about that accompanies so much action in Smollett. Taking for granted the fact, then, that every form in Smollett is apt to be diffuse and every category which one may reasonably apply to Smollett's fiction is apt to be cluttered by the simultaneous presence of a number of other categories, it is still possible to describe Roderick's game. It is as a combination of *agon* and *mimicry* that that game, and the typical game elsewhere in Smollett's picaresque fiction,[5] can best

4. *Man, Play, and Games*, pp. 14–23.
5. By "elsewhere in Smollett's picaresque fiction," I mean in *Roderick Random* and *Peregrine Pickle*. Robert Donald Spector's *Tobias George Smollett* (New York, 1968) seems to me an interesting attempt to make sense of the Smollett canon as a unified whole. But is it not procrustean in its insistence that *all* the fiction is picaresque? For example, Spector describes Matt Bramble as "a picaro in the sense that Smollett uses him as an observer of society and that his observations are carried on as a result of the typical picaresque journey device" (p. 130), a use of literary category that strikes me as being imprecise and unpersuasive. I find neither *Sir Launcelot Greaves* nor *Humphry Clinker* picaresque and have not treated them. *Ferdinand Count Fathom* is a difficult case, for its first two-thirds are as picaresque as the earlier two novels. Yet

be described; *mimicry* superimposed upon *agon*. The *agon* between Roderick and the captain, the doctor, and the parson is that classic picaresque struggle between the brighter, quicker, more clever picaro and institutional power. We know that Roderick, like every other picaro, will gain temporary victories but no substantial change. The captain will go on being tyrannical, the surgeon indifferent, and the parson full of casuistry. It is the triumph of Roderick to survive, *agon* by *agon*, against such institutional stupidity. But it is *not* enough, after all, to survive. In the act of surviving, which is, in itself, a game, Roderick plays at another game only tangentially related to survival. It is as if a chess player, in the act of winning a game of chess, were to occupy himself between moves by mugging, grimacing, and mocking the gestures of his opponent. If we remind ourselves, however, that Roderick's is no chess game but a grim business carried out in a cruel, repressive world in which no victory is more than temporary, the function of Roderick's *mimicry* becomes clear. Roderick plays his *agons* to stay alive; he mimics to *be* alive. And in the free invention of his *mimicry*, he transcends his cloddish antagonists, his limitations of choice, and his brutal world.

II

The shape of the picaresque event is determined to a large extent by its nature as a game. Or rather, in the case of Smollett, the shape of the event is determined by the somewhat discordant

---

the nature of its games is quite different from what I take to be the norm in *Roderick Random* and *Peregrine Pickle* and thus I have rather arbitrarily excluded it from consideration. Note the phrases, for example, that are used by Smollett to characterize the element of *mimicry* in one of Fathom's *agons:* "Fathom acted a very expressive pantomime"; "he began to act the part of a very importunate lover"; "he mimicked that compassion and benevolence which his heart had never felt"; "For by this time he had artfully concentrated and kindled up all the inflammable ingredients of her constitution." (*Ferdinand Count Fathom,* I, pp. 200–204). Here the *mimicry*, rather than being the free invention that Caillois defines and Roderick exhibits, is vicious, pragmatic, opportunistic, very much in the service of Fathom's agonistic ends. Fathom's monotonous and cynical feigning is a very different kind of game from Roderick's and I have chosen not to try to include it in my analysis.

nature of its games, especially Smollett's peculiar combination of *agon* and *mimicry*. Of all of Caillois's categories, *agon* is apt to strike one as the most thoroughly circumscribed by rules. Any number of *agons*, for example, require a disinterested party, an umpire or a referee, for the express purpose of administering rules. Such *agons* as chess and fencing have vast protocols and elaborate lore accumulated around them. And even such crude agonistic confrontations as Indian wrestling still inevitably carry with them the obligation that they be conducted in some kind of mutually acceptable form. *Mimicry*, on the other hand, exhibits all of the characteristics shared by other forms of play, as Caillois points out, with one exception: that it is free of rules. It consists of incessant invention. Other pairs of Caillois's categories fit more easily and naturally together than do *agon* and *mimicry*, *agon* and *alea*, for example: it is easy to think of any number of games containing significant elements both of skill and chance. But *agon* and *mimicry* in certain ways pull the participant, and of course the writer as well, in opposite directions. And it is a special triumph of Smollett's art that he is able to reconcile the claims of two such different play impulses, the first tending toward symmetry, regularity, and ultimately, tedium, the other tending toward freedom, spontaneity, and, ultimately, incoherence.

The combination of the two is contained with particular purity in chapter li of *Peregrine Pickle*. Pickle and a certain Knight of Malta, having seen a performance of *Le Cid* by Corneille, argue over the comparative merits of the French and English stages.

Our hero, like a good Englishman, made no scruple of giving the preference to the performers of his own country, who, he alleged, obeyed the genuine impulses of nature, in exhibiting the passions of the human mind; and entered so warmly into the spirit of their several parts, that they often fancied themselves the very heroes they represented; whereas the action of the Parisian players, even in their most interesting characters, was generally such an extravagance in voice and gesture, as is nowhere to be observed but on the stage. To illustrate this assertion, he availed himself of his talent, and mimicked the manner and voice of all the principal performers, male and female, belonging to the French comedy, to the admiration of the chevalier, who, having complimented him upon this surprising modulation, begged leave to dissent in some particulars from the opinion he had avowed.[6]

Presently the argument resumes, although the responses of Pickle tend to be overwhelmed by the learning, the pseudo-learning, and the verbosity of the knight. The *mimicry* of Pickle does not substantially alter the shape of the event, which follows an agonistic logic of challenge and response; the conventions of the *agon* are those of the debate, respect for evidence, rhythm between the generalization and the supporting instance, certain features of a public, oratorical rhetoric. But the position of the *mimicry* allows it to dominate the event; and the values which the *mimicry* carries alter every value that follows.

Those values can be roughed out with such words as "energy," "spontaneity," "élan"; unlike the learning of the knight, which is made to seem self-congratulatory, pedantic, and quite forced, the *mimicry* of Pickle is made to seem uncontrived and "natural." M. A. Goldberg has analyzed Smollett's novels by positing a correspondence between their thematic structure and the ideas of the Scottish common-sense philosophers.[7] Certainly the antitheses which Goldberg finds—reason and passion, imagination and judgment, art and nature, social- and self-love, primitivism and progress—are at play in Smollett's works; and there is no doubt that such antitheses are sufficiently stylized and intellectualized that it is defensible to describe the novels' value structures with the aid of "ideas" found outside of the novels, in philosophy. But in Smollett's novels, like anybody else's, there are values and values. What I mean by the values of the *mimicry* of Pickle as opposed to those of the pompous knight is a good deal more sub-intellectual, or supra-intellectual, than the large thematic patterns which Goldberg finds with the aid of Scottish common sense. In the long run, Pickle may come to be the embodiment, one may feel, of passion, or imagination, or nature. In the short run, it doesn't matter. What does matter is that he is alive.

More than his vitality, Pickle's *mimicry* has a dimension that draws its power from the attribution to it of supernatural qualities.

6. *Peregrine Pickle,* II, p. 120.
7. *Smollett and the Scottish School* (Albuquerque, 1959).

His *mimicry*, that is, seems at once perfectly explainable and also magical. Smollett's world is full of people who seem to be what they are not, but Pickle is one person who can transform himself before our eyes into someone else without compromising his integrity of self. And although Smollett does not render the mimicry with any amplitude, it is certainly his intention (note the diction: "male and female," "admiration of the chevalier," "this surprising modulation") to make Pickle's performance seem an extraordinary presentation, virtuoso, unaccountable, unique, and in its way magical.

Such *mimicry* as Pickle's, moreover, acts as the concrete representation of the picaro's nerviness, his cockiness, his colossal gall. Erving Goffman has chosen to take seriously the idea of "the action" as it is contained in that cant phrase "where the action is." "Action," as he defines it, "is to be found wherever the individual knowingly takes consequential chances perceived as avoidable." [8] Given characters so imprudent as Roderick Random and Peregrine Pickle, every *agon* is *un*avoidable. They are bound to suffer humiliation, bound to burn for revenge, bound to be provoked, bound to fight. I have argued that their *mimicry* is a necessary mode of their continued self-assertion. But in any ordinary causal sense, their *mimicry*, unlike their *agons*, is avoidable, perceived as such by the reader and, insofar as we can infer their mental states, perceived as such by the characters. Their *mimicry* is a kind of chance-taking, always likely to expose them to additional hostility, always likely to fail in its effects, exposing them to still more ridicule. And the consequences of such *mimicry* may very well be, and often are, triumph and increased confidence, or, on the other hand, embarrassment, futility, a punch in the nose. The mimicry of Smollett's picaros is a splendid instance of Goffman's "action." And to see it as such is to see a linkage between Smollett's picaros and those driven characters of Goffman's essay, the gamblers, the hustlers, the vandals, the criminals, the professional athletes, the skydivers, the mountain climbers, for whom the events of routine experience are not enough and for whom the artificial production of an additional series of events with their own very real peril becomes a personal necessity.

8. *Interaction Ritual* (Garden City, N.Y., 1967), pp. 149–69.

Judged by the agonistic rules that govern the debate between Pickle and the chevalier, the latter wins, easily and decisively. But judged by the complex of values contained in Pickle's *mimicry*, the chevalier's victory is a hollow one. The *mimicry* is a small part of the total episode. But its function as a correlative for the high spirits of the hero and as a conveyor of those of his values which we are certainly expected to endorse make the *mimicry* far more important than its apparent prominence would lead us to believe. Not all *mimicry*, to be sure, is performed by Smollett's picaros. In chapter xlvi of *Roderick Random*, for example, Roderick's new acquaintance Ranter mimicks Roderick's "air, features, and voice." Somewhat later, he makes an elaborate series of mock representations to Roderick's companion Wagtail, who becomes, as the chapter continues, the butt of several others' mimetic ingenuity. Roderick, throughout the chapter, is either victim or spectator, never the chief mime. Yet even though the personages change about, the values attached to certain actions remain substantially the same. People who play at identity are always distinct from people who assume a false identity for self-serving purposes. And the person who plays at identity is likely to be, however morally reprehensible, an interesting person, vital and alive.

Pickle and Pallet at one point in their travels approach Antwerp and the city, being the birthplace of Rubens, reminds Pallet of his idol.

He swore . . . that he already considered himself a native of Antwerp, being so intimately acquainted with their so justly boasted citizen, from whom, at certain junctures, he could not help believing himself derived, because his own pencil adopted the manner of that great man with surprising facility, and his face wanted nothing but a pair of whiskers and a beard to exhibit the express image of the Fleming's countenance. He told them he was so proud of this resemblance, that, in order to render it more striking, he had, at one time of his life, resolved to keep his face sacred from the razor; and in that purpose had persevered, notwithstanding the continual reprehensions of Mrs. Pallet, who, being then with child, said, his aspect was so hideous, that she dreaded a miscarriage every hour, until she threatened, in plain terms, to dispute the sanity of his intellects, and apply to the chancellor for a committee.[9]

9. *Peregrine Pickle,* II, pp. 187–88.

Pallet's *mimicry* becomes the subject of the chapter. More is made of Pallet's imagined resemblance to Rubens. Ultimately he travels to the tomb of Rubens where he falls onto his knees in apparent adoration, to the considerable dismay of those at the church. Here is an example of *mimicry* which is patently ludicrous from start to finish. The most obvious reason that Pallet's *mimicry* is ludicrous is that he is no descendant of Rubens in any sense but is rather an unmitigated fraud, a terrible painter, and the butt of some of Smollett's coarsest humor. But the other reason is that he does not play. His *mimicry* is not his way of expressing his vitality, as it is with Roderick or Ranter; it is his pathetically serious way of seeking to express his own self-image, an assertion of appearance as if it represented essence. *Mimicry* which is not play comes close to the pathological.

The *mimicry* in Smollett's version of picaresque, then, is the chief conveyer of a complicated set of values: energy, vitality, quickness of invention, joy, and, more than all of these, a kind of personal stability, integrity, and authenticity. In a kind of fiction in which every character is more or less flat and every analysis is more or less perfunctory, the way we know who the characters are and the way we know that they have real human substance is through their modes of play. The bare structure, on the other hand, the rhythm and movement of the novel is provided by its successive *agons*. There are events in Smollett that are more or less pure *agon,* more or less pure *mimicry,* or neither, being perhaps melodramatic vignette without anything of the game about them. But ordinarily *mimicry* and *agon* interact in a fairly limited number of ways and these can first be set forth by returning to the pattern of Pickle's theatrical *mimicry*.

Pickle's theatrical *mimicry* precedes the main substance of the *agon,* and as the *agon* continues, Pickle does not return again to his *mimicry*. The *mimicry,* occurring at the beginning of the episode, provides Pickle with a means for "winning," at least in the eyes of the reader, for no amount of dialectical skill can really triumph over so splendid a mimetic talent. In the episode cited earlier, Roderick Random *mimics,* plays dead, at the end of the episode. He had already "won" against the captain, the parson, the disease itself, and his *mimicry* is a kind of triumphant foolishness, a parting shot not really at Morgan so much as at life itself. A third option allows Smollett to integrate the two, so that a character uses his *mimicry* as an agonistic tactic, playing back and forth between his strength and skill on the one hand and his mocking and posturing on the other. The use of *mimicry* at the beginning of an *agon*, as a kind of value base, the use of *mimicry* at the end of an *agon* as a self-defining gesture, and the integration of *mimicry* and *agon*, Stephen Potter fashion—these are the three basic structures of countless events in Smollett. And limited though these basic paradigms may be, individual instances are capable of demonstrating large dimensions of subtlety and considerable areas of aesthetic choice.

Chapter xlv of *Roderick Random* is rich and diverse enough to demonstrate a number of such choices. After the usual preliminary episodic business of settling into a location, Roderick goes to a playhouse "where I saw a good deal of company, and was vain enough to believe that I was observed with an uncommon degree of attention and applause." Imagining himself to be the center of so much admiration, Roderick

rose and sat down, covered and uncovered my head twenty times between the acts; pulled out my watch, clapped it to my ear, wound it up, set it, gave it the hearing again; displayed my snuff-box, affected to take snuff, that I might have an opportunity of showing my brilliant, and wiped my nose with a perfumed handkerchief; then dangled my cane, and adjusted my sword-knot, and acted many more fooleries of the same kind, in hopes of obtaining the character of a pretty fellow, in the acquiring of which I found two considerable obstructions in my disposition, namely, a natural reserve, and jealous sensibility.[10]

As a base for the play of values that is to follow, such *mimicry* is superb, showing, as it does, Roderick's vitality, his passionate wish to define and assert himself together with the gaucherie and the naïveté that makes it all ridiculous and, above all, the honesty toward himself, the insight into his own ridiculousness, the "natural reserve" that makes the passage rather touching to read, and, incidentally, one of the less picaresque events of the novel. As the

10. *Roderick Random*, II, p. 72.

play proceeds, Roderick is moved by the plight of the heroine and shares her tears, although he notices that no one else is similarly moved. And once again, Smollett has it both ways: Roderick's identification with the tragic situation on the stage is amusing and naïve; yet his susceptibility to the heroine's distress is very much related to his ability to mime—both depend upon an implicit *Einfühlung,* a rich responsiveness to the imagination of what it means to be someone else—and thus Roderick is not only more ridiculous, he is also more admirable, more interesting, more fully human than all of those facile and self-controlled popinjays who surround him in the boxes of the playhouse.

After the play is finished, Roderick encounters an attractive woman and persuades her to accompany him to a tavern. Roderick learns that she is a whore, but as he discovers this, he and the woman exchange tactic and move, precisely that kind of game I have described in which the agonistic structure is integrated with a continuing play of *mimicry.* The episode of the playhouse whore is followed by several pages of coffee house conversation on that most typical of Smollett's subjects, the merits of the English versus the merits of the French. There is, throughout the conversation, much agonistic maneuvering, much bluster and pretense, much *mimicry,* although Roderick himself observes more than he participates. Ultimately the chapter works toward its last event, in which Roderick and an acquaintance argue over points of Latin grammar and diction, finally conversing "a full two hours, on a variety of subjects" in Latin. In one sense, the ultimate *mimicry* consists of an utterly persuasive representation of another person. But in another quite legitimate sense, the ultimate *mimicry* consists of the sustained conversation (not merely schoolboy disputation) in another language, that language being the product of a culture detached from oneself by several centuries.

It is hard to imagine any system of analytical concepts being brought to bear on that chapter. It is harder still to imagine any critic who judges fiction according to its apparent structural control finding the chapter to be anything but a dismal failure, a sequence of some four main encounters without thematic unity and without even causal necessity. Yet it is a richly expressive chapter and is by no means so disunified as it may seem. For playing across every *agon* is an intermittent, quite unpredictable, but closely related series of *mimicries*, containing Roderick at the center and Roderick at the periphery, presenting Roderick, at the end of the chapter, as mimetic virtuoso and Roderick, at the beginning of the chapter, as mimetic fool. To see only the structure of the successive *agons* is to understand the chapter's events at their crudest level. To see *agon* and *mimicry* interrelated, on the other hand, is to understand the events as closely though not sequentially related vehicles for the arrogance and effrontery, the imagination and ingenuity, the energy and vitality, which is the particular source of power in Smollett's version of picaresque.

III

All picaresque novels show face-to-face relations with emphasis upon dissembling, fraud, disguise, and trickery. And to that extent all picaros are skilled mimes. Yet for Defoe's Roxana, to choose a contrast close to Smollett, such dissembling consists of assuming names not her own, wearing clothing that disguises her class or nationality or identity, suppressing her emotions, lying with a straight face. Nothing that she does, however, is comparable to the splendidly exuberant *mimicry* of Smollett's heroes. Smollett's picaros are not typical of their kind, and the difference lies, as A. A. Parker has pointed out, in the basic goodness of their impulses,[11] a difference that has more than a little to do with their modes of play. "Good" and "bad" are not very relevant categories when applied to the worlds of *Lazarillo de Tormes* or *La Vida del buscón*. In an absolute sense, everybody is bad, the picaro among them. But in Smollett, however fallible or even sometimes cruel his picaros may be, they are generally enraged by evil, compassionate toward the oppressed, honest in the long run if not the short, basically decent. Indeed, Parker maintains that *Roderick Random* is not picaresque at all since it is the world that is wicked in contrast to the hero, who is very far from that "delinquency" which Parker finds common to picaros within the European tradition.

11. *Literature and the Delinquent: The Picaresque Novel in Spain and Europe, 1599–1753* (Edinburgh, 1967), p. 127.

Up to this point I have stressed the expressive value of *mimicry* in making concrete the vitality of Smollett's picaros. Insofar as they tend to be distinguishable from other picaros by their comparative goodness, it is appropriate to ask whether their *mimicry* is not merely a function of their vitality but also of their goodness. As a kind of coda to the present discussion, I wish to suggest that it is. Their games, taken together, contain examples of gratuitous malice, insignificant foolishness along with many *agons* in which their antagonists are unmistakably evil. The point is that even when their games are least ostensibly moral, we never forget that they are basically decent, capable of compassion and remorse. Above all, we never forget the controlling values of Smollett, who hated sham and exploitation with an uncompromising fierceness. Thus I mean to suggest that there is a special resonance in Smollett's picaresque games that is the result of the fact that they exist in relation to the implied limits of certain ethical imperatives.

Neither the historical richness of Huizinga's *Homo Ludens* nor the anthropological richness of Caillois's *Man, Play, and Games* suggests that play has had, and certainly had in the eighteenth century, an ethical dimension. In fact both Huizinga and Caillois, by stressing the gratuitousness of play, implicitly deny its ethical dimension. Caillois further discusses certain tendencies which overtake the play impulse, debasing it, and the idea of measuring play by ethical criteria would certainly be one such. Caillois is perfectly right: if we play because it is "good for us," we *are* debasing the play impulse. And Huizinga is also right: the extraordinary evidences of the play impulse in culture *haven't* anything to do with moral worth. Yet if we shift our perspective somewhat, we are easily enough persuaded that certain kinds of play are vicious and exploitative, hence "bad" or other forms of play are intolerably coarse, dehumanizing, in some other sense, "bad." What kind of games does a good man play? If we didn't think so anyhow, Smollett would demonstrate for us that the question is absurd, that almost any kind of play is possible without compromising one's basic goodness. Yet other fictional settings can as easily demonstrate that play has consequences that cannot finally be separated from the moral world in which it occurs: the manipulative and mendacious games in Samuel Butler's novels, for example, or those games in Evelyn Waugh's that succeed in trivializing the whole of life.

Hugo Rahner has undertaken a study of play, theological in its orientation, which begins by assembling a number of ancient valuations of play: Plato and Plotinus, Tertullian and Origen, Aristotle and Augustine, and above all Aquinas.[12] What emerges from Rahner's study is a synthesis of certain pagan and Christian views of play in history and a remarkable meditation on God at play in the creative act. From the *Nicomachean Ethics* of Aristotle and later from early patristic writings, Rahner revives the ethical concept of "eutrapelia." The "eutrapelos," as Rahner summarizes Aristotle, is the man whose fondness for the playful exists in balance and harmony with his valuation for the serious. "This person," writes Rahner,

stands between two extremes, the description of which is particularly important as showing how Aristotelian ethics emerged from the cult and politics of the city-state—a description which Aquinas later took over. The one extreme is the "bomolochos," the poor wretch who hung about the altar of sacrifice in the hope of snatching or begging an odd bit of meat; in a broader sense, one who was ready to make jokes at every turn for the sake of a good meal and himself to be made the butt of cheap gibes. The opposite extreme was the "agroikos," the "boor," whose coarse stiffness was despised by the "asteios," the highly cultured Athenian citizen.[13]

The means by which Rahner shows the transition of this Aristotelian grace and balance into Christian thought is less important for our purposes than the fact that such a transition does exist, that there is a long, impressive continuity in ethical thought, both Christian and non-Christian, which values play while recognizing the ethical perils in its excess.

Even if it could be demonstrated—which it cannot—that Smollett knew and loved the tenth book of the *Nicomachean Ethics*, that would not, I think, establish very much about the values of his fiction. Rahner's treatment does not at all provide the material

12. *Man at Play,* trans. Brian Battershaw and Edward Quinn (London, 1965).
13. *Man at Play,* pp. 93–94.

for a possible "source." What it does provide is the idea that "eutrapelia," in one form or another, is a fairly constant virtue in ethical thought, that it is based so firmly in the cultural patterns of the West that it appears in philosophical writers of widely varying temperaments and world views. To put the matter another way, Rahner's treatment both codifies and confers great dignity upon an idea that is accessible to the common moral sensibilities of great numbers of people who have not read Aristotle and Aquinas. The general accessibility of the idea becomes especially apparent in the eighteenth century since the modes of play in the period are often highly developed and the introspective records of individual people in the period, their letters, journals, and private papers, tend often to be preserved and often to be extraordinarily honest and perceptive. There is scarcely a figure of consequence in literary eighteenth-century England who did not strive daily for "eutrapelia"; we are aware of the importance of the play impulse because it carries over into literature of the first rank more often than in other periods and we are aware of the efforts to keep such play impulses in balance because writers like Boswell tell us how difficult it is. And, as such writers in the eighteenth century make clear, striving for "eutrapelia" comes not merely out of social constraint but out of an implicit conviction of the union of play and ethics.

Of Smollett himself, no reader of the Noyes edition of the letters can fail to have been moved by the last letters in the collection. After the countless personal assaults and defenses, the literary wars, the ills real and imagined of the preceding pages, Smollett prepares to die and describes himself in a letter to Dr. John Hunter which is at once self-deprecatory and dignified, tough and affectionate, stoic and playful.

With respect to myself, I have nothing to say, but that if I can prevail upon my wife to execute my last will, you shall receive my poor carcase in a box, after I am dead, to be placed among your rarities. I am already so dry and emaciated, that I may pass for an Egyptian mummy, without any other preparation than some pitch and painted linen. . . .[14]

14. *The Letters of Tobias Smollett, M.D.*, ed. Edward S. Noyes (Cambridge, Mass., 1926), pp. 108–9.

The last letter of the collection is only a fragment, undated but evidently written before Smollett's daughter died in 1763.

Many a time I do stop my task and betake me to a game of romps with Betty, while my wife looks on smiling and longing in her heart to join in the sport; then back to the cursed round of duty.[15]

The easiest way to state the most widely held ethical ideal in the eighteenth century is to invoke the phrase that the eighteenth century often invoked itself, "to live well and to die well." The phrase can mean all things to all men, but to Smollett it meant the coexistence of wit and compassion, of "duty," as he puts it himself, and "romps."

Consider, then, the examples of *mimicry* I have cited as being characteristic of Smollett's picaros. In the first he tricks his best friend, who had thought him dead, but no sooner does he trick him than he is struck with remorse. Although it is proper for Roderick to celebrate his being alive and understandable that he should mock the muddle-headed solicitousness of Morgan, it all becomes, in the act, very close to vicious buffoonery: Roderick soothes the shock of Morgan the moment he has realized the impact of his *mimicry*. Pickle imitates the actors of the French stage in his disputation with the Knight of Malta not only out of high spirits, not only out of a sense of contest and a knowledge of his own mimetic talent, but out of an implied impulse toward balance in play. Roderick checks his own *mimicry* at the playhouse precisely out of his own insight that he has been excessive and foolish. As Smollett's picaros always know, although they do not say it, to play badly is to become distorted and grotesque, to join that gallery of living caricatures that forms the human background of the novels.

Pickle's first recorded act, at age nine months, is to contrive an alarming expresssion of mock pain, apparently for the malicious joy of seeing his elders try to relieve him of some non-existent pin prick. His last recorded act is to spurn a visiting nobleman who had once behaved contemptuously toward him, by pretending that

15. *Ibid.* p. 110.

he is not Mr. Pickle at all. Despite his marriage and good fortune at the end no one would argue that he achieves "eutrapelia." There is scarcely a page of the novel (somewhat less so with Roderick Random), in which he is not boorish, coarse, or cruel. Yet it is also true that there is scarcely a page in either *Roderick Random* or *Peregrine Pickle* in which we are not aware of the judgment, either of Smollett or of the picaros themselves, that they are in danger of behaving boorishly, playing to excess. Of Pickle's infant mimicries, for example, we understand that he was treated with gratuitous cruelty in his infancy and that he has been surrounded by grotesques from his very birth; that he should play in a malicious manner is hardly surprising. Yet his games are "a peculiarity of disposition," described with ironic understatement at every point. And no one who reads of the anxiety that Smollett tells us his mock discomfort arouses in his mother is likely to find the infant Pickle's exploitation of her tenderness altogether amusing.

It would be a mistake, I think, to systematize the restraints that act upon the play of Smollett's picaros. Their guilt or embarrassment or remorse is always momentary, always highly specific; they improvise their moral response to experience. Smollett's narrative judgments of them are likely to be problematic, embedded in his rhetoric, every bit as *ad hoc* as their views of themselves, and just as unsystematic. The texture of Smollett's rhetoric, for example, is filled with man-beast images, which serve, among other things, to remind us of the sub-human possibilities that are always open to his human character, open, certainly, to his exuberantly mimetic picaros who are always in danger (to choose one of Smollett's own favorite beast metaphors) of becoming baboons. And the action of the novels is filled with reminders that the picaros, being skilled mimes, could lie, cheat, steal, and gamble so as to lay waste around them if they wished; but their play most often succeeds against the vain and the arrogant and they never become the vicious and indiscriminate confidence men which they have every native skill to become. In short, Smollett so constructed the characters of the picaros as to keep them in a perpetually unbalanced tension between their lust for game on the one hand and their moral constraint on the other.

Being comic characters set in the repetitive structure of episodic works, Smollett's picaros repeat certain paradigmatic events as the books proceed but they do not change. The unbalanced tension is never resolved. To the end, they are more aggressive than conciliatory. If we were ever persuaded that Roderick Random or Peregrine Pickle had achieved "eutrapelia," we would, I suspect, be disappointed. It is hard to imagine that their perfectly earnest wish for the good life, a life responsive to their own best judgment and their own sensitivity to the distress of others, should ever entirely temper their lust for *agon* and their delight in *mimicry*. They do not achieve "eutrapelia" not only because of the structure of the books in which they appear but because "eutrapelia" is a moral ideal difficult to attain. To play strenuously, ingeniously, and joyfully while keeping that play in a morally responsive balance with the whole of one's life, that is the possibility that lies behind Smollett's picaresque events. *Humphry Clinker* is, in a sense, a realization of such an ideal. But in the picaresque novels, "eutrapelia" is as difficult to achieve as Smollett knew it to be in actual experience.

The Two Worlds of *Ferdinand Count Fathom*

—◆—

T. O. TREADWELL

Two conflicting views of the function of the heroes of novels
may be seen to have been held by English writers and critics
throughout the 1750's. The principle that the purpose of fiction,
whether in prose or verse, is to imitate human nature, was un-
questioned, but as to the fidelity of imitation proper in the novel a
dispute arose. It was argued on the one hand that the novelist ought
to represent human nature as it is commonly observed in the world.
This may involve the depiction of "low" characters and actions,
but it will provide an accurate guide to the temptations and dangers likely to be encountered in the journey through life. William
Park has pointed to John Cleland's 1751 review of *Peregrine
Pickle*, which provides an excellent summary of this position: [1]

If we consider then in general, before we come to particular application, the true use of these writings [comic romances], it is more to be
lamented that we have so few of them, than that there are too many.
For as the matter of them is chiefly taken from nature, from adventures, real or imaginary, but familiar, practical, and probable to be met
with in the course of common life, they may serve as pilot's charts, or
maps of those parts of the world, which every one may chance to travel
through; and in this light they are public benefits. Whereas romances
and novels which turn upon characters out of nature, monsters of perfection, feats of chivalry, fairy-enchantments, and the whole train of

1. See William Park, "Change in the Criticism of the Novel after 1760,"
Philological Quarterly, XLVI (1967), 34, 35–36.

the marvellous-absurd, transport the reader unprofitably into the clouds, where he is sure to find no common footing, or into those wilds of fancy, which go for ever out of the way of all human paths.[2]

For those who share this view, the effectiveness of the novel as a "pilot's chart" allowed any sort of material, however "low," to be brought within its scope. Thus Ralph Griffiths can praise Cleland's own *Memoirs of Fanny Hill* as a morally improving work because it shows in their true light the pitfalls that await the unwary:

The author of *Fanny Hill* does not seem to have expressed any thing with a view to countenance the practice of any immoralities, but meerly to exhibit truth and nature to the world, and to lay open those mysteries of iniquity that, in our opinion, need only to be exposed to view, in order to their being abhorred and shunned by those who might otherwise unwarily fall into them. . . . Vice has indeed fair quarter allowed it; and after painting whatever charms it may pretend to boast, with the fairest impartiality, the supposed female author concludes with a lively declaration in favour of sobriety, temperance, and virtue.[3]

Cleland and Griffiths emphasize the didactic effectiveness of plot— the ability of the novelist to expose his characters to the snares set for virtue in the world, and by this means to warn his readers against them. Another group of novelists and critics were concerned with the potency of fictional characters—the creation by the novelist of models to be imitated. The clearest expression of this view is probably to be found in Samuel Johnson's fourth *Rambler* (1750):

Many writers, for the sake of following nature, so mingle good and bad qualities in their principal personages, that they are both equally con-

2. *Monthly Review*, IV (1751), 356–57. Cleland has been identified as the author of this review by Benjamin Christie Nangle in his *The Monthly Review: First Series, 1749–1789* (Oxford, 1934), p. 49.
3. *Monthly Review*, II (1749–50), 432. The fact that Griffiths was the publisher as well as the reviewer of Cleland's work may explain his praise of it, but his view of it as a "pilot's chart" novel is the interesting point of his remarks. *The Memoirs of Fanny Hill* is an abridgment, and to some extent an expurgation, of Cleland's *Memoirs of a Woman of Pleasure* (1748) which had also been published by Griffiths. See the Appendix to David Foxon's *Libertine Literature in England, 1660–1745* (London, 1964), pp. 52–63.

spicuous; and as we accompany them through their adventures with delight, and are led by degrees to interest ourselves in their favour, we lose the abhorrence of their faults, because they do not hinder our pleasure, or, perhaps, regard them with some kindness, for being united with so much merit. . . . In narratives, where historical veracity has no place, I cannot discover why there should not be exhibited the most perfect idea of virtue; of virtue not angelical, nor above probability, for what we cannot credit, we shall never imitate, but the highest and purest that humanity can reach, which, exercised in such trials as the various revolutions of things shall bring upon it, may, by conquering some calamities, and enduring others, teach us what we may hope, and what we can perform.[4]

Johnson's opinion was probably in Samuel Richardson's mind when, in "A Concluding note by the editor" appended to the last volume of *The History of Sir Charles Grandison* (1753–54), he admitted that, "Human Nature as it *is*," is indeed sometimes corrupt, but asked, "need pictures of this be held out in books?"[5]

The adoption of one or the other of these theories about the didactic aim of the novel has an obvious reflection in the final form of the work. If the novel is conceived as a chart for guiding the reader safely through the shoals and rapids of villainy, then it must clearly expose its heroes and heroines to as many of the assaults and temptations of the villainous as is consistent with probability. It will thus be episodic and geographically discursive, following its characters up and down the social scale as they are punished or rewarded for their conduct in the adventures through which they pass. If the novel sets out to exhibit a virtuous man or woman for the edification and imitation of its readers, its range will be deeper and less broad. Its ambience will be rather domestic than peripatetic, and it will develop through the interaction of a relatively small number of characters with one another, rather than through their reactions to the environments in which they find themselves. It is to these formal aspects of the two theories of the role of the novel that Johnson referred when, speaking of Fielding and Richardson, he distinguished between "characters of manners" and "characters of nature." "Characters of manners are very

4. *The Works of Samuel Johnson, Ll.D.* (Oxford, 1825), II, pp. 18, 19–20.
5. *The History of Sir Charles Grandison* (Oxford, Blackwell, 1931), VI, p. 329.

entertaining; but they are to be understood, by a more superficial observer, than characters of nature, where a man must dive into the recesses of the human heart." [6]

These differing views on the proper portrayal of human nature in the novel underlie the quarrel between the partisans of Richardson and Fielding which occupied the English novel-reading public throughout the middle years of the eighteenth century, and there can be little doubt that the publication of *Roderick Random* in 1748 placed Smollett squarely among the novelists who were seen to paint "Human Nature as it *is*." Martin Battestin has drawn attention to a pamphlet published in 1748 which, while highly praising *Joseph Andrews*, finds that *Random* too faithfully pictures the grosser aspects of human nature.[7] "There are many free Strokes that please, because they are true and agreeable to Nature; but some Truths are not to be told, and the most skilful Painters represent Nature with a Veil." [8] Catherine Talbot, in a letter to Elizabeth Carter dated 15 February 1748, speaks of "that strange book Roderick Random! It is a very strange and a very low one, though not without some characters in it, and I believe some very just, though very wretched descriptions." [9] Smollett had anticipated this sort of reaction from some of his readers, and he included in the Preface to *Random* a justification for the "mean scenes" in which his hero is engaged on the grounds that the "humours and passions" can be observed more clearly when they are "undisguised by affectation, ceremony, or education." [10] Roderick himself, although labeled by his creator an embodiment of "modest merit," [11] clearly does not represent the highest and purest

6. Boswell, *Life of Johnson*, ed. G. B. Hill, revised L. F. Powell (Oxford, 1934), II, p. 49.

7. Martin C. Battestin, "On the Contemporary Reputations of *Pamela, Joseph Andrews*, and *Roderick Random:* Remarks by an 'Oxford Scholar,' 1748," *N & Q*, CCXIII (1968), 450–52.

8. Quoted by Battestin, pp. 451–52. Compare Johnson's dictum in *Rambler* 4, "It is justly considered as the greatest excellency of art, to imitate nature; but it is necessary to distinguish those parts of nature, which are most proper for imitation." *Works*, II, p. 18.

9. *A Series of Letters between Mrs. Elizabeth Carter and Miss Catherine Talbot* (London, 1808), I, p. 166.

10. *The Adventures of Roderick Random*, I, x.

11. *Roderick Random*, I, ix.

form of virtue that humanity can reach. Still less so does the hero of *Peregrine Pickle* (1751), or the unfortunate Lady Vane, whose interpolated "Memoirs," as Howard S. Buck has shown,[12] attracted most of the attention which Smollett's second novel received. Summarizing the contemporary reaction to the first two novels, a student of the history of Smollett's reputation writes, "Thus at the very beginning we find two notes struck—Smollett's fidelity to life and his lowness—whose variations seem to have been inexhaustible."[13] That *Random* and *Pickle*, especially the former, were hugely popular is undeniable, but it is equally clear that they were seen to fall into that class of novels which dealt with human nature as it is rather than as it ought to be, and that they were condemned accordingly by those who took the other view of the responsibility of the novelist.[14]

Modern critics have tended to emphasize the essential similarity between the novels of Richardson and Fielding, and have pointed out that most ordinary readers throughout the latter half of the eighteenth century enjoyed reading the novels of both schools.[15] Nevertheless, it seems clear that, while *Tom Jones* and *Roderick Random* were very widely read, the weight of critical opinion inclined toward the Johnsonian, or Richardsonian, view of the novel.[16]

12. Howard Swazey Buck, *A Study in Smollett, Chiefly "Peregrine Pickle"* (New Haven, 1925), pp. 48–52.

13. Fred W. Boege, *Smollett's Reputation as a Novelist* (Princeton, 1947), p. 3.

14. For other contemporary instances of the association of Smollett with the school of Fielding, see Lady Mary Wortley Montagu, *Complete Letters*, ed. Robert Halsband (Oxford, 1965–67), III, pp. 9, 66; the quotation from the *Magazine of Magazines* for April 1751 in *Henry Fielding, the Critical Heritage*, ed. Ronald Paulson and Thomas Lockwood (London and New York, 1969), p. 271; and *An Essay on the New Species of Writing Founded by Mr. Fielding*, ed. Alan D. McKillop, Augustan Reprint Society Publication no. 95 (1962), pp. i–ii. It has recently been argued, not, in my view, very convincingly, that the novels of Smollett's middle period were written as a conscious attempt to imitate Fielding's technique. See Tuvia Bloch, "Smollett's Quest for Form," *Modern Philology*, LXV (1967), 103–13.

15. See, for example, William Park, "Fielding *and* Richardson," *P M L A*, LXXXI (1966), 381–88, and Alan D. McKillop, *Samuel Richardson, Printer and Novelist* (Hamden, Conn., 1960), pp. 230–31.

16. For evidence in support of this assertion, see Frederic T. Blanchard, *Fielding the Novelist* (New Haven, 1926), pp. 126–39.

It is in the context of this critical climate that the form and structure of Smollett's third novel, *The Adventures of Ferdinand Count Fathom*, must be approached, for it represents not so much a continuation or a mutation of the techniques established in the first two novels as it does a reaction to the criticism those novels had attracted. As a result, *Fathom* can be read as a unique, if not altogether successful, attempt to combine within one book the didactic techniques of the novel of manners and the novel of nature.[17] That Smollett had been stung by those critics who had dismissed *Random* and *Pickle* as "low" works may be inferred from the long and bitter apostrophe which he inserted into the first chapter of *Fathom:*

And here it will not be amiss to anticipate the remarks of the reader, who, in the chastity and excellency of his conception, may possibly exclaim, "Good Heaven! will these authors never reform their imaginations, and lift their ideas from the obscene objects of low life? Must the publick be again disgusted with the groveling adventures of a waggon? Will no writer of genius draw his pen in the vindication of taste, and entertain us with the agreeable characters, the dignified conversation, the poignant repartee, in short, the genteel comedy of the polite world?"

Have a little patience, gentle, delicate, sublime, critic; you, I doubt not, are one of those consummate connoisseurs, who in their purifications, let humour evaporate, while they endeavour to preserve decorum, and polish wit, until the edge of it is quite wore off; or, perhaps of that class, who, in the sapience of taste, are disgusted with those very flavours, in the productions of their own country, which have yielded infinite delectation to their faculties, when imported from another clime; and damn an author in despite of all precedent and prescription . . .

Yes, refined reader, we are hastening to that goal of perfection, where satire dares not shew her face; where nature is castigated, almost even

---

17. Johnson's terms are used as convenient shorthand descriptions of the two views of the novel summarized above. I am, of course, aware that they cannot be defended as serious characterizations of the novels of Fielding and Richardson, and that they express only one aspect of Johnson's views on this subject. For a convenient summary, see Robert E. Moore, "Dr. Johnson on Fielding and Richardson," *P M L A*, LXVI (March 1951), 161–81.

to still life; where humour turns changeling, and slavers in an insipid grin; where wit is volatilized into a meer vapour; where decency, divested of all substance, hovers about like a fantastic shadow; where the salt of genius, escaping, leaves nothing but pure and simple phlegm; and the inoffensive pen for ever drops the mild manna of soul-sweetning praise.[18]

These caustic and sarcastic effusions can be said, at least, to show the kind of criticism by which Smollett had been wounded, and the plan of *Fathom*, as outlined in the preface, can be seen to be consciously heroic in response to it. The plan is conceived, to begin with, in dramatic terms. Smollett justifies his use of a villainous protagonist by appealing to the precedents of Shakespeare's Richard III and Congreve's Maskwell, contrasting them with, "Almost all the heroes of this kind, who have hitherto succeeded on the English stage" (I, 4). Evil characters like Fathom, Smollett goes on to say, are didactically effective because the vision of their downfall and punishment arouses in the reader the impulse of fear, "which is the most violent and interesting of all the passions" (I, 4), and which is therefore obviously to be taken seriously (the serious tenor of the passage is reinforced by the echo of Aristotle in the idea). Opposed to the evil protagonist, and counterbalancing the fearful emotions which his fate is designed to provoke, is a hero figure, the embodiment of the virtues, whose function is to "amuse the fancy, engage the affection, and form a striking contrast which might heighten the expression, and give a *Relief* to the moral of the whole" (I, 5). A summary of the didactic motives underlying the novel concludes the Preface:

If I have not succeeded in my endeavours to unfold the mysteries of fraud, to instruct the ignorant, and entertain the vacant; if I have failed in my attempts to subject folly to ridicule, and vice to indignation; to rouse the spirit of mirth, wake the soul of compassion, and touch the secret springs that move the heart; I have at least, adorned virtue with honour and applause; branded iniquity with reproach and shame, and carefully avoided every hint or expression which could give umbrage to the most delicate readers. (I,5)

18. *The Adventures of Ferdinand Count Fathom*, I, pp. 10, 12.

Both moral techniques receive mention here. The novel fulfills the function of a pilot's chart or map in order to "unfold the mysteries of fraud," but the novelist intends also to "touch the secret springs that move the heart," to produce, that is, a novel of nature in Johnsonian terms. Since Smollett has chosen to make his protagonist a villain, and to balance him schematically with a virtuous deuteragonist, the two techniques which we have called those of manners and of nature will polarize themselves accordingly, the villain assuming by example the didactic function of warning the unwary against the artifices of his kind and instructing the ignorant in the way of the world, while the hero can be left to assume the role demanded by Johnson and Richardson, exhibiting "the most perfect idea of virtue" for the edification of the judicious. This polarization is, as we should expect, the principle upon which the novel is constructed. *Fathom* encompasses two fictional worlds, which correspond to the didactic functions which the two chief characters fulfill. At certain points in the story the two worlds touch each other, but the reconciliation of one with the other is morally impossible, given a fictional universe in which good must triumph and evil be punished. These two worlds within the novel are built around the figures of Fathom, the villain, and Renaldo, Count de Melvile, the hero, and they may conveniently be labeled the "world of satire" and the "world of romance."

I have called the fictional milieu in which Fathom's adventures take place "satiric" because the manner in which it fulfills its moral purpose corresponds approximately to the technique of satire, although satire itself is only one of the elements involved in it. This is the world in which Smollett endeavors "to unfold the mysteries of fraud, to instruct the ignorant, and entertain the vacant." It encompasses a good part of Europe, ranging up and down the social scale. It has a characteristic diction of its own, the chief element of which is irony. It is a public world, the characters who move within it functioning not as individuals but as members of society.

The world of romance within the novel contains characters who are either heroic and good from the start or who suffer heroically and learn goodness as a result. It is consequently equipped to provide models of good conduct for the reader to emulate. Like the satiric world, it is geographically far-ranging, but its scale is much narrower. It is a private world, and the few characters inhabiting it are drawn from society's upper ranks. The diction in which it is described is hyperbolical and ornate.

Fathom's particular kind of villainy, as M. A. Goldberg has pointed out,[19] owes less to Milton's Satan than to Hobbes and Mandeville; that is to say that his evil deeds are not self-generating and self-sufficient, but rely for their effectiveness on the cupidity and corruption of the society in which he moves. We learn of Fathom that:

He had formerly imagined, but was now fully persuaded, that the sons of men preyed upon one another, and such was the end and condition of their being. Among the principal figures of life, he observed few or no characters that did not bear a strong analogy to the savage tyrants of the wood. One resembled a tyger in fury and rapaciousness; a second prowled about like a hungry wolf, seeking whom he might devour; a third acted the part of a jackall, in beating the bush for game to his voracious employer; and a fourth imitated the wily fox, in practising a thousand crafty ambuscades for the destruction of the ignorant and and [sic] unwary. The last was the department of life for which he found himself best qualified, by nature and inclination, and he accordingly resolved that his talent should not rust in his possession. (I,57–58)

The more corrupt the society in which he finds himself, therefore, and the more ignorant its members, the more scope Fathom will have for the exercise of his capacities, and the society in which he is most successful, and which therefore becomes the hub of the satiric world within the novel, is England.

The idea of foreignism is crucial in *Fathom*, and the mindless contempt with which aliens are treated by Englishmen provokes an undercurrent of bitterness which runs throughout the novel, and which must have its source in Smollett's experience as a Scotsman in London.[20] That he felt himself to be an alien in En-

19. *Smollett and the Scottish School: Studies in Eighteenth-Century Thought* (Albuquerque, 1959), p. 91.
20. Resentment of the treatment of Scotsmen in England is a minor theme in *Roderick Random*. See especially I, chap. xiii.

gland, at least during his early years of residence there, can be inferred from *Fathom*, and is stated explicitly in a letter from Smollett to his friend Alexander Carlyle, written in 1753, the year in which *Fathom* was published:

I do not think I could enjoy life with greater relish in any part of the World than in Scotland among you and your friends . . . I am heartily tired of this land of indifference and phligm where the finer sensations of the soul are not felt, and felicity is held to consist in stupifying Port and overgrown buttocks of Beef—Where Genius is lost, learning undervalued, Taste altogether extinguished, and Ignorance prevail, to such a degree that one of our Chelsea club asked me if the Weather was good when I crossed the sea from Scotland, and another desired to know if there were not more Popes than One, in as much as he had heard people mention the Pope of Rome, an expression which seemed to imply that there was a Pope of some other place.[21]

The first English citizen to appear in *Fathom*, apart from Fathom's mother, a camp-follower who supplements her earnings by killing and robbing the wounded after a battle, is a visitor to Paris, and Smollett begins his description of him by emphasizing that his suspicious xenophobia is not a personal idiosyncrasy, but a national characteristic:

The baronet's disposition seemed to be cast in the true English mould. He was sour, silent and contemptuous; his very looks indicated a consciousness of superior wealth, and he never opened his mouth, except to make some dry, sarcastic, national reflection: nor was his behaviour free from that air of suspicion which a man puts on, when he believes himself in a croud of pickpockets whom his caution and vigilance set at defiance. (I,131)

The theme of English xenophobia is reintroduced when Fathom, having at length arrived in the land of his ancestors, boards the London stage-coach at Canterbury. His fellow passengers, "understanding the sixth seat was engaged by a foreigner, determined to profit by his ignorance," and, "with that politeness which is pecu-

21. Quoted in Lewis Mansfield Knapp, *Tobias Smollett, Doctor of Men and Manners* (Princeton, 1949), p. 115.

liar to this happy island" (I, 186), they make him the victim of a practical joke. The rude insularity of Englishmen is referred to most specifically by Fathom's accomplice, Ratchkali, the Tyrolese gamester. The passage is interesting because it emphasizes the inclusion of the Scots and Irish among those whom the English despise as "foreign." We are surely very close to Smollett's own experience here:

One would imagine, that nature had created the inhabitants, for the support and enjoyment of adventurers like you and me. Not that these islanders open the arms of hospitality to all foreigners without distinction: on the contrary, they inherit from their fathers, an unreasonable prejudice against all nations under the sun; and when an Englishman happens to quarrel with a stranger, the first term of reproach he uses, is the name of his antagonist's country, characterized by some opprobrious epithet; such as a chattering Frenchman, an Italian ape, a German hog, and a beastly Dutchman; nay, their national prepossession is maintained even against those people with whom they are united, under the same laws and government; for, nothing is more common than to hear them exclaim against their fellow-subjects, in the expressions of a beggarly Scot, and an impudent Irish bog-trotter. (I,207–8)

Ratchkali goes on to point out how this aspect of the English character can be turned to the confidence-man's advantage, the sense of national superiority thus undermining itself and so containing within itself the seeds of the satirist's revenge. That England is the chief goal and haven of the adventurers of Europe has been stressed throughout. It is, "the land of promise, flowing with milk and honey, and abounding with subjects on which [Fathom] knew his talents would be properly exercised . . . the Canaan of all able adventurers" (I, 110). The biblical parallel is repeated later in the volume when Fathom, from the harbor of Boulogne, "surveyed the neighbouring coast of England, with fond and longing eyes, like another Moses reconnoitring the land of Canaan from the top of mount Pisgah" (I, 183). Like Caesar, however, Fathom has difficulty getting ashore after his voyage. He slips while leaping out of the boat which has carried him ashore, and his hands, appropriately enough, are the first parts of him to touch this promised land. "Upon this occasion, he, in imitation of Scipio's behaviour on the cost [sic] of Afric, hailed the omen, and grasping an handful of the sand, was heard to exclaim in the Italian language, 'Ah ha, old England, I have thee fast' " (I, 184). Some of the qualities that render the English, as described by Ratchkali, the prime dupes of Europe are laudable ones: honesty makes them credulous, for example, and love of privacy keeps them from prying (I, 209), but these excellencies of character are not apparent in Fathom's experience as his career develops.

For England turns out to be somewhat different from the paradise of gullibility imagined by Fathom and described by the Tyrolese, and among her citizens are found the crafty and vicious as well as the credulous and simple. The English in *Fathom* are either fools or knaves, and the two qualities are united and summarized in the splendid figure of Sir Stentor Stile, one of the finest of Smollett's grotesques:

While [Fathom] thus enjoyed his pre-heminence, together with the fruits of success at play, which he managed so discreetly, as never to incur the reputation of an adventurer; he one day, chanced to be at the ordinary, when the company was surprised by the entrance of such a figure as had never appeared before in that place. This was no other than a person habited in the exact uniform of an English jockey. His leathern cap, cut bob, fustian frock, flannel waistcoat, buff breeches, hunting-boots and whip, were sufficient of themselves to furnish out a phaenomenon for the admiration of all Paris: but these peculiarities were rendered still more conspicuous by the behaviour of the man who owned them. When he crossed the threshold of the outward door, he produced such a sound from the smack of his whip, as equalled the explosion of an ordinary cohorn; and then broke forth into the hollow of a foxhunter, which he uttered with all its variations, in a strain of vociferation, that seemed to astonish and confound the whole assembly, to whom he introduced himself and his spaniel, by exclaiming in a tone something less melodious than the cry of mackarel or live cod, "By your leave, Gentlevolks, I hope there's no offence, in an honest plain Englishman's coming with money in his pocket, to taste a bit of your Vrench frigasee and ragooze." (I,143–44)

Sir Stentor is here clearly a representative of a stock eighteenth-century comic type, of which Squire Western before him and Tony Lumpkin afterwards are obvious other examples. But his raw bumptiousness is counterfeit, and he turns out to be a consummate sharper. He strips Fathom of all his money and effects, and is later seen, "dressed in the most fashionable manner, and behaving with all the overstrained politesse of a native Frenchman" (I, 153).

Nearly all the English people in *Fathom* partake of one or the other aspect of Sir Stentor's character. They are credulous fools, the dupes of their own pretensions, like the fashionable folk in London to whom Fathom sells worthless jewels and antiques (I, ch. xxxii), or the set of people who credit him with profound medical knowledge (I, ch. xxxv, and II, chs. l–liii), or else they are cunning villains, like Mr. and Mrs. Trapwell (II, ch. xxxvi), or the attorney whom Fathom hires to defend him when he is sued by Trapwell (II, chs. xxxvii–xxxviii), or Doctor Buffalo, the rich quack who effects Fathom's final ruin (II, chs. liv, lvi).

As the English people in *Fathom* are either fools or knaves,[22] so the foreigners, within the "romance" sections of the novel, are virtuous nearly without exception. What is more, the fact of their being foreign is frequently gratuitous in terms of the plot of the novel. After Fathom attempts to rape Monimia, the heroine, she is rescued by Madame Clement, a Frenchwoman living in London;[23] the moral balance requires that Monimia's savior be, like herself, an alien in England. Similarly, the doctor who tends Monimia throughout her illness, a minor character in terms of the plot, is described as, "a humane man, and a foreigner" (II, 106), qualities that, within the romance world of *Fathom*, are virtually synonymous. Madame Clement is, "a humane gentlewoman" (II, 101); the only man who will lend Renaldo the money he needs to travel to Vienna and claim his patrimony is Joshua Manasseh, a Jew, and therefore, by English law at the time, an alien.[24] The

22. For other anti-English passages in *Fathom*, all of them authorial interjections and irrelevant to the movement of the plot, see I, pp. 11–12; I, p. 43; I, p. 190; and II, p. 170.

23. Madame Clement is introduced only as "a merchant's widow in opulent circumstances" (II, p. 102), but she has a French name, and Monimia meets her at a French chapel (II, pp. 97, 101). She is called "the French lady" later in the novel (II, p. 215).

24. It has been argued that Smollett's portrait of a benevolent Jew in *Fathom* is less the result of humanitarianism than an attempt to support the promoters of the Jewish Naturalization Bill. See Tuvia Bloch, "Smollett and the Jewish Naturalization Bill of 1753," *American Notes & Queries*, VI (1968), 116–17.

officer who befriends Renaldo on his journey is an Irishman; Renaldo himself is Hungarian, but his father, whose generosity had been responsible for Fathom's advancement, "was originally of Scotland" (I, 18). Monimia, *alias* Serafina, and her father, Don Diego, are Spaniards. The romance world, in which these characters move, is remarkably private and self-contained. It has almost no contact with the society of England within the framework of which it placed, and it is therefore untouched by the values of this society which form the chief concern of the "satiric" parts of the novel.[25] The social world of England is unworthy of Renaldo and Monimia, a fact which is emphasized at the close of the novel when the lovers have been married, and their return to material prosperity has been achieved. Renaldo does not introduce his bride to his former acquaintances, "because not one of them had formerly treated her with that delicacy of regard which he thought her due" (II, 284–285). As for Monimia:

The fame of her beauty was immediately extended over this immense metropolis, and different schemes were concerted for bringing her into life. These, however, she resisted with unwearied obstinacy. Her happiness centred in Renaldo, and the cultivation of a few friends within the shade of domestic quiet. (II,285)

As *Fathom* closes, Renaldo, Monimia, and Don Diego set sail for the Continent, Don Diego for Spain, and the others, "to reside in the Low Countries 'till his return" (II, 288). The romance characters have triumphed over Fathom and the England which has provided so much scope for his talents. They have lived in a private world of virtue and honor within the vicious and dishonorable society around them, and having resisted the attempts of this society to destroy them, they move away from it.[26]

But Fathom's England, too, has its self-contained enclave of

25. The romance world is unremittingly foreign. Even the old woman into whose keeping Fathom delivers Monimia and who acts as his pander is "widow of a French refugee" (II, p. 76). The man with whom Renaldo plays chess in a coffee house until thoughts of Monimia distract him, an absolutely inconsequential character, is "an old French refugee" (II, p. 78).

26. They intend to return (II, p. 284), but this intention, within the novel, at least, is vague and unfulfilled.

exiles, and we meet them in one of the greatest prison scenes in the eighteenth-century novel. As we might expect, most of the characters described are foreigners. The prison scene in *Fathom* is constructed around the historical figure of Theodore de Neuhoff, the former king of Corsica, who had been imprisoned in the King's Bench for debt in 1749.[27] The story of de Neuhoff's life in England moves Smollett to reflect again on the English attitude toward strangers:

The English of former days, alike renowned for generosity and valour, treated those hostile princes whose fate it was to wear their chains, with such delicacy of benevolence, as even dispelled the horrors of captivity; but, their posterity of this refined age, feel no compunction at seeing an unfortunate monarch, their former friend, ally and partizan, languish amidst the miseries of a loathsome gaol, for a paultry debt contracted in their own service. (II,30)

Of the five members of Fathom's "club" within the prison, four are foreign. De Neuhoff himself was born in Metz, and his companions include Major Macleaver, an Irishman, Sir Mungo Barebones, a Scot, and an anonymous French chevalier. The fifth member, Captain Minikin, is, presumably, an Englishman. These characters are, of course, comic, as befits their place in the "satiric" portion of *Fathom*, but they are endowed with a certain dignity as well, and this places them apart from most of Smollett's caricatures. Sir Mungo Barebones, for example, the mad biblical scholar, is a brilliantly grotesque figure, but Smollett's description of him passes from the comic into the pathetic:

Yet this figure, uncouth as it was, made his compliments to our adventurer in terms of the most elegant address, and in the course of conversation, disclosed a great fund of valuable knowledge. He had appeared in the great world, and bore divers offices of dignity and trust, with universal applause: his courage was undoubted, his morals were unimpeached, and his person held in great veneration and esteem; when his evil genius engaged him in the study of Hebrew, and the

27. See André Le Glay, *Theodore de Neuhoff, Roi de Corse* (Monaco and Paris, 1907), pp. 361–75.

mysteries of the Jewish religion, which fairly disordered his brain, and rendered him incapable of managing his temporal affairs. (II,32)

Within the context of comedy, the prison, like the expatriate world presided over by Madame Clement, is a place of humanity and honor. The king takes a kindly interest in Sir Mungo's lunatic scheme, and the duel by *assa foetida* fought between Major Macleaver and Captain Minikin, while grotesque, is fought out of a regard for female delicacy, and the result is accepted with good will. Unlike the free citizens of England, the inhabitants of the prison accept foreigners in a spirit of toleration. Captain Minikin says of the French chevalier, "the truth is, I believe his brain is a little disordered, and he being a stranger we overlook his extravagancies" (II, 25). The virtues of tolerance and humanity are liabilities in a society which rewards the corrupt, and those who possess these virtues are imprisoned for debt—they are failures, that is to say, in society's terms. Renaldo and Monimia reject the corrupt England depicted in *Fathom*, and are thus heroic, figures of romance. The inhabitants of the prison have lived and moved in this England, and must thus be figures of comedy, but they have failed, and are therefore endowed with a kind of heroism of their own.

The constant emphasis on the corrupt nature of society in England, which is demonstrated both directly in the actions of her citizens, and by contrast with the conduct of the foreign "romance" characters, furnishes *Fathom* with most of its satiric bite, but it also serves to deflate the grandeur of Fathom's villainy. The preface has prepared us for a confrontation between virtue and vice in the persons of Renaldo and Fathom, but England becomes the real villain of the novel, and this seriously weakens Fathom's effectiveness as a character. For an arch-fiend, designed by his creator to terrify readers away from the "irremediable gulph" of iniquity (I, 4-5), dealing in cheap antiques and practicing medicine without the proper qualifications seem tame occupations, and Fathom's diabolism comes more and more to depend on his seductions. Ronald Paulson has pointed out that the five seductions or attempted seductions in the novel show Fathom in an increasingly villainous light as the women involved become progressively more innocent.[28] But even here, as Paulson points out, Fathom succeeds only by playing upon the weaknesses of his victims, and the sense of outrage at his callousness is tempered by the reader's awareness of Elinor's vanity and Celinda's silly superstitiousness. Both stories are "pilot's charts" in Cleland's sense, and their function is not so much to mark Fathom's progress in degradation as to warn young ladies that men were deceivers ever. At the close of the Celinda episode, Smollett makes this quite explicit:

This being the case, the reader will not wonder that a consummate traitor, like Fathom, should triumph over the virtue of an artless innocent young creature, whose passions he had entirely under his command. The gradations towards vice are almost imperceptible, and an experienced seducer can strew them with such inticing and agreeable flowers, as will lead the young sinner on insensibly, even to the most profligate stages of guilt. All therefore that can be done by virtue, unassisted with experience, is to avoid every trial with such a formidable foe, by declining and discouraging the first advances towards a particular correspondence with perfidious man, howsoever agreeable it may seem to be: for, here, is no security but in conscious weakness. (I,234)

The apogee of Fathom's wickedness is, of course, his attempt to seduce Monimia, and this fails because she has no weaknesses for him to play upon. He attempts to rape her,[29] but is overawed by her courage, and gives up his plot, having "lost no time in bewailing his miscarriage" (II, 108). Like Roderick Random and Peregrine Pickle, Fathom remains largely unchanged by his adventures and by the various milieux in which they occur. All three characters pass through a number of vicissitudes of fortune, and having

---

28. *Satire and the Novel in Eighteenth-Century England* (New Haven, and London, 1967), p. 228.

29. The relationship between sex and violence is very close in *Fathom,* and it might almost be said that Renaldo succeeds in rape where Fathom fails. Notice the images used to describe the consummation of his marriage with Monimia:

he hailed the signal, entered the apartment, and like a lion rushing on his prey, approached the nuptial bed, where Serafina, surrounded by all the graces of beauty, softness, sentiment, and truth, lay trembling as a victim at the altar, and strove to hide her blushes from his view. (II p. 265) eventually come to understand the vanity of the world, all three withdraw from it. The heroes of the earlier novels, having wed the heroines and gained the birthrights out of which they had been cheated, move off to a private rural paradise where they will live out the pastoral dream of country squirearchy, away from the snares and pitfalls of the world.[30] Fathom, too, is married, and proceeds to, "a cheap country in the north of England" (II, 281), where his penitence can be worked out in decent poverty and toil. Renaldo and Monimia have never been part of the world through which Roderick, Peregrine, and Fathom pass, their private paradise-world having coexisted with the larger one, been threatened by it, and finally having conquered it. They too, as we have seen, move away.

The spiritual regeneration of men through contact with a better world than their own is the chief theme of *Humphry Clinker*, but it is also illustrated, perfunctorily, in *Fathom*. Both Don Diego and Fathom himself are purged of their vices through contact with Monimia and Renaldo, and the didactic effectiveness of the Richardsonian moral technique is therefore established; but this process does not involve any reconciliation between the satiric and romantic aspects of the novel. The absolute separation of the two worlds is insisted upon.

This separation of the two worlds of *Fathom* is emphasized, as we might expect, in the style in which each is expressed. The characteristic diction of the parts of the novel presided over by Fathom is ironic; in the passages concerning the romantic adventures of Renaldo and Don Diego, it is hyperbolical. The phrase "knight-errant," for example, is applied, obviously ironically, to Fathom and Ratchkali (I, 107), to Sir Stentor Stiles and Sir Giles Squirrel, the confidence men (II, 8), and to Sir Mungo Barebones and the French chevalier (II, 36); it is applied, seriously, to Renaldo during the fairy-tale adventure in which he rescues his mother from the tower where his wicked step-father is keeping her prisoner (II, 175). Here the term is used to underscore the nobility of Renaldo's actions, but its effect is hyperbolical in that it marks

30. This is a very common process in the eighteenth-century novel, and its significance is ultimately mythical, as Fielding understood when he named Squire Allworthy's house, Tom Jones's true inheritance, "Paradise Hall."

the movement of the plot into the romantic milieu of ladies imprisoned by ogres in towers. Smollett provides a real knight-errant
in *Sir Launcelot Greaves,* and is forced to make him at least partially mad.[31] The style of *Fathom* moves between the ironic and
the romantic, and there is very little in between, precisely because
the worlds these styles describe are mutually exclusive and irreconcilable. Irony and hyperbole are balanced at opposite ends of the
scale of diction and are therefore appropriate for a novel as polar-
ized in conception as *Fathom.* The principal ironic device employed is the mock-heroic, the mode with which the novel opens.
Fathom's mother, the camp-follower, is compared with Semiramis,
Tomyris, Zenobia, and Thalestris (I, 23), while the infant Fathom
himself, having been suckled on gin, "improved apace in the ac-
complishments of infancy; his beauty was conspicuous, and his
vigour so uncommon, that he was with justice likened unto
Hercules in the cradle" (I, 14). The scene in the King's Bench is
mock heroic in conception, rendered pathetic by the circumstance
of the ex-king's historical fall from power. The duel by *assa
foetida* within the prison is in the same tradition as the heroic
games of the *Dunciad.* The mock-heroic functions ironically by
emphasizing the contrast between pretension and action and thus
deflating both. The style itself implies the standard by which the
matter it describes is found wanting. The hyperbolic, romance
style employed in *Fathom,* like the mock-heroic, is "high," its elevation serving to mark the contrast between its subject matter and
the ordinary world of the day-to-day. It, too, implies a heroic
standard, but its standard is fulfilled by the characters it describes.
Out of the context of character, therefore, the styles are similar.
Compare, for example, the following passages:

"Light of my eyes, and empress of my soul! behold me prostrate at
your feet, waiting with the most pious resignation, for that sentence
from your lips, on which my future happiness and misery must altogether depend. Not with more reverence does the unhappy bashaw kiss

31. Smollett refers to Renaldo's "Quixotism" in dashing to the rescue of the
girl who has eloped with her father's clerk (II, p. 258). The ex-king of Corsica
has "a spirit of Quixotism" which maintains him in the confidence of being
restored to his throne (II, p. 30). Smollett had been engaged on his translation
of *Don Quixote* at least as early as 1748, see Knapp, *Tobias Smollett,* p. 44.

the Sultan's letter that contains his doom, than I will submit to your fatal determination. Speak then, angelic sweetness! for, never, ah never will I rise from this suppliant posture, until I am encouraged to live and hope. No! if you refuse to smile upon my passion, here shall I breathe the last sighs of a dispairing lover: here shall this faithful sword do the last office to its unfortunate master, and shed the blood of the truest heart that ever felt the cruel pangs of disappointed love." (I,67–68)

"Can I then trust the evidence of sense? And art thou really to my wish restored? Never, O never did thy beauty shine with such bewitching grace, as that which now confounds and captivates my view! sure there is something more than mortal in thy looks! where hast thou lived? where borrowed this perfection? whence art thou now descended? Oh! I am all amazement, joy and fear! thou wilt not leave me! no! we must part again: by this warm kiss! a thousand times more sweet than all the fragrance of the east! we never more will part. O this is rapture, extasy, and what language can explain!" (II,228)

The first of these passages is taken from Fathom's speech to the vain and concupiscent jeweler's daughter, Wilhelmina, whose seduction he is about to accomplish, while the second forms part of Renaldo's effusion upon finding Monimia restored to him, as he thinks, from the grave. The style of both passages is "high"; we readers never talk like this, even in our moments of passion, and the fact that Wilhelmina, unaware of this, is impressed by Fathom's words renders her a figure of comedy. We know what Wilhelmina and Fathom are like, and the inappropriateness of such terms as "angelic sweetness" to her and of such gestures as the threat of suicide to him places the diction within the realm of the mock-heroic. The style exposes its objects. The second passage is equally remote from the diction of ordinary life, but here it is sincere. The fact that we do not talk like Renaldo merely emphasizes the gulf between our world and his. Renaldo's style is appropriate to his station; the novelist's problem is to give him a character which will justify the style.

There is, to be sure, a difference between the two passages, even when taken out of context. Fathom's speech, ornate as it is, is more prosaic than Renaldo's, which is perpetually at the point of breaking into verse.[32] Just as the romance world in *Fathom* triumphs over the satiric world that surrounds and threatens it, so the true heroic style overcomes the mock-heroic. Fathom's speech of penitence at the end of the novel is delivered in a style indistinguishable from Renaldo's:

"Is there no mercy then for penitence! is there no pity due to the miseries I suffered upon earth! save me, O bountiful heaven! from the terrors of everlasting woe; hide me from these dreadful executioners, whose looks are torture: forgive me, generous Castilian. O Renaldo! thou hadst once a tender heart. I dare not lift my eyes to Serafina! that pattern of human excellence who fell a victim to my atrocious guilt; yet, her aspect is all mildness and compassion. Ha! are not these the drops of pity? yes, they are tears of mercy: they fall like refreshing showers upon my drooping soul! ah murthered innocence! wilt thou not intercede for thy betrayer at the throne of grace!" (II,276–77)

Fathom's world, the world of English society, has been conquered both in plot and diction, and the last view we have of this monster of ingratitude, covetousness, and lust shows him bathing the hand of Renaldo with tears. The novel thus ends with both its didactic intentions accomplished. The reader has been warned not to be duped by plausible confidence-men or deceived by artful seducers, and has been granted a vision of proper conduct embodied in the actions and sentiments of a worthy hero and heroine. *Fathom* belongs in the realm of comedy; it ends, fulfilling Byron's definition, with marriages all around, and it invokes the sense of new lives and fresh beginnings of which marriage is symbolic. But the effect of the novel, taken as a whole, is pessimistic. The bitterness behind it is intense, and while it is directed chiefly, as we have seen, at England and the English, it at times goes deeper than nationalism. The list of personal failings included in Smollett's ironic dedication of the novel to himself are evidence

32. Renaldo's lamentation at Monimia's supposed grave produces the same effect, and parts of it can indeed be written as verse, e.g.:

"cold! cold and withered are those lips that swelled with love, and far out-blushed the damask rose! and ah! for ever silenced is that tongue, whose eloquence had power to lull the pangs of misery and care!" (II, p. 217)

that he was under no illusion as to the perfection of his own character, while of the general race of men he tells us, in an authorial
aside:

Success raised upon such a foundation [as a reputation for incompe-
tence], would, by a disciple of Plato, and some modern moralists, be
ascribed to the innate virtue and generosity of the human heart, which
naturally espouses the cause that needs protection: but I, whose
notions of human excellence are not quite so sublime, am apt to believe it is owing to that spirit of self-conceit and contradiction, which
is, at least, as universal, if not as natural, as the moral sense so warmly
contended for by those ideal philosophers. (II,137)

If Fathom is not altogether right, "that the sons of men preyed
upon one another, and such was the end and condition of their
being" (I, 58), he is very nearly so, as the greater part of the novel
makes clear. The pessimism implicit in this view ought structurally to be balanced by a final optimism engendered by the actions of the heroic characters, but the world of the heroic, as we
have seen, is beleaguered in *Fathom*, and although it triumphs, it
does not reform the world of the satiric but escapes from it.

The dualistic structure of *Fathom*, then, arises out of an attempt
to reconcile the satiric adventure novel of the *Random-Pickle* type
with the "higher" species of fiction, the chief practitioner of which
was Richardson. This experiment takes the form of the creation of
two protagonists, each of whom figures as the hero of a fictional
world appropriate to one of these two novelistic types. The two
worlds are sharply distinguished and are brought into conflict, but
this conflict is finally divisive, and the separation of the ethoi of
romance and satire is irreconcilable. Renaldo, Monimia, and Don
Diego can change the character and destiny of Fathom, but from
the society in which Fathom moved so freely they will remain
foreign by virtue of the humanity which in the novel is often
synonymous with foreignness. It is this irreconcilability which
renders the effect of *Fathom* finally pessimistic. The duality of the
novel is a formalistic experiment, but it is also a reflection of a
dark and bitter view of human nature, a view in which the generous and good are outnumbered and besieged.

In Smollett's last and greatest novel, we again are shown characters at odds with society and with each other, but *Humphry Clinker* is a novel in which the process of regeneration is unifying rather than divisive. As if to emphasize that the pessimism of *Fathom* is not the last word, Smollett gives Fathom and Renaldo a place in *Humphry Clinker*, a place in which the process of regeneration is shown at work. In accordance with the novel's central metaphor of health,[33] Fathom has become a healer, a country apothecary dedicated to the conscientious and disinterested service of the poor. By rescuing Renaldo and Monimia from an attack by highwaymen, Fathom both manifests his repentance and pays off the debt of gratitude which he owes, and the two worlds of *Fathom* are at last reconciled in the figure of the daughter of Fathom and Elinor, who is named after Monimia, and taken up by her.[34]

But this is irrelevant to a study of *Fathom*, however neatly it completes and harmonizes that work, and the interest which the earlier novel holds for us must lie in its quality as a unique formal experiment, an experiment infused with bitterness, and enlivened by the hard, brilliant satiric style which is at once the projection and the justification of Smollett's spleen.

33. For a discussion of the theme of spiritual and physical health in *Humphry Clinker*, see B. L. Reid, "Smollett's Healing Journey," *The Virginia Quarterly Review*, XLI (1965), 549–70.
34. *The Expedition of Humphry Clinker*, ed. Lewis M. Knapp (London, 1966), pp. 165–71.

The Economy of *Humphry Clinker*

BYRON GASSMAN

EVER since Henry James mastered the art of fiction, one of the most popular ways to assert a novel's excellence has been to demonstrate how every element of it relates to a pervasive purpose or vision and how all elements are molded into significant form by a controlling point of view. Perhaps one of the reasons Smollett has remained in a somewhat lower firmament than Fielding, Richardson, and Sterne is the difficulty of submitting a novel such as *Humphry Clinker* to the kind of analysis that produces scholarly articles entitled "The Unity of *Such and Such*" or "Meaning and Point of View in *So and So.*" Written at the end of one of the most diversified careers in English literary history, *Humphry Clinker* was used by Smollett to resurvey many of the subjects he had interested himself in during the nearly twenty-year period when he was one of the busiest writers on the literary scene of London. With material ranging from crude practical jokes to sentimental reunions, from an analysis of the British constitution to a merry account of Scottish funeral customs, from well-limned character sketches to animadversions on unhealthful sanitary conditions, the novel has almost always struck readers and critics as a veritable grab-bag of British life in the mid-1700's, filled with gusto when analyzed piecemeal, but unyielding to any attempt to define a synthesizing principle.

In a remark typical of many earlier comments on *Humphry Clinker,* George Saintsbury hit exactly this note in his introduction to the novel. After commenting on Smollett's lack of method, he observed that "the distinguishing excellence of *Humphry Clinker* is the excellence of the particulars" and went on to speak of its "cheerful divagation from pillar to post." [1] Most scholarship and criticism of the twentieth century has implicitly endorsed Saintsbury's observations by undertaking to illuminate or explicate particular elements of the novel,[2] although there have been recent attempts to provide holistic views of it.[3] Persuasive and useful as these latter have often been, when they are examined alongside the complete work, it is clear that there is much material from the grab-bag that no system-oriented view of the novel can fully account for.

Not only are the materials of *Humphry Clinker* manifold, but the purposes to which Smollett puts them may easily be viewed as at least threefold. In the first place, as announced by the prefatory correspondence, *Humphry Clinker* shares with the collections of travel letters so popular during the eighteenth century the purpose of disseminating information on geography, history, customs, and manners. But *Humphry Clinker* is obviously more than a perceptive journalist's account of travels through England and Scotland, more than a companion volume to Smollett's own *Travels* and the other works referred to in the prefatory correspondence. It finds its way into the novel section of our literary history because, simultaneously with his reporting, Smollett effects the creation

1. *The Works of Tobias Smollett*, ed. George Saintsbury (New York, n.d.), VI, pp. xi, xvii–xviii.
2. Characteristic and very well known are Knapp's discussion of the autobiographical elements, Martz's of certain descriptive passages, and Kahrl's of travelogue materials: Lewis M. Knapp, "Smollett's Self-Portrait in *The Expedition of Humphry Clinker*" in *The Age of Johnson* (New Haven, 1949); Louis L. Martz, *The Later Career of Tobias Smollett* (New Haven, 1942); George M. Kahrl, *Tobias Smollett: Traveler-Novelist* (Chicago, 1945).
3. Probably the most striking of these is M. A. Goldberg's discussion of *Humphry Clinker* as "A Study in Primitivism and Progress" in *Smollett and the Scottish School* (Albuquerque, 1959). Along similar lines are David L. Evans, "*Humphry Clinker*: Smollett's Tempered Augustanism," *Criticism* IX (1967), 257–74; and B. L. Reid, "Smollett's Healing Journey," *Virginia Quarterly Review* XLI (1965), 549–70. All of these suggest a reading of *Humphry Clinker* as a journey of reconciliation. The notion of the action of *Humphry Clinker* as a kind of archetypal pilgrimage may perhaps be traced to Robert Gorham Davis's introduction to the Rinehart edition (New York, 1950).

of a company of characters to delight the reader by their actions and reactions. The creation of entertaining characters and incident, and the interaction of the two, is a second very evident purpose of the work. Moreover, the novel goes beyond the scope of the usual travel book of the mid-eighteenth century by adding a marked note of criticism and didactic commentary on the English milieu of the 1760's, and the reader can identify this didactic purpose as a third basic strand in the variegated fabric of the novel.

Since *Humphry Clinker* is so clearly a multi-purpose work, incorporating a wide variety of heterogeneous materials, one always runs the risk of appearing overingenious in trying to lay out some formal principle which gives significance to the work as a whole or in trying to identify some controlling idea which functions as a basis for structural unity. Nevertheless I believe it possible to show that Smollett, in writing *Humphry Clinker,* did handle disparate material and diverse aims in such a way as to achieve, if not a unified work, at least a fairly economical one, one in which his purposes of reporting, characterizing, and moralizing are neatly interfused and his diverse materials tellingly exploited.

In choosing to describe the "economy" of *Humphry Clinker,* I desire to label as conveniently and precisely as words allow two related qualities of the novel. In one respect, I am trying to suggest something not so tightly handled as the term *unity* would suggest, something with more loose ends, with more variety—one can hardly think of Henry James taking time out of *The Ambassadors* to discourse on French marriage customs—but nonetheless suggesting some sense of perceptible structure and, even more, an effective manipulation of function.[4] And still more precisely, I should like the term to suggest that quality we designate when we use *economy* to describe thrifty management, the husbanding of resources to make every expenditure produce the best possible return.[5]

The achievement of *Humphry Clinker* in these senses may well be approached by briefly noting some of the problems Smollett

4. Cf. *OED* definition 8: "The organization, internal constitution, apportionment of functions, of any complex unity."
5. Cf. *OED* definition 4: "Careful management of resources, so as to make them go as far as possible."

had in the structure and handling of material in the earlier novels. The single purpose, "to represent modest merit struggling with every difficulty to which a friendless orphan is exposed," [6] and single career of *Roderick Random*, for example, seem to have encouraged Smollett into a spendthrift extravagance of incident and attitude, a proliferation of episodic discontinuity that makes difficult any serious attempt at structural or thematic synthesis. Alan McKillop pinpointed a similar problem of economy in point of view with his comment on *Roderick Random* that "the story is not controlled throughout by an effective commentator, a voice of reason." [7] Indeed *Roderick Random* seems liable to most of the difficulties of control to which first-person fictional memoirs are prone: the difficulty of distinguishing between the thoughts and reactions of the moment (as an incident occurs) and the reflections upon it as the incident is supposedly written down years afterwards, and the difficulty of the actual author in validating or commenting on the values and attitudes of his narrator. In *Roderick Random* the reader is often confused by the shifting moral awareness of Roderick—and the same confusion is equally troublesome in *Peregrine Pickle* even when Smollett turns to a third-person narrative and produces a more perceptible plan. At one moment the hero may strike the reader as a young man of keen ethical sensitivity, a straightforward spokesman for his creator, and at the next moment as a crude barbarian, delighting in the pain of his fellow creatures and quite insensitive to any niceties in the demands of justice or mercy, a person for whom neither the author nor the reader could be expected to have much sympathy.

As Tuvia Bloch recently pointed out, a continuing problem for Smollett, even after he gave up the first-person point of view of *Roderick Random*, was that of maintaining a consistent and thus, for the reader, an interpretable stance toward his narrative and his characters. Unlike Fielding, Smollett found it difficult to distance his characters by ironic style.[8] He often moves from a dis-

---

6. "The Preface" to *Roderick Random*.
7. Alan Dugald McKillop, *The Early Masters of English Fiction* (Lawrence, Kansas, 1956), p. 152.
8. Tuvia Bloch, "Smollett's Quest for Form," *Modern Philology* LXV (1967), 109–10.

tancing rhetoric to an unmediated reaction that leaves the reader in uncertain territory. Thus the implied economy that may arise from the steady view of an informing creative intelligence frequently fails to develop in Smollett's first four novels. Such a wavering point of view becomes a considerable hindrance to the creation of any coherent moral underpinning to a novel. If one has trouble in sustaining a single point of view or in giving one's putative narrator consistency, then some additional or substitute device is needed for straightening out perspective.

Paradoxically it was Smollett's decision to turn from the basically single point of view used in his earlier novels and to let his last novel take shape as the work of several letter-writers that provided the device on which the economy of *Humphry Clinker* depends. At first glance, one might expect that, having had trouble with a single point of view, Smollett might find a multiple point of view entailing an even greater expenditure of unassimilated effort and posing the danger of a *Clarissa*-like prolixity. But in the event, it enabled Smollett to evolve a consistent, interpretable stance toward his characters, their actions, and their society, and to achieve his purposes with an economy that would do full credit to the proverbial thriftiness of his homeland. The author of *Roderick Random* and *Peregrine Pickle* is like a juggler with only one ball to handle: he can be fairly extravagant and even uncoordinated in his motions and still engage his audience's attention by keeping the ball moving. The author of *Humphry Clinker* is like the juggler with numerous paraphernalia: he must be much more economical in his movements, not only trying to avoid uncoordinated movements but often making the same motion simultaneously serve the purposes of balancing, catching, and throwing.

The most obvious feature of Smollett's multiple point of view is the manner in which each letter-writer characterizes himself through his reaction to the sights and scenes encountered on the expedition. At the same time that the reader is being given typical data about the social customs of Bath or the mushrooming growth of London, he is being intimately introduced to the personality of the observer. A characteristic instance is Win Jenkins's letter describing her impressions of London. Here the reader finds some good first-hand reporting about the tumult of London streets, the

sights of the Tower of London, and the entertainment at Sadler's
Wells, data about the London of the 1760's that is good primary
material for the modern historian.[9] But all is described in a delightfully malapropian prose that effectively delineates Win's
character. When she remarks, "I have seen the Park, and the
paleass of Saint Gimses, and the king's and the queen's magisterial
pursing, and the sweet young princes, and the hillyfents, and pye-
bald ass, and all the rest of the royal family" (WJ–June 3), the
reader has actually been given an accurate account of what the
traveler might have seen in Saint James's Park, but the ludicrous
confusion with which it is told is also a piece of superb characterization. In the letters of Matthew Bramble the physical layout and
the social routines of Bath are as fully reported as in most of the
travel journals of the time. But the descriptions are strained
through the imagined writer's sensibility in such a way as to
acquaint us equally and simultaneously with Bath and Matthew
Bramble. Of the famous Bath balls, Bramble grumbles that he
"could not help wondering that so many hundreds of those that
rank as rational creatures, could find entertainment in seeing a
succession of insipid animals, describing the same dull figure for a
whole evening, on an area, not much bigger than a taylor's shop-
board" (MB–May 8). Highly individualized in its expression, such
a statement nonetheless is substantially accurate as a report of Bath
assemblies.[10]

The effect of characterization by means of personalized reporting
is particularly noticeable when two letter-writers, most often
Bramble and Lydia Melford, react to the same sight or event. In
the early portions of the novel, Lydia's point of view is often used
by Smollett to neutralize somewhat Bramble's crabbed observations. Bramble's "pretty baubles" (MB–Apr. 23) at Bath become
"sumptuous palaces" (LM—Apr. 26) in Lydia's eyes. Bramble characteristically complains of "the dirt, the stench, the chilling blasts,
and perpetual rains" (MB—Apr. 20) at the Hot Well. The next

9. The usefulness of the letters of the Bramble party to modern historians
is well illustrated by consulting the entry *Smollett* in such works as Sir Walter
Besant, *London in the Eighteenth Century* (London, 1903); and Rosamond
Bayne-Powell, *Eighteenth-Century London Life* (New York, 1938).
10. Cf. Oliver Goldsmith's account of Bath balls in *The Life of Richard
Nash* in *Collected Works*, ed. Arthur Friedman (Oxford, 1966), III, p. 304.
Goldsmith's account follows closely an earlier one by John Wood.

day the impressionable Lydia rapturously writes, "The air is so pure; the Downs are so agreeable . . . the weather so soft . . . the prospect so amusing" (LM—Apr. 21). For Bramble, Vauxhall is "a composition of baubles, overcharged with paltry ornaments, ill conceived, and poorly executed" (MB—May 29). For Lydia, in the very next letter, it is "a spacious garden, part laid out in delightful walks . . . part exhibiting a wonderful assemblage of the most picturesque and striking objects" (LM—May 31). In setting Bramble's and Lydia's accounts of Vauxhall and Ranelagh together, one hardly knows whether more praise should go to the masterful job of reporting the temper and tempo of these haunts of pleasure or to the creative skill that brings to life the characters through whose words the report is made. In the last analysis the praise goes to Smollett's genius which makes his method at once serve both purposes.

Thus while managing a clear account of topographical and historical data, habits, customs, manners, travel anecdotes—the type of material to be found in any travel-book of the day—Smollett is also creating a small gallery of individualized letter-writers who command interest in their own right. At least this is true with Matthew Bramble, Tabitha Bramble, Lydia Melford, and Winifred Jenkins. It is not so true in the case of the fifth letter-writer, Jeremy Melford, who remains considerably less individualized, keeping free of the situations that embarrass and distress the others. He is tolerant and amused, but seldom carried away into excesses of pleasure or displeasure, excitement or disgust, as are his fellow-writers. He is, in brief, a good reporter, narrating events without the embroidery of personal animus or affectation, describing scenes with affable objectivity, and, in direct contrast with the others, keeping his own personality and opinions fairly well in the background.

Smollett makes efficient use of the objective point of view provided by Jery Melford in working out the economy of *Humphry Clinker*. The reader's appraisal of the characters of his fellow-travelers is validated as they are seen, not through their own sensibility or the idiosyncratic accounts of others, but through a point of view not grossly individualized. Jery's letters are highly useful in letting the reader see his traveling companions in action. It is perhaps oversimplified but nevertheless generally accurate to say that the letters of Bramble, Lydia, Tabitha, and Win are letters of reaction, those of Jery, letters of action. Jery himself does suffer some loss of vitality thereby. Bramble's early characterization of him as "a pert jackanapes, full of college-petulance and self-conceit" (MB—Apr. 17) and the early episodes of the challenge to Wilson and the affair with Miss Blackerby offer hints from which a new Peregrine Pickle might have developed, but nothing much materializes from these hints. However, the loss of another *Peregrine Pickle*—arguably Smollett's most verbose performance—and a certain pallidness in Jery's character are compensated for by the narrative efficiency achieved through the straightforward and well-paced reporting of events in Jery's letters. Without violating his conception of an epistolary novel, Smollett gains Richardson's effect of letting his work form itself from the interplay of his characters' reactions while also, through Jery's letters of action, providing a means for effective propulsion of the narrative. Unimpeded by the generous indignation, the gross resentment, or the humane sentiments that seemed at times in the earlier novels to work at cross purposes with the Smollettian vivacity, Jery becomes Smollett's most efficient and effective narrator. Availability of the other four letter-writers relieves him of some of the tasks that created awkwardness and uncertainty in Smollett's earlier narrative voices. In addition, a resource is provided for a well-handled playing back and forth between narrative action and character reaction and comment that makes *Humphry Clinker* a model of how to manage a grab-bag of material and purpose in fictional form.

One way in which Smollett characteristically employs this resource to good advantage may be demonstrated by an early episode in the book. Bramble ends his first few letters with requests to Dr. Lewis to relieve the misfortunes of various dependents, thus revealing an apparently charitable disposition. Tabitha, in her first letter, is totally concerned with her own comforts and her own profits on the Bramble estate, thus exposing an apparently selfish character. The impressions gained by the reader from these self-revealing letters are confirmed by events when Jery reports the little scene in which his uncle tries secretly to relieve the distress of an ensign's widow with a twenty-pound note, only to have Tabitha pounce on the pair, snatch the note, and accuse her brother of concupiscence. Later Bramble voices a complaint about the noise and tumult of Bath, while Jery actually narrates the confused and noisy reception they meet upon their arrival. Bramble is dismayed by the mean state of the literary world of London; Jery relates his experiences with a motley group of literary hacks who have Sunday dinner with Smollett. It is Jery who keeps the narrative moving, who gets the travelers from place to place. It is he who narrates most of the memorable and typically Smollettian adventures: the evening spent with Quin, Ulic Mackilligut's encounter with Tabitha's dog, the meeting with Humphry on the road between Bath and London and the exposure of his bare posteriors, the fire in the inn at Harrowgate, the cawdie festival in Edinburgh, the practical jokes of Sir Thomas Bullford. Most of those events in which the interest lies more in the event itself than in the narrator's reaction are customarily given to Jery Melford.

The usefulness of the difference between the highly individualized, subjective point of view of Bramble and the objective point of view of Jery in weaving diverse material into the fabric of *Humphry Clinker* is equally noticeable when we direct our attention to the didactic purposes of the work. To any reader of the novel it soon becomes obvious that Matthew Bramble has assumed for himself the role of moralist and social critic among the travelers, but it is perhaps not so immediately obvious how seriously Smollett intended his readers to respond to Bramble's criticisms of English society. It is at least possible for the reader to consider Bramble's querulous denunciations as merely another characterizing device, emphasizing again his peevish and eccentric disposition. But even assuming that the reader is more convinced by the humors of Bramble's character than by the soundness of his moral judgments, and that the reader concludes his pronouncements to be mere eccentricities to be smiled at rather than pondered over, there is another source of didactic effect that acts as a corroboration of Bramble's pronouncements. This source is Jery's objective reporting of events and situations which carry with them an implicit moral or comment on society. A very obvious example occurs while the travelers are at Bath. Bramble is constantly complaining about the heterogeneous society at Bath and asserting that the mixture of all classes can only lead to the vulgarization of them all. His nephew, in conversation with him, opines that it tends to polish the inferior ones. The question is resolved the next day when a general tea-drinking is turned into a near riot; the guests charge the dining tables at the sound of a bell, and both the aristocracy and the mob debase themselves. Regardless of how little convinced the reader may have been by Bramble's fears, the event itself, as reported by Jery, resolves the difference of opinion. Later Bramble's frequently voiced suspicions of the *nouveaux riches* are confirmed when Jery reports how the newly affluent Paunceford ungenerously neglects his old benefactor Serle. Again when the travelers arrive in London, Bramble reprehends the political system of the day and complains about self-serving factions, venal office holders, and prostitute ministers. His complaints are dramatized when Jery encounters some of the "great men of the kingdom" at a high festival at court, particularly the bumbling Duke of Newcastle, whose ridiculous and fulsome behavior, as reported by Jery, bears out most of Bramble's criticisms.

A further didactic emphasis wrought through alternating points of view is provided occasionally by the coincidence of Lydia's opinion with Bramble's. As indicated above, Lydia is used, especially in the early parts of the novel, to soften Bramble's harsh pronouncements and leave a more neutral impression of sights and events viewed by the travelers. But occasionally her viewpoint is used to reinforce some pronouncement by Bramble, and when this occurs the reader becomes even more conscious of the importance of the pronouncement to the didactic contours of the book. When Humphry is discovered preaching Methodism, Bramble takes him to task in a typical outburst: "Heark-ye, Clinker, you are either an hypocritical knave, or a wrong-headed enthusiast" (JM—June 10). Later in the book, Lydia comments on her aunt's Methodist activities: "She has been praying, preaching, and catechising among the methodists, . . . and pretends to have such manifestations and revelations, as even Clinker himself can hardly believe. . . . God forgive me if I think uncharitably, but all this seems to me to be downright hypocrisy and deceit" (LM—Sept. 7). The reader of course expects a harsh verdict from the mouth of Bramble, but he is not quite prepared for so severe a judgment as Lydia delivers, and, as a result, the indictment of Methodism from the usually uncritical young girl comes with even more persuasive force. Similarly Bramble's frequent reiteration of the evils of life in the city as compared with the felicities of rural life at Bramble-ton-hall may not strike the reader with full force because of Bramble's propensity to complain. But Bramble's complaints are given increased emphasis in enforcing the didactic aims of the novel when Lydia, who is charmed and delighted by almost all that she encounters, nevertheless expresses herself thus: "I wish my weak head may not grow giddy in the midst of all this gallantry and dissipation; though, as yet, I can safely declare, I could gladly give up all these tumultuous pleasures, for country solitude, and a happy retreat with those we love" (LM—May 31). Thus Bramble's moralizing and his criticism of the social values of Bath and London are given additional validity by the comments of the person in the letter-writing group who is usually most different from him in her reactions and impressions. When a crotchety but charitable old man and an impressionable but good-hearted young girl agree in their judgment, as Lydia and Bramble do on several issues, they may still both be wrong, but the agreement multiplies the chances that their judgment is sound.

The value of multiple point of view in establishing the validity and economy of both the reporting and the moralizing of *Humphry Clinker* may be further emphasized by considering what might have been the result had Smollett restricted his work to one letter writer, say Matthew Bramble. In such a case, *Humphry Clinker* might well have turned out to be another *Travels through France and Italy,* the idiosyncratic impressions of a hypersensitive and hypochondriacal traveler, interesting and readable no doubt, but without the telling and structurally consolidating force that contrasting and corroborating points of view provide. And the reader, after a certain amount of exposure to the crabbed remarks of Bramble, unrelieved by the malapropian versions of Tabitha and Win, unmodified by the impressions of Lydia, unconfirmed by the objective accounts of Jery, might well react as Sterne did to the learned Smelfungus of the *Travels:* "I'll tell it, cried Smelfungus, to the world. You had better tell it, said I, to your physician." [11]

The preceding comments on the economy engendered by Smol-

11. Laurence Sterne, *A Sentimental Journey Through France and Italy,* World's Classics ed. (London, 1928), p. 51.

lett's use of multiple point of view are in general much more applicable to the English section of the novel than they are to the Scottish section. In fact the value it had for Smollett can be pointed up by contrasting the English letters with the Scottish ones. Tabitha writes no letters at all from Scotland, and Lydia writes only one at the conclusion of the tour through the northern kingdom; in this she pays only the briefest of compliments to the politeness of the Scots and the beauties of Loch Lomond. Only from two letters written by Win Jenkins does the reader get any of the interplay between new sights and the female personality that blended the reporting and characterizing functions in the English letters. The dissevering of these functions becomes even more obvious in the Scottish letters of Matthew Bramble. The mellowing effect of Scotland on Bramble has often been remarked; the crabbed critic of Bath and London suddenly becomes the admirer of Edinburgh, Glasgow, and Loch Lomond.

But the apparent change in Bramble occurs partly because in the Scottish letters Smollett does not characterize him by individual tone and diction to the extent that he did in the English letters. Bramble characteristically complains briefly about sanitary conditions in Edinburgh, and the reader can detect the Bramble acid punctuating many of his remarks. But there are numerous descriptive paragraphs and even pages in which Bramble goes on merely retailing typical travel data in an unindividualized tone of approval, unmodified by any subjective reaction that would distinguish his report from the accounts of Scotland written by Defoe or Pennant or Smollett himself as editor of *The Present State of All Nations*.[12] Especially after leaving Edinburgh, Bramble often seems merely a convenient peg for Smollett on which to hang facts and observations, and the idiosyncrasies of his point of view are not so neatly exploited as in the earlier parts of the journey. The economy of the novel weakens, and it becomes for many pages little more than the compilation of pedestrian travel letters it was originally announced to be.

In Scotland Jery Melford continues to write his genial reports of

12. Martz, Chaps. V–VI, points out the extent to which Smollett derived his description of Scotland in *Humphry Clinker* from materials in *Present State,* which in turn were often derived from other published accounts.

events such as the cawdie dinner, the rough voyage on the return from the excursion into Fife, and the festive Highland funeral at which the corpse is left behind, but even in his letters we get long factual passages which are little different from the conventional travel report. In brief, because in the Scottish section of the novel there is less emphasis on self-characterization as well as on the type of characterization that was so brilliantly developed in the early letters by multiple reflection from one point of view to another, and because Smollett apparently weakens in his ability to interlock reporting and moralizing from letter-writer to letter-writer, most readers, finishing the Scottish letters, are apt to feel that there has been some loss of creative control over material and purpose, a control that was exercised in the earlier part of the book by imaginative handling of several points of view.

When the travelers return to England, their interest in sights and scenes, an interest which has been strong throughout the novel and especially dominant in Scotland, begins to fade, and they turn their attention to their own affairs. What little conventional plot the novel has is wound up with the revelation of Humphry's parentage and the triple wedding. One additional element in the final pages of the novel is, however, worthy of comment because it demonstrates again how Smollett uses objective reporting to reinforce subjective reaction and didactic purpose. In his letter of June 8, about one-third of the way through the novel, Bramble pours forth his accumulated dislike for urban living with a point-by-point contrast between his "town grievances, and . . . country comforts." At Brambleton-hall, the air is pure, the food and drink wholesome, the amusements innocent, and friends and dependents honest and trusty. In London, the air is putrid, food and drink contaminated, amusements insipid or corrupting, and "your tradesmen are without conscience, your friends without affection, and your dependents without fidelity." In the final section of the novel, the Bramble party meets two of Matthew's old friends, Baynard and Dennison. Baynard is on the verge of ruin because of a wife who has forced him into the vortex of fashionable living centered in the ostentatious city. Dennison, on the other hand, is in a prosperous and happy situation because he has refused to be enticed by the luxury and show of the city and has been content to husband judiciously his rural resources. The situations of Baynard and Dennison, reported in the last series of letters, are clearly objective confirmations of the many strictures on English society made by Bramble during his stays in Bath and London. A certain symmetry thus emerges from the rambles of *Humphry Clinker* by using the objective reports of the careers of Baynard and Dennison in the last part of the novel to verify the criticism of English society which threaded its insistent way through the subjective reactions of Bramble in the first part.

It seems likely that Smollett, aware of his rapidly deteriorating health, sensed that *Humphry Clinker* was to be his last opportunity to get into print a multitude of ideas and experiences that he had accumulated over the years and that were energizing still his imagination. The reader can speculate, but he cannot actually know in what terms Smollett viewed the problem of giving fictional form to this multitude of material demanding expression. Quite possibly he was not particularly conscious of any formal problem and was quite content to work up his material in such a way as to suggest Hazlitt's fine phrase, "the most pleasant gossiping novel that ever was written." [13] Hazlitt's response has been that of many readers, both casual and scholarly, and it suggests a perspective useful to keep in mind in any study of the novel: *Humphry Clinker* is too much of a "gossiping novel," too much of a pleasant potpourri of events, persons, data, observations, criticism, satire, and moralizing ever to submit to the kind of analysis that discovers a single unifying principle dictating form and content to a work of fiction. But in spite of this amorphous quality, the case can be made that Smollett effectively blended his variegated materials and diverse aims by his use of multiple point of view. Never a master of form, Smollett was a master of material, and by his fortunate discovery or adoption of a multiple point of view, he brilliantly and effectively assembled the materials and ideas of a lifetime into *Humphry Clinker* to produce one of the enduring delights of English fiction.

13. William Hazlitt, *Lectures on the English Comic Writers* in *Complete Works*, ed. P. P. Howe (London, 1931), VI, p. 117.

Smollett as a Caricaturist

GEORGE KAHRL

I

"Ludicrous writing in general is extremely subject to the injuries of time." So wrote James Beattie in 1764 in his *Essay on Laughter and Ludicrous Composition*,[1] observing how laughter so often originates in the discovery, the surprise at the incongruities in traditions, fashions, manners, classes, nationalities, and professions. For contemporaries "there are few incongruities to which *custom* will not reconcile us";[2] furthermore, many incongruities coexist in social contexts so momentary and subtle as to be missed by later generations. Hence, the antiquarianism and footnotes, the analysis of the literary historian and critic, even the remarks of the humorist himself defeat that momentary insight into an incongruity which is the genesis of laughter. In no form of "ludicrous composition" does the transient wit so quickly fade as in caricature; even the term itself has been so distorted or expanded in meaning, particularly in the second half of the eighteenth century, that it retains little more than pejorative associations.

None of the eighteenth-century humorists has been more "subject to the injuries of time" and place than Tobias Smollett. His predilection for the grotesque was more in the Scottish character than the English, and much of the laughter that was relished by

1. (Edinburgh, 1776), p. 461.
2. *On Laughter and Ludicrous Composition*, p. 417.

contemporaries became increasingly offensive with the passing of the century. Without undertaking to recapture the moment, to track down the allusions, to illuminate the manners, one may enrich the reading of Smollett by some familiarity with the spirit and artistry of caricaturing as it flourished in its Continental origins and in the first half of the century, and in turn by cultivating an understanding not only of the contemporaneity of the subject matter of Smollett's prose fiction, but more of his attainments as a caricaturist.

Art historians agree that caricature as a distinct genre arose and was perfected in practice and theory in the seventeenth century, first in Italy and then in France. From the outset the Carracci brothers were recognized as the founders, notably Annibale (1560–1609), an exceptionally accomplished artist with wide influence in several genres; hence his critical epitome of caricature best serves as the first step in definition.

Is not the caricaturist's task exactly the same as the classical artist's? Both see the lasting truth beneath the surface of mere outward appearance. Both try to help nature accomplish its plan. The one may strive to visualize the perfect form and to realise it in his work, the other to grasp the perfect deformity, and thus reveal the very essence of personality. A good caricature, like every work of art, is more true to life than reality itself.[3]

From Carracci's practice and the work and theories of other Italian (such as Leonardo and Bernini) and later French caricaturists, the historical concept of caricature might be analyzed as follows:

1. Caricature in origins and subsequent development was first and last the portrait of what was known and recognizable as a public figure, a type, class, profession, trade, or nationality. The Carracci brothers and others began with amusing and kindly

3. E. H. Gombrich and Ernst Kris, *Caricature* (London, 1940), pp. 11–12; also E. H. Gombrich, *Art and Illusion* (London, 1961), Chapter X, "The Experiment of Caricature"; Kris, *Psychoanalytic Explorations in Art* (New York, 1964), Part III, "The Comic"; Martin Foss, *Symbol and Metaphor in Human Experience* (Princeton, 1949), *passim;* Bohun Lynch, *A History of Caricature* (London, 1926); Werner Hofmann, *Caricature: from Leonardo to Picasso,* trans. from German (London, 1957).

sketched portraits of friends, acquaintances, public figures. Annibale searched through the streets of Bologna for recognizable
types of trades, classes, nationalities—proto- and stereotypes—for
schemata faces. The pleasure was not in the perception of an individual projected by a novelist or dramatist, but in the perception
of an essential and a dominating deficiency, a contrast between
recognized normalities and contradictory aberrations.

2. While the caricature was a highly skilled simplification and
heightening, the picture consistently gave the impression of an
informal, rather off-hand—*capriccio*—sketch, the term being derived from the Italian *caricare*, translated into French as *portrait
chargé*. Later the descriptive terms *ritratto ridicolo* and *outré* were
added. The overcharging of a blemish or defect, natural or acquired, afforded insight into a character that was more true, more
perceptive than a direct imitation or transcript. Almost the direct
opposite of realism, a caricature is highly artistic and stylized.

3. Caricaturing assimilated the grotesque in medieval art that
represented human qualities or characters in the form of animals
or domestic utensils. With a decline in the grotesque, there was
a great upsurge in the study and elaboration of the wide range
in human physiognomy, an extraordinary development of portraiture in the seventeenth century, with the schematizations of
the combinations and meanings of features, such as Le Brun's
Traité sur les passions (1667) and G. B. della Porta's *De Humana
Physiognomonia* (1586), well known in the early eighteenth century in English translation.[4] The face became the focus of characterization, perfected, for example, by Garrick in his acting.

4. Finally, the appeal of caricature was not to a sense of beauty
or to the grotesque, but to laughter. All art in diverse ways makes
a comment, a criticism, and an evaluation; there is an element
of aggressiveness in all art, but the aggressiveness is transformed
into the aesthetic sphere. The caricaturist by skillful selection,
simplification, proffers a congruity in incongruities that surprises,
and the truth of the revelation, the laughter, affirms values. When
the comment tips over into rejection, the result is satire. In caricature "aggression has remained in the aesthetic sphere and thus

4. See also James Granger, *A Biographical History of England* (London,
1769); Arthur M. Hind, *Engraving in England in the Sixteenth and Seventeenth Centuries* (Cambridge, 1952–64).

we react not with hostility but with laughter." [5] In modern critical terms, the ego is no longer threatened and through aesthetic distance we gain a psychological security. Often, however, with the lapse of time the combativeness of the artist or the writer, is forgotten or subordinated by the more enduring aesthetic qualities, and what was created as a satiric print survives as a caricature, a shift in evaluation from satire to caricature that has produced so many contradictions, for example, in the criticism of William Hogarth, about whom Smollett wrote, "Hogarth is an inimitable original with respect to invention, humour, and expression." [6]

Caricatures were generally sketched in red chalk or crayon and were not preserved with all the solicitude for more finished paintings; hence, only a few of the originals of Carracci, Bernini, Ghezzi, and the early caricaturists survive. Further, reproduction was not by copying, as with oils, but by engraving, and the transformation of the informal to the formal and the conventionalized practices of engravers obliterated some of the simplicity of the originals; only later did some of the caricaturist-engravers learn to catch and preserve this simplicity. With the flourishing of engraving, print selling became lucrative, and engraved pictures of all sorts were available for rich and poor alike. Some dealers, such as Matthew and Mary Darly,[7] specialized in caricatures and satiric prints, and pieces which were originally issued in separate sheets were gathered into folios, thereby preserving for us much that was ephemeral in the single caricature.

Although Englishmen who traveled, artists who studied abroad, and Continental engravers who migrated to London were all familiar with Continental caricature, the first prints published in England were from copies made by Arthur Pond, engraved and sold by John Boydell from 1736 to 1745, and assembled in what is, now, a rare folio. No summary or description of the twenty-five prints will serve so well as a reproduction of the table of contents to cover the range in artists, subjects, medium, and point of view;

5. Kris, *Psychoanalytic Explorations in Art,* p. 203.
6. *The Present State of All Nations* (1758), II, p. 230.
7. See their *A Political & Satyrical History* (London, 1765) with a short introduction on "The Difference between Character & Caricature."

the reproduction of five of the prints may convey some sense of the collection as a whole.[8]

Another folio of twenty-four engravings, such as English travelers found abroad and imported, was published by Matteo Oesterreich in Rome in 1750–51, from caricatures drawn by Pier Leone Ghezzi (1674–1755), who for years made a living by accepting commissions to do caricatures of visitors to Rome. (The general interest in the fashionable clientele was transitory, and the folio is now most rare.) The two folios by Boydell and Oesterreich indicate the range of caricaturing as a genre: the persons are identified, even with dates; the engravings are of drawings; examples of the better known artists are included; the pictures concentrate on a skillful simplification and heightening of deformities; and the appeal is not satiric but kindly and comic.

Even though his attention and drawings were concentrated on political satire, the Marquis of Townshend is often considered to have been the first practitioner of caricature in England. As the century wore on, an almost overwhelming number of satiric prints was issued by artists and engravers. As Thomas Gray remarked in May 1742: "the Wit of the times consists in Satyrical Prints, I believe, there have been some Hundreds within this Month; if you have any hopeful young Designer of Caricaturas, that has a political Turn, he may pick up a pretty Subsistance here." [9] This accumulation of satiric prints was first studied in 1873 by F. G. Stephens in his *Catalogue of Prints and Drawings in the British Museum,* and more recently by Mary Dorothy George in *English Political Caricature to 1792* (Oxford, 1959) and *Hogarth to Cruikshank* (London, 1967). The "aggressive imagery of propagandist art does not aim at the achievement of aesthetic effect," [10] as everyone realizes who has pursued the course of even a minor public figure—such as Smollett was as a journalist in support of the Bute administration—through the dreary waste of ephemeral political satire. Paradoxically, William Hogarth, the dominant figure in

8. See plates VII–XII, and for an account of the folio see Henry M. Hake, "Pond's and Knapton's Imitations of Drawings," *The Print Collector's Quarterly,* IX (1922), 325–49.
9. *The Correspondence of Thomas Gray,* ed. Paget Toynbee and Leonard Whibley (London, 1935), I, p. 207.
10. Kris, *Psychoanalytic Explorations in Art,* p. 192.

English caricature, confused the distinction between satire and caricature. On the one hand he professed and endeavored to avoid caricature because of its foreign origins, its cultivation by the non-professional dilettante, and because of its concentration on imperfections rather than on what was natural and beautiful. His aggressive moral evaluations disposed him toward satire; nevertheless, his temper and skill as an artist drew him over into comedy and authentic caricature, or as Frederick Antal has remarked, Hogarth "as a critic and satirist . . . often slid imperceptibly from a most decided realism to what is almost its direct opposite—caricature." [11] Like the Continental artists and caricaturists, Hogarth was absorbed in the range of human features, and some of his early pictures were almost exercises in the modification of features such as the *Chorus of Singers* (1732), the *Laughing Audience* (1733), and *Scholars at a Lecture* (1737). Some of the faces would have been identifiable by contemporaries, since well-known people often sat, for example William Fisher, of Jesus College, Oxford, who agreed to be drawn as the reader in *Scholars at a Lecture*.[12] Hogarth's prevailing attitude toward subjects as well as individuals was early evident in *A Midnight Conversation* (1733). In four lines of verse below the engraving, he protested:

> *Think not to find one* meant Resemblance *there*
> *We lash the* Vices *but the* Persons *spare*
> Prints *should be* prizd *as* Authors *should be* read
> *Who sharply smile prevailing Folly dead.*

The "Persons," however, contemporaries, and biographers have ever been more persuaded by Hogarth's practices than by his protestations, and the "reading" of Hogarth's graphic works early and late has included the identification of the "Persons." Even more controversial has been the diversity of emphasis on *"sharply"* as against *"smile,"* sharpness subordinating the comic into rejection and satire. Then, Hogarth's acceptance of a commission to execute the caricature, in every characteristic of the genre, *Taste in High Life* (1742), has further convinced "readers" as well as the dilet-

11. Frederick Antal, *Hogarth and His Place in European Art* (London, 1962), Chapter VII, "Expression and Caricature," p. 129.
12. Ronald Paulson, *Hogarth's Graphic Works* (New Haven, 1965), II, p. 172, to which I am greatly indebted in this study.

tante that Hogarth disdained to accept and enjoy himself as a
caricaturist.

Against this interpretation of his works, Hogarth protested in the
print *Characters and Caricaturas* (1743) where he diversified some
one hundred male faces in profile. In the lower part of the composition he reproduced three "characters" after Raphael and four
"caricaturas" after Ghezzi, Carracci, and Leonardo. To enforce
the distinction and to defend and enhance his role as a "comic
history painter," Hogarth gratefully cited Fielding's famous tribute
to him in the Preface to *Joseph Andrews:* that he was an exact
copier of nature. Ten years later, Hogarth returned to his attack
on the "phizmongers" in his expanded critical manifesto, the
Analysis of Beauty, where in the longest chapter, "Of the FACE,"
he developed the old truism that "the face is the index of the
mind," and that "imperfections are easier to be imitated than
perfections." [13]

Finally, in the fourth and revised version of *The Bench* (1758),
he reverted to *"the different meaning of the Words* Character,
Caracatura *and* Outrè [sic] *in Painting and Drawing":*

> . . . *to express* [the first] *with any degree of justness in Painting, re-
> quires the utmost Efforts of a great Master. Now that which has, of late
> Years, got the name of* Caracatura, *is, or ought to be totally divested of
> every Stroke that hath a tendency to good Drawing; it may be said to be
> a Species of Lines that are produc'd rather by the hand of chance than
> of Skill; for the early Scrawlings of a Child which do but barely hint an
> Idea of an Human Face, will always be found to be like some Person or
> other, and will often form such a Comical Resemblance as in all proba-
> bility the most eminent* Caracaturers *of these times will not be able to
> equal with Design, because their Ideas of Objects are so much more
> perfect than Children, that they will unavoidably introduce some kind
> of Drawing.*

Early and late, Hogarth's practice belied his prejudices and
protests against the increasing dominance of caricature in art and

13. ed. Joseph Burke (Oxford, 1955), esp. pp. 134–35; Alexander Cozens,
Principles of Beauty, Relative to the Human Head (London, 1778), p. 9:
"But there are more degrees of deformity than of beauty, as there are a
greater number of irregular forms than regular."

writing. Many of the heads in the earlier pictures certainly heighten defects, not perfection or beauty. Hogarth's attitude was more kindly than satiric, and though moral disapprobation was a more powerful emotion with Hogarth than laughter, in confronting the deformities and the distortions, we tend to be less distressed and to reject less. *The Gate of Calais, or The Roast Beef of Old England* (1749), though expressing Hogarth's resentment of his treatment in France and his fervid patriotism, was accepted in his own day, and has been ever since, as a caricature in the full perfection of the genre. Hogarth certainly considered *Simon Lord Lovat* (1746) and *John Wilkes Esq.* (1763), more as portraits than caricatures; yet, in each he caught the essence of personality in deformity. Even if he did not do it consciously, Hogarth effectively projected his own pugnacious English nature in his dog Trump who sits with him in the famous self-portrait, *Gulielmus Hogarth* (1749). Hogarth produced his ultimate caricature when he took the plate of his self-portrait, obliterated his "natural" likeness and then in porte-crayon depicted Charles Churchill as a bear and entitled the plate *The Bruiser* (1763). All the personal and political bitterness between Hogarth and Charles Churchill has now become irrelevant. We enjoy *The Bruiser,* the amiable bear, and the dog Trump, as caricature within the primary distinction and perfection of the genre, the interpretation of human faults or blemishes in the form of animals. It is a fitting climax to long knowledge and practice of caricaturing that in the *Tailpiece to the Catalogue* (1761) Hogarth should draw, and Grignion engrave the connoisseur (who long had aroused the deepest resentment in Hogarth) as a monkey.

Although Hogarth professed to reject caricaturing and thought of himself as a satirist, yet with all his popularity and influence, Hogarth did not impede the progress of caricaturing that culminated in Cruikshank and Rowlandson. "From the 1730's, personal caricature, good-humoured and intimate, became fashionable among English dilettanti in Italy and was much influenced by the caricatures of Ghezzi." [14] Early in his career Reynolds painted

14. Mary Dorothy George, *English Political Caricature to 1792*, I, p. 11. Mrs. George's Chapter VI, "Hogarth and English Caricature—Mid-Century Developments," is one of the best interpretations of Hogarth I have seen.

half a dozen caricatures, three while he was in Rome in 1751, which are now in the National Gallery of Ireland. In his notebook he recorded his subjects and then did the pictures which were commissioned by some of the subjects who appeared in them. His best known was the parody of the *School of Athens,* one of the twenty-one figures being Thomas Patch, about whom more follows. The subjects and owners, aristocracy and travelers in the English colony in Rome, were gratified by the caricatures, not offended, but James Northcote reports that:

I have heard Reynolds himself say that, although it was universally allowed he executed subjects of this kind with much humour and spirit, he yet held it absolutely necessary to abandon the practice; since it must corrupt his taste as a portrait painter, whose duty it becomes to aim at discovering the perfections only of those whom he is to represent.[15]

The English artist who worked more in response to the cultivated tastes of the English connoisseurs and more in accord with the artistic concepts of the Continental caricaturists, was Thomas Patch (1725–1782). While a medical student in Exeter, Patch tried his hand at drawing, just as Smollett had tried his at occasional verse in Glasgow.[16] "The offence caused by [Patch's] caricatures of his fellow townsmen was still remembered" more than sixty years later. He turned to the study of painting in Rome; in 1749 he was joined by Reynolds, but for reasons not clearly known, he was banished from Rome in 1756 and settled in Florence, becoming for many years a member of the English colony of which Sir Horace Mann had long been the patron. Patch was in great demand as a caricaturist, but he always had the consent of the person he was portraying. First, he made single sketches of individuals, later assembling the sketches in groups of as many as twenty in paintings of which engravings were then made. But he always included himself as the most marked caricature. The titles are indicative of many eighteenth-century caricatures in art and fiction: *The Punch Party* (1760), with a key for the fifteen figures;

15. *The Life of Sir Joshua Reynolds* (London, 1818), I, p. 46.
16. Lewis M. Knapp, "Early Scottish Attitudes toward Tobias Smollett," *Philological Quarterly,* XLV (1966), 262–69.

The Musical Party (1774), eleven figures without a key but readily identified in the English colony; *A Gathering at Sir Horace Mann's House,* containing the figures of fourteen well-known English travelers; and *A Caricature Group* (1763?) which includes Mann and Garrick. In Patch's own words:

After seven years laborious Observation on this curious Study [of the human face] he had found out ye Means of knowing at Sight what a Man's profession was, in what country he was born, and in what situation of that Country—what his religion was and to what sect of that religion he belonged—what his situation in Life was respecting Marriage etc.,

The study was to be illustrated in six copper plates, unfortunately lost before publication. In his caricatures Patch made "a kindly and humorous commentary on his subject by a trifling exaggeration of their distinguishing characteristics," generally in profile that "facilitates the exaggeration of facial characteristics." His chief concern, expressed in words he took from Machiavelli, was to show *come il mondo è guasto.* The identity of his subjects is of interest only to social historians; his skill as a painter, especially his studies of the human face, sustained the popularity of his pictures for a long time.[17]

By the third quarter of the century caricaturing was so developed and flourishing as to dispose Francis Grose, the antiquarian and lexicographer of the vulgar tongue, to publish *Rules for Drawing Caricaturas: with an Essay on Comic Painting* (1788).[18] This was a history as much as a manual, replete with "analytical diagrams" of the nose, lips, chins, and facial proportions, assigning a term to each variation. For example, the head in the fifth figure, plate III: "the contour is convexo-concavo; nose snubbed, mouth blubbered, chin double, eyes goggle, eyebrows pent-housed." [19] To be sure, a rather pedestrian performance but all the more indica-

17. F. J. B. Watson, "Thomas Patch (1725–1782): Notes on His Life, Together with a Catalogue of His Known Works," *The Walpole Society,* XXVIII (1940), 15–31.
18. See Arthur Clayborough, *The Grotesque in English Literature* (Oxford, 1965), pp. 6–9.
19. *Rules for Drawing Caricaturas* (London, 1778), p. 15.

tive of current practices and tastes.[20] He rates Coypel, the illustrator of *Don Quixote,* and Hogarth as the most successful, for example. He points out that "many human faces have striking resemblances to particular animals," and cites Hogarth's *Gate of Calais* and *The Bruiser;* in fact "on examining divers of Hogarth's designs, we find he strongly adopted the principle here laid down." [21] Grose, in his opening paragraph, reasserts the essential tradition:

The art of drawing Caricatura is generally considered as a dangerous acquisition, tending rather to make the possessor feared than esteemed; but it is certainly an unfair mode of reasoning, to urge the abuse to which any art is liable, as an argument against the art itself.

James Beattie, however, as a philosopher and a man of letters, understood better the amplitude and merits of the comic spirit in art and literature, the graphic works of Hogarth and the prose fiction of Tobias Smollett, to whom he specifically alludes several times.[22] In one concise passage, Beattie assimilates the genre into the classical perspective:

Aristotle, Cicero, and Quintilian, all admit, that bodily singularities may be laughable; and, according to the first of these authors, that is a ridiculous countenance, in which there is deformity and distortion without distress. Any feature, particularly one of the middle features, a nose, a mouth, or a chin, uncommonly large, may, when attended with no inconvenience, tempt one to smile; as appears from the effect of caricatura in painting.[23]

The singularities may be laughable, but in caricature, incongruities are essential, and Beattie continues to develop and illustrate the magisterially important proposition that "the greater the number of relations, as well as of contrarieties, that take place in

20. For a contrasting handbook see Cozens's *Principles of Beauty, Relative to the Human Head,* in plates and text basic to any consideration of portraiture in art and literature.
21. *Rules for Drawing Caricaturas,* pp. 15, 24.
22. *On Laughter and Ludicrous Composition,* pp. 350, 367, 431, 475.
23. *Ibid.* p. 353.

any ludicrous assemblage, the more ludicrous it will generally appear." [24]

II

Seventeenth- and eighteenth-century artists both in portraiture and caricature studied and interpreted the variations in human features in the terms of pictorial art and thereby created conventions of characterization that were adopted and translated into the prose of novelists in the descriptions of appearances and actions, and gradually became absorbed into the medium of speech itself. Furthermore, artists both established and confirmed traditional categories and classifications of personalities and developed the antithesis between the beauty of perfection on the one hand and the aesthetic appeal of imperfections or deformities, on the other: the irrational and evil deformities in satire, the physical abnormalities and the demonic in the grotesque, and the tolerable and humorous imperfections in caricature. I have sought to concentrate only on the last of these, though caricature often tips over into satire and the grotesque. The focus on Hogarth's caricature here is made not because of his pervasive influence on artists and writers alike, often remarked on and studied,[25] but to establish a stance, a perspective, a critical category in order to give a context to Tobias Smollett as a caricaturist. Smollett, because he was forced to subsist by journalism, was more sensitive to the cultural demands of his public, to the subjects, the artistry, and appeal of caricature; yet he survives not as an historical curiosity but as a writer of durable values, best grasped in some of our modern terminology.

The popularity in the 1740's of caricatures and satiric prints,

24. *Ibid.* p. 354.
25. More recently by Robert Etheridge Moore, *Hogarth's Literary Relationships* (Minneapolis, University of Minnesota Press, 1948) in his chapter on Smollett. Some studies have been made of Rowlandson's and Cruikshank's illustrations of Smollett's novels, but not of his contemporary illustrators such as Darly, Bunbury, and Hayman. A. S. W. Rosenbach, *A Catalogue of the Works Illustrated by George Cruikshank and Isaac Cruikshank* (Philadelphia, 1918); Edward C. J. Wolf, *Rowlandson and His Illustrations of the 18th Century English Literature* (Copenhagen, 1945); Albert M. Cohn, *Bibliographical Catalogue of the Printed Works Illustrated by George Cruikshank* (London, 1914).

LES CARICATURES DE M. POND,

EN DEUX PARTIES.

PUBLIÉES PAR

JEAN BOYDELL, GRAVEUR, Rue de CHEAPSIDE,

A LONDRES.

Prix QUINZE CHELINS en Feuille.

PREMIERE PARTIE, CONTENANT DOUZE ESTAMPES.

PEINTRES.

ANN. CARRACHE. 1. Deux PHILOSOPHES.

C. MARATTI. 2. TÊTE de Profil, avec des LUNETTES fur le NEZ, en Crayon rouge.

DITTO. 3. Ditto, un SINGE, en Crayon rouge.

WATTEAU 4. Le Docteur MISAUBIN, "Prenez des Pilules."

C. GHEZZI. 5. H. P. SEB. RESTA, Célébre Amateur du Deffein, mort à ROME l'An 1714.

DITTO. 6. CHAIRCUITIER.

DITTO. 7. Le Sieur CAV. TOMASO.

DITTO. 8. Le Docteur B.

DITTO. 9. Le Docteur TOM BENTLEY.

DITTO. 10. Deux célébres Antiquaires, STOCH & SABBATINI.

DITTO. 11. Le GOUVERNEUR voyageant avec fon PUPILE.

DITTO. 12. Madame PETIT & fon CUISINIER.

SECONDE PARTIE, CONTENANT TREIZE ESTAMPES:

LE GUERCHIN. 13. Le CORDONNIER, en Crayon rouge.

F. MOLA. 14. Une FIGURE avec des LUNETTES.

C. MARATTI. 15. TÊTE de Profil, en Crayon rouge.

LE FAGE. 16. La Caricature de LE FAGE.

DITTO. 17. Celle de Car. GHEZZI.

DITTO. 18. CARNACCI, Acteur du Théatre du VALLON dans le Tems du CARNAVAL de l'Année 1738, que tout ROME alla voir en Foule, à caufe de fon Jeu & de fa Voix.

DITTO. 19. POLICHINELLE attaqué de la GOUTTE, Ditto, du Cabinet de M. le Duc de DEVONSHIRE.

DITTO. 20. Le même, qui enfeigne à lire à fes Enfants.

TUSCHER. 21. VIEILLARD qui n'eft pas trop réchauffé, &c.

DITTO. 22. La Caricature du célébre Cav. DILLE.

A. POND. 23. VINUM NON FACIES BONUM BIBENDO. MART.Lib.v.

C. GHEZZI. 24. FIGURE Affife.

DITTO. 25. TÊTE de Profil.

PLATE VI—Table of Contents for *Les Caricatures de M.* [Arthur] *Pond, publiées par Jean Boydell, graveur, Rue de Cheapside, à Londres, 1740–42.* (By kind permission of The Fitzwilliam Museum, Cambridge, England.)

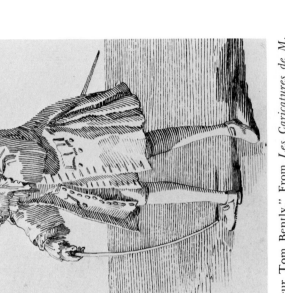

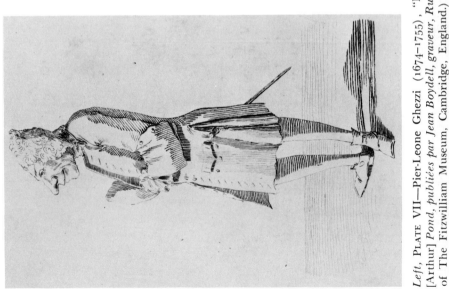

Left, PLATE VII—Pier-Leone Ghezzi (1674–1755), "Le Docteur Tom Bently." From *Les Caricatures de M. [Arthur] Pond, publiées par Jean Boydell, graveur, Rue de Cheapside, à Londres, 1740–42.* (By kind permission of The Fitzwilliam Museum, Cambridge, England.) *Right*, PLATE VIII—Raymond La Fage (1651–1690), "Carnacci, acteur du théâtre du Vallon dans le Tems du Carnaval de l'Année 1738, que tout Rome alla voir en Foule, à cause de son Jeu & sa Voix." From *Les Caricatures de M. [Arthur] Pond, publiées par Jean Boydell, graveur, Rue de Cheapside, à Londres, 1740–42.* (By kind permission of The Fitzwilliam Museum, Cambridge, England.)

PLATE IX—Raymond La Fage (1651–1690), "Polichinelle attaqué de la Goutte." From *Les Caricatures de M.* [Arthur] *Pond, publiées par Jean Boydell, graveur, Rue de Cheapside, à Londres, 1740–42.* (By kind permission of The Fitzwilliam Museum, Cambridge, England.)

Top left, PLATE X—Annibale Carracci (1560–1609), "Deux Philosophes." From *Les Caricatures de M.* [Arthur] *Pond, publiées par Jean Boydell, graveur, Rue de Cheapside, à Londres, 1740–42.* (By kind permission of The Fitzwilliam Museum, Cambridge, England.)

Bottom left, PLATE XI—Karl Marcus Tuscher (1705–1755), "Vieillard qui n'est pas trop réchauffé." From *Les Caricatures de M.* [Arthur] *Pond, publiées par Jean Boydell, graveur, Rue de Cheapside, à Londres, 1740–42.* (By kind permission of The Fitzwilliam Museum, Cambridge, England.)

Above, PLATE XII—Pier-Leone Ghezzi (1674–1755), "Bernardino Luchesini Bolognese." From *Raccolta di XXIV Caricature, disegnate collà penna dal celebre Cavaliere P. L. Ghezzi,* Mathias Oesterreich, sculp., Dresden, 1750. (By kind permission of The British Museum.)

Left, PLATE XIII—P. L. Ghezzi, "Dottore che tasta il Polso." From *Raccolta di XXIV caricature di Matthaeus Oesterreich*, (sculps), Dresden, 1750. (By kind permission of The British Museum.)

Right, PLATE XIV—P. L. Ghezzi, "Abbate Napoletano." From *Raccolta di XXIV caricature di Matthaeus*

Left, PLATE XV—P. L. Ghezzi, "Cercante Cappuccino." From *Raccolta di XXIV caricature di Matthaeus Oesterreich* (sculps), Dresden, 1750. (By kind permission of The British Museum.)

Right, PLATE XVI—P. L. Ghezzi, "Decano." From *Raccolta di XXIV caricature de Matthaeus Oesterreich* (sculps), Dresden, 1750. (By kind permission of The British Museum.)

PLATE XVII—P. L. Ghezzi, "Petruccella servitore." From *Raccolta di XXIV caricature di Matthaeus Oesterreich* (sculps), Dresden, 1750. (By kind permission of The British Museum.)

which occasionally later depicted Smollett himself, cultivated the habit in the public of anticipating and recognizing individuals artistically or fictionally disguised. Smollett, feeling frustrated and abused as a Scottish physician and writer in London, attempted to appeal to this fashion in his first novel, *Roderick Random* (1748). By his narrative of the then recent Carthagena Expedition, the subject of much public controversy, his inclusion of public figures, his obvious satiric thrusts, his insistent autobiographic perspective, Smollett invited—initially among his Scottish readers—the identification of the individuals he had in mind. He, on second thought, was apprehensive on this score and protested in his Preface: "Every intelligent reader, will, at first sight, perceive I have not deviated from nature, in the facts, which are all true in the main, although the circumstances are altered and disguised to avoid personal satire." Within six months of the publication of *Roderick Random,* Smollett, disturbed by the indignation of Scottish acquaintances, protested in a private letter to Alexander Carlyle, on June 7, 1748: "I am not a little mortified to find the characters strangely misapplied to particular men whom I never had the least intention to ridicule. . . . I shall take this opportunity therefore of declaring to you, in all the sincerity of unreserved Friendship that no person living is aimed at in all the first part of the Book." [26]

Be that as it may, though this proviso may have exempted or mollified Scottish acquaintances, the personal satiric impact of the novel was such that Smollett inserted in the Dublin edition of 1754 an "Apologue" containing a defense in the metaphor of the caricaturist:

A Young painter indulging a vein of pleasantry, sketched a kind of conversation-piece, representing a bear, an owl, a monkey, and an ass; and to render it more striking, humourous and moral, distinguished every figure by some emblem of human life.

Bruin was exhibited in the garb and attitude of an old, toothless, drunken soldier; the owl perched upon the handle of a coffee-pot, with

26. Lewis Mansfield Knapp, *Tobias Smollett, Doctor of Men and Manners* (Princeton, 1949), pp. 99–100. I regret that in this study I have too often assumed rather than acknowledged my indebtedness to Professor Knapp.

spectacle on nose, seemed to contemplate a newspaper [and so on; some persons, however] affirmed the resemblance was too palpable to be overlooked. . . .

Christian reader, I beseech thee, in the bowels of the Lord, remember this example whilst thou art employed in the perusal of the following sheets; and seek not to appropriate to thyself that which equally belongs to five hundred different people. If thou should'st meet with a character that reflects thee in some ungracious particular, keep thy own counsel; consider that one feature makes not a face, and that tho' thou art, perhaps, distinguished by a bottle nose, twenty of thy neighbours may be in the same predicament.[27]

Smollett's subjective defenses are almost irrelevant. He held to no settled canons in his writing; instead he appropriated and exploited everything in the tradition of prose fiction that at the moment he thought might entertain, instruct, reform, and be read. Even within one novel the progress is more spontaneous than structured; the very process of writing generated what followed from chapter to chapter, and his attitude toward characters wavered. Nevertheless, despite all the variations and exceptions, some consistent attitudes and practices emerge.

First of all Smollett habitually made a sharp and generally consistent distinction between satire and caricature, between those characters he rejected and those characters he accepted with tolerant laughter, sympathy, and an understanding of human imperfections. It is, however, far less effective to point up satire by subjecting the innocent and virtuous to the iniquities of a system of oppressors than it is to make the caricature the medium of satire rather than its object. Smollett is not consistent in distinguishing the object from the medium, but it is caricature as an art form in itself and not as a medium of satire, that I wish to pursue mostly in *Roderick Random* and *Peregrine Pickle,* in the composition of which Smollett developed the skills and qualities that were to culminate in the perfection of *Humphry Clinker.* I am not undertaking a comprehensive survey of all the novels; I am endeavouring only to establish and apply a critical category, in the hope of inducing and assisting others to pursue an analysis of the

27. Quoted from the 1766 edition.

passages in Smollett's novels upon which I have not touched. With some minor exceptions and modifications, Smollett did not characterize the objects of his satire by description of features, by dialogue, or by distinguishing actions. In the initial seven chapters of *Roderick Random,* until Roderick reaches London, there is a succession of faceless, stereotyped characters with such names as Gawky, Syntax, Potion, Rifle, Shuffle, later Oakum, Crampley, and Mackshane; not individualized in appearance, in dialogue or action. In the long satiric interlude of Melopoyn, the nameless characters are to be recognized by reference to the conduct of public figures. On the other hand, Smollett almost invariably introduces a caricature with a description of the face and appearance, such as Lieutenant Bowling, Isaac Rapine, Beau Jackson, and Lavement, the last a caricature in the manner of Ghezzi.

Caricature was primarily pictorial. When the subjects and the interpretations of these subjects were assimilated to another medium—to prose fiction—equivalencies in language had to be developed and perfected. Henry Fielding equated caricature with style, mistakenly with the burlesque style which he employed for narrative detachment and comment, not characterization. One embarks on a scrutiny of any style with trepidation, recalling how Longinus warned that the "enterprise is . . . an arduous one. For the judgement of style is the last and crowning fruit of long experience." Assuming some familiarity with Smollett and quoting a few short passages, I shall endeavor, nevertheless, to point out some rhetorical features of Smollett's literary caricaturing.[28]

Smollett's initial effective modulation of style into caricature occurs in the dialogue of Lieutenant Bowling. Following a description of his appearance, a brief narrative of his dispatching the dogs that attacked him, his defiance of Gawky, their owner, and his armed servants, Bowling speaks out:

Lookee, brother, your dogs having boarded me without provocation, what I did was in my own defence. So you had best be civil, and let us shoot ahead, clear of you. . . . Lookee, you lubberly son of a w--e, if

28. For a fuller and more comprehensive study of Smollett's style, see Albrecht B. Strauss's essay "On Smollett's Language: A Paragraph in *Ferdinand Count Fathom," English Institute Essays* (New York, 1959), pp. 25–54.

you come athwart me, 'ware your ginger-bread-work. I'll be foul of your quarter, d--n me. . . . None of your jaw, you swab—none of your jaw . . . I shall trim your lac'd jacket for you.—I shall rub you down with an oaken towel, my boy—I shall.[29]

Restricted by a naval career of actions and not words, he verbalizes all communications in the metaphors of sea life; his dialogue is colloquial rather than literate in the sense that his verbal concepts are expressed in groups of words rather than in one; he resorts to repetitions and profanity to compensate for his insecurity with language; his periods are broken up into the cadence of impetuous assertiveness. Even from so brief an introduction, a reader immediately thereafter recognizes Bowling whenever he speaks, such recognition being the true test of characterization by style. Here is an eloquence, however, a garrulity heightened beyond the command of any "natural" or "realistic" seaman, but highly stylized in the sense that caricature is an artifact. This same style, with appropriate modifications, characterizes all Smollett's seamen who are struggling to cope within the limitations and the deformity of their sea life with life ashore; with landsmen, bureaucracy, matrimony, the law, the manners of a way of life more complex and universal.

Crab speaks only briefly, but in his own manner. The Latin tags of the innkeeper are more in character than his exorbitance; Captain Weazel has a command of all the eloquence of Theophilus Cibber's acting Pistol, and Lavemont is the first of a succession of foreigners handicapped by his unfamiliarity with the English and their language. Second only to Bowling and Rattlin is the explosive dialogue, more like a monologue, of Morgan, the Welshman. Again, a few lines from Morgan's first appearance are sufficient to identify him ever afterwards:

Splutter and oons! you lousy tog, who do you call my master? get you gone to the doctor, and tell him my birth, and education, and my abilities; and moreover, my behaviour is as good as his, or any shentleman's (no disparagement to him) in the whole world—Got pless my soul! does he think or conceive, or imagine, that I am a horse, or an ass, or

29. *Roderick Random*, I, pp. 12–13.

a goat, to trudge backwards and forwards, and upwards and downwards, and by sea, and by land, at his will and pleasures?—Go your ways you rascallion, and tell doctor Atkins, that I desire and request, that he will give a look upon the tying man, and order something for him if he be dead or alive, and I will see him take it by and by, when my craving stomach is satisfied, look you.[30]

Here the style is in harmony with the substance. Morgan's Welsh accent and allusions, more frequent later on, are amusingly tolerated, not out of any sentiment for Welsh nationalism but because they offset the professional subordination he has suffered from an appetite that has often come before duty. The deliberation of synonymous elaboration rather dignifies his subordinate dependence; his oaths and his exclamations are of a religious cast to ally his life with a larger framework of values; the cadence of the periods is a projection of patient suffering. " 'As for a shentleman in distress . . . I lofe him as I lofe my own powels; For Got help me! I have had vexation enough upon my own pack.' "[31]

A portrait, however, is limited to an individual arrested in repose, or in a moment of time; the caricaturist must surmount this limitation by selecting a moment of cumulative action. In eighteenth-century terms, "beauty and character of the face consist in form and colour; but that passion and grace depend upon action."[32] Or in modern terminology, "expression in life and physiognomic impression rest on movement no less than on static symptoms, and art has to compensate for the loss of the time dimension by concentrating all required information into one arrested image."[33] Hogarth, in his chapter on action in the *Analysis of Beauty*, struggled with this limitation. Prose fiction, on the other hand, is organically the narration of action over a period of time, segmented into episodes, but controlled by an evolving plot. Both painters and writers, Hogarth and Smollett especially, were tempted to crowd the moment, the episode, with "realistic" violent action rather than to select and develop one action. Furthermore, the amplification, in particular the heightening of action, notably in

30. *Ibid.* I, pp. 204–5.
31. *Ibid.* I, p. 207.
32. Cozens, *Principles of Beauty*, p. 5.
33. Gombrich, *Art and Illusion*, p. 345.

caricature, transcends the limitations of the natural laws of physics, physiology, and probability, and the human body survives falls, accidents, fights, and catastrophes that would maim and kill in "real" life. The characters are also more energetic, more emotional, more profane. Every reader of *Roderick Random* will perceive how Smollett intensified the action to appeal to the brutal action of pantomime, such as the beating of the schoolmaster, the violence of the press gang, the adventuring in London and later in France. On the other hand, by selecting and heightening the action artistically he attained the detached laughter of the acceptance of human limitations, as in the carriage episodes on the road to London and, best of all, in the action in the naval battles. Rather than try to illustrate how Smollett transcended sensationalism to achieve a calming simplicity, I offer a rather brief episode that might have been written by Smollett, but is actually to be found in a rejected passage of Hogarth's *Analysis of Beauty*, doubtless inserted by Morrell.

Even storys of the utmost Horror . . . become matter of laughter and jest, as the known story of the wounded man in a sea fight [who] having [first] had his leg shot off had also afterwards his head shot off unknown to the bearer by a cannon ball as he [was] carried down to the surgeon, unknown to the Bearer, the surgeon being angry . . . [at the absurdity of] bringing a man to be cur'd [without] a head the fellow who brought the body, returnd for answere in a pet damn him he told me it was his leg.[34]

    Smollett did attempt a caricature of one woman, the female virtuoso who employed Roderick following his shipwreck on the Somerset coast. Critics and artists repeatedly warned that features must not be exaggerated until they became repulsive and grotesque, nor certain physical habits or necessities dwelt upon in the manner of the Dutch painter. With the female virtuoso, Smollett failed in both regards: she is little more than a miscellany of eccentricities and offensive habits that are neither amusing nor tolerable. Almost equally infelicitous are Smollett's attempts to

34. *Analysis of Beauty*, p. 180. Compare the amputation episode in *Roderick Random*, I, pp. 208–10.

describe, reveal through dialogue, or project into action any qualities of what the eighteenth century denominated as beauty. Reynolds gave up caricaturing for fear it would corrupt his sense of
beauty; Hogarth basically rebelled against caricature all his life to
preserve his sense of human perfections. Late in the novel, when
Roderick surprises Narcissa in the garden, and she swoons from
surprise, the narrator exclaims:

O! that I were endowed with the expression of a Raphael, the graces of
Guido, the magic touches of a Titian, that I might represent the fond
concern, the chastened rapture, and the ingenuous blush, that mingled
in her beauteous face, when she opened her eyes upon me, and pronounced, "O heaven! is it you?" [35]

The passage fails for two reasons. First of all Smollett, by in-
voking the great names in the idealizing of the sublime and the
beautiful, presumably hoped to accomplish by allusion what he
should have attempted himself; or else Smollett's sense of perfection or beauty was of natural phenomena such as a vibrant, healthy
female or the spontaneous generosity of the uncorrupted such as
Strap. There is no center or quality of disciplined virtue or perfection in Narcissa, and here as elsewhere Smollett lapses into
ready-made formulas and clichés when he introduces the subjects
of beauty and virtue into his fiction. Though he aspired in Roderick "to represent modest merit struggling with every difficulty
to which a friendless orphan is exposed, from his own want of experience, as well as from the selfishness, envy, malice, and base
indifference of mankind," we are not persuaded or enlightened.
Melopoyn is hardly more than pathetic, Thomson an abstraction.
    In the development of Strap, however, Smollett attempted to
combine both perfections and imperfections. In the Scottish chapters, Strap is no more than a classmate in the chastisement of the
schoolmaster, but once Roderick meets up with Strap on the road
to London, Smollett began to sense the potentialities of Strap as
a rather simple-minded, industrious, loyal barber with a propensity
to apprehension and terror. As the narrative progresses Smollett
fails again and again to translate into controlled dialogue and ac-

35. *Roderick Random*, II, pp. 281–82.

tion Strap's wholly admirable emotions of surprise at good fortune, his generosity, and loyalty; instead these are dissipated in a tumult of hyperbole. Late in the third volume Smollett as much as admits again his failure to cope with virtue when Roderick undertakes with Strap's money to court and marry an heiress: "it would require"—Smollett writes—"the pencil of Hogarth to express the astonishment and concern of Strap." [36] Readers resent in the final chapters Strap's humiliations in the sea fight under Bowling and also the reward of his long-suffering and loyalty and generosity in the marriage to the cast mistress, Miss Williams.

On the other hand, Smollett is far more effective in perfecting Strap's apprehensions and fears. Not until the arrival in London of the pair does Smollett describe Strap's appearance:

Strap was habited in . . . a short crop-eared wig that very much resembled Scrub's in the play, and the knapsack on his back, added to what is called a queer phiz, occasioned by a long chin, an hook nose and high cheek bones, rendered him on the whole a very fit subject of mirth and pleasantry.[37]

In the same way that Cibber's playing the role of Pistol was the inspiration for the caricature of Captain Weazel, Garrick's favorite role as Scrub in Farquhar's *The Beaux' Stratagem* was the original of Strap. A study has yet to be made, so far as I can discover, of the affinities and reciprocal influences of caricature and acting; the influence, for example, of the harlequins in the *commedia dell' arte* whose "performance[s] consisted simply of a series of extravagant capers, of violent movements and outrageous blackguardisms." [38] Also to be taken into account were the extraordinary pantomimes of John Rich and Henry Woodward; the acting of humour and low comedy characters, or in the "entertainments" of Samuel Foote at the Haymarket. Indeed, at all times actors have been tempted by a dangerous capacity for parody, and

36. *Ibid.* II, p. 109.
37. *Ibid.* I, p. 86.
38. Cyril W. Beaumont, *The History of Harlequin* (London, 1926), p. 50. Smollett remarked in *The Present State of All Nations* (II, p. 229): In England pantomime is "exhibited in a variety of surprising scenes, supposed to be the effects of sorcery wrought in favour of Harlequin and his mistress Columbine."

the great Samuel Johnson trembled in fear of Foote. Garrick often expressed a preference for acting low characters, and owed much, in his role as Scrub, to Hogarth.

When threatened by danger, or misfortune, or the supernatural, Strap in apprehension and fear reacts with all the uninhibited emotions and actions of a low comic character, of harlequin and the pantomimes of the popular stage. From the moment he triumphs with a Latin tag over the Latin-quoting landlord, Strap surmounts his shortcomings and fears with the wit of Horace, with rather incongruous proverbs of his own concoction, and with flights of allusion, all assimilated into a style that is his own. The climax is not in the action but in the word:

"I am a poor but honest cobbler's son—my mother was as industrious a woman as ever broke bread, till such time as she took to drinking, which you very well know—but everybody has failings—*humanum est errare.*—Now, for myself, I am a poor journeyman barber, tolerably well made, and understand some Latin, and have a smattering of Greek —but what of that? perhaps I might also say that I know a little of the world—but that is to no purpose—though you be gentle and I simple, it does not follow but that I who am simple may do a good office to you who are gentle.—Now this is the case—my kinsman the school-master —perhaps you did not know how nearly he is related to me—I'll satisfy you in that presently—his mother and my grandmother's sister's nephew—no, that's not it—my grandfather's brother's daughter—rabbit it! I have forgotten the degree: but this I know, he and I are cousins seven times removed." [39]

Thus in substance and manner, simplicity is heightened and understood. We have Smollett's word that "the character of Strap (who I find is a favourite among the ladies everywhere) is partly taken from life," from "my neighbor John Lewis, Bookbinder" in Chelsea. So flattering and sentimental was the kindly and humorous caricature that in succeeding years at least four other persons were championed as the model for Strap—a response that more than any other evidence sets the stamp of ultimate success on a caricature. [40]

39. *Roderick Random*, I, pp. 133–34.
40. Knapp, *Tobias Smollett*, pp. 100–2.

III

Smollett's second novel, *Peregrine Pickle* (1751), is an anomalous and digressive piece of prose fiction that might support any critical theory or tempt one to digress from a controlling argument. In a study of Smollett as a caricaturist, however, it affords an opportunity to mark the disparity between the transience of the journalistic realism of passing events and social adventuring in contrast to the imaginative and enduring values of expressionism in caricature.

Smollett in *Peregrine Pickle* (working ostensibly as a moralist to expose the manifold wickedness of society) scrambled together a kind of compendium of private resentments, the satire of public figures, memoirs, and caricatures. The personal allusions, comments on contemporaries, the inserted journalistic narratives of Lady Vane and Daniel MacKercher, all won the novel some immediate notoriety. And much scholarly research has been expended in identifying the public figures Smollett had in mind and the events to which he alludes, some of the distortions of which he later regretted and modified.[41] The action is also the type of action a journalist seeks: the confrontation of antagonistic schematic types, trades, professions, and nationalities, culminating in the drubbing or humiliation of one of the protagonists. Peregrine himself, though endowed with little more than a succession of legacies that opened the "sluices of his natural benevolence," [42] is not an evolving or ingratiating character; rather a fight promoter, the stager of confrontations, never passing up provision for a return bout, gratuitously exposing the baseness in others. Even Smollett deplores, unconvincingly, his own creation, and barely one-tenth of the way through the novel, Smollett pauses to reflect on Peregrine; but readers soon recognize that the passage is equally applicable to Smollett himself: "howsoever preposterous and unaccountable that passion may be, which prompts persons, otherwise

41. Howard Swazey Buck, *A Study in Smollett, Chiefly "Peregrine Pickle"* (New Haven, Yale University Press, 1925), *passim.*
42. *Peregrine Pickle,* I, p. 192.

generous and sympathising, to afflict and perplex their fellow-creatures, certain is it that our confederates [Peregrine and Smollett] entertained . . . a large proportion of it." [43]

The injuries of time have all but obliterated the contemporaneity of *Peregrine Pickle,* the current knowledge of the navy, of public figures, of subjects, episodes, social patterns assumed by Smollett as common knowledge. All this background is now the province of the historian, the biographer, and the editor. We must grope and conjecture about how much Smollett knew of Captain, later Commodore Daniel Hore, Captain John Bover, and boatswain Thomas Smale, their naval careers in the Carthagena Expedition, and later their friendships and personalities; also of the extraordinary house for retirement, "Bellefield," in Cheshire, which Hore built after the model of a ship and where he continued the nautical routine ashore. How much did Smollett's readers know about these men? [44] Did Hore, Bover, and Smale ever recognize themselves in the caricatures? We do not know. What was familiar to readers in the 1750's is almost discovery for us, and what was enjoyed as caricature in full is now almost only a kind of grotesque comical fantasy. Even much of the subtle artistry is lost to us in Smollett's appropriating the roles of Quin, Cibber, Garrick, and others in the comedy characters of Shakespeare, Jonson, and Farquhar.

Yet a residue, an impersonal and timeless narrative survives, and we are caught up immediately by the opening scene—the first act as it were—of *Peregrine Pickle.* The dramatic exposition by the innkeeper, exactly in character, prepares for the entrance of Commodore Hawser Trunnion, Lieutenant Jack Hatchway, and Boatswain Tom Pipes; the piping of the docking, with descriptions of the appearances of each, the order of seating, the pantomime, the dialogue, the curtain coming down with the piping and chorus of "The Boatswain's Whistle," all in the metaphor, the idiom, of the sea, survive to us as caricature—as one of the great episodes in English literature. This is not realism or

43. *Ibid.* I, p. 98.
44. George M. Kahrl, *Tobias Smollett, Traveler-Novelist* (Chicago, 1945), Chapter III, "A Retired Admiral."

naturalism, or at the other extreme a *tour de force,* a farce, but insight into human values, the triumph of the human spirit over the "perfect deformity."

In comparison with the turbulence and passion elsewhere in *Peregrine Pickle* how can the human spirit enrich a routine, even a banal, evening at a commonplace public house? Of the five persons present, two are in retirement, one is silent, another accomplishes one short response to a question. First there is the nameless "loquacious publican" who is a publican because of his insatiable interest in all that goes on in the community, manifest in his tireless and indiscriminate retailing of circumstantial details. Yet he is aware that as a publican he must not take sides or become involved; hence his narrative is a perilous balance between curiosity and indifference, the catch-phrase, "as the saying is," being his formula of detachment. He has not the imagination to use metaphors; his idioms are localisms, but not dialectal; the diction almost as colorless as the publican himself. In almost every line, however, there is the conflict between a yearning for intimate relations in the community and the politic anonymity of a publican. "For my part, Master, I believe much may be said on both sides of the question; thof to be sure, the devil is always going about, as the saying is." [45]

Commodore Hawser Trunnion is a victim of his own hasty temper, and a distorter of his failures into an idealized image of himself as a vigorous and heroic naval officer. He now lives in a defensive isolation in the Garrison insulated by preserving the naval routine with his former naval companion Hatchway and servant Pipes. He asserts this fiction of his life in a richness of naval metaphor—in the dialect of the life he had lived as boy and man until retired as incompetent at the age of thirty. Like the excerpt from Sturmy that Swift inserted into the narrative by Gulliver of a storm at sea, Trunnion's cant or jargon becomes more effective as it becomes more unintelligible to a reader; Trunnion talks and repeats not to persuade others, but to sustain himself, and yet he has the saving wit, when Hatchway sardonically deflates his pose, to laugh at his own weakness. The substance of the conversation that evening in the public house is secondary and

45. *Peregrine Pickle,* I, p. 9.

expository. The personalities revealed in the dialogue are supreme, and like every work of art they are more true to life than reality itself.

To sustain a narrative, initiated and carried forward by such a trilogy of protagonists was the ultimate opportunity of the novelist, and Smollett again and again rises to the challenge, superbly in the preposterous wedding of Trunnion, and in the deathbed scene when Trunnion transmutes his life into his own terms; even the echoes of Falstaff do not distract, but are absorbed into the vision. Smollett lapses lamentably, however, into episodes engineered by Peregrine to perplex and agitate the Commodore, and again fails to translate the emotions of frustration and rage into action or even an eloquence that is more than hyperbolic profanity. At a loss how to handle one of the turbulent confrontations, Smollett confesses, "it would be a difficult task for the inimitable Hogarth to exhibit the ludicrous expression of the commodore's countenance, while he read this letter [supposedly from a repudiated nephew]. It was not a stare of astonishment, a convulsion of rage, or a ghastly grin of revenge, but an association of all three, that took possession of his features." [46] The succession of practical jokes too often violates or subordinates characters to no clear purpose other than to animate the scene and raise a laugh at the expense of trust or goodwill. To make fools out of masters and tutors, out of Keypstick and Jolter, will always please the immature; a spinster is a stock figure of the most heartless laughter, yet somehow Smollett treats Jolter and Mrs. Trunnion with the sympathy of caricature as the narrative progresses. With the potentialities of Garrison, the Pickles, and Peregrine's schooling exhausted, Smollett turns to a satire of the Grand Tour, resuscitated and animated only by the introduction and expansion of the caricatures of William Hogarth and Mark Akenside.

As much as biographical studies enrich the enjoyment of the two caricatures, it is of far more significance that Smollett transcended his models to perfect two incongruous, recurring types of human personalities, not in isolation but in association and conflict, in accord with Beattie's observation that "the greater the number of relations, as well as of contrarieties, that take place in

46. *Ibid.* I, p. 102.

any ludicrous assemblage, the more ludicrous it will generally appear." [47] The Physician and Pallet contrast the incongruities of several human imperfections: ignorance versus learning; impetuosity versus solemnity; rashness versus deliberation; the moderns versus the ancients; the incongruities of false enthusiasm. If there was any vanity, it was in Smollett, in the display of classical learning in the Physician, and though in the "entertainment in the manner of the ancients," his source was limited to *Apicci Coelii de Opsoniis et Condimentis, Sive Arte Coquinaria,* nonetheless, to have assimilated Apicius showed some measure of erudition. [48]

IV

Smollett's caricatures are more of types than of individuals, though the models for his characters may have been persons now little more than names in Smollett scholarship. Akenside and Hogarth were public figures and their lives and works were known in varying degrees over the years, quite apart from their probable caricatures in *Peregrine Pickle.* More recently Howard Buck in "Smollett and Dr. Akenside" and Ronald Paulson in "Smollett and Hogarth" [49] have repaired the injuries of time to these two men, and we are now in a better position to comprehend Smollett's re-creation of both into the caricatures of the Physician and Pallet.

Intrinsic to caricaturing, each was a prominent figure, Hogarth the most famous artist in London; Smollett touched only on their careers and not their private lives. Some contemporaries and biographers in the eighteenth century commented on the identity of Akenside in the Physician; but no one until Paulson seems to have commented on parallels between Hogarth and Pallet, though it does not follow that some of the parallels were not obvious then or later. Of the personal reactions of the two men, we know nothing. Hogarth as a caricaturist, even of himself, doubtless would not have been offended (and he was quick to resent); he would have more likely welcomed the notoriety. We are probably

---

47. *On Laughter and Ludicrous Composition,* p. 354.
48. Kahrl, *Tobias Smollett, Traveler-Novelist,* pp. 44–49.
49. *Journal of English and Germanic Philology,* XXXI (1932), 10–26; *Studies in English Literature,* IV (1964), 351–59.

mistaken in assuming that the caricatures were provoked by Akenside's reflections on Scotland or Hogarth's friendship with Fielding. As far as is known, Smollett had no intimacy with either; the
caricatures are impersonal. Smollett presents Akenside as "a
young man, in whose air and countenance appear all the uncouth
gravity and supercilious self-conceit of a physician piping hot from
his studies . . . a mere index-hunter, who held the eel of science
by the tail." [50] He rather neglects Akenside as a physician, though
he calls him by that title, but he concentrates on Akenside as a
classicist, a poet, and an enthusiast for republicanism. The pedant
has at all times been a stock character in comedy, not at the expense
of his learning but his manner. He is "a person who is simplified,
cut and dried to a formula, using his environment as a means for
his one and only purpose . . . he lives the proposition of identity." [51] The Physician, afflicted perhaps only subconsciously by
his incapacities and failure as a physician, compensates in his
poetry and classical learning. His manner is the defect that Smollett projects into action; he must develop "the proposition of
identity," beginning with his dress and solemnity, his manner
of expounding his learning—Smollett is good at this—the repeated
interjection of the classical erudition, superbly dramatized in the
"Entertainment in the Manner of the Ancients," and more subtly
in the Physician's courting martyrdom, the transcendent identity
of the ineffectual.

In Pallet we get even more of the incongruities between the two
levels of his character. Pallet also is asserting an identity, to conceal his little learning, ignorance of artistic canons, incompetence
at historical painting; in a measure of resentment of the low estate of artists against the esteem for scholars and poets. Smollett
was never more adept at projecting into a caricature the inverse
of the blemish or defect of a character who by an irony of human
nature reveals his flaw in the assertion of a self-created image.
Pallet is conspicuous in appearance; his insecurity and ignorance
are projected in an almost buffoonish assurance, a cultivated vivacity in dialogue, aggressive actions, best dramatized in his manners and comments on visits to patrician art galleries. Smollett

50. *Peregrine Pickle*, II, pp. 55–58.
51. Foss, *Symbol and Metaphor in Human Experience,* pp. 140ff.

at times heightens the portrait with some general traits of ignorant English artists abroad and includes episodes that may not have been biographical—some touches, perhaps, from a nameless artist that he had met in Paris in 1750. But he never touches on those achievements for which Hogarth was famous.

In the last analysis, however, no matter who the subject or what the medium, the ultimate achievement for both the artist-author and the reader is the refinement of style; only this gives durability to a book and in this only are art and writing intrinsically creative. In caricaturing, the style or manner that appeared unlabored, rather off-hand—*capriccio*—perfected only after great effort yet giving no sense of travail, was most sought after and prized. I find much of Smollett's fluency in *Roderick Random* and *Peregrine Pickle* (especially when Peregrine is upstaged) self-conscious, manipulated, a mixture of comment and narrative, and a hypnotic variation of elegant formulas and clichés. In caricaturing, on the other hand, Smollett progressively evolved an immediacy and animation, a discrimination in style not mannered, but modulated to the differentiation in characters. Smollett ceased to narrate, but allowed his characters to speak, as it were, first the seamen, and then the humbler characters, in a style organic to the character—for example, Strap, the Physician, and Pallet—and with a heightened informality that graces the subject. There are some touches of this quality in *Sir Launcelot Greaves,* but Smollett the novelist rose to the full command of the informal style in *Humphry Clinker,* where spontaneity, intrinsic to the familiar letter, and *capriccio* are imperative.

Although Smollett may have raised the curtain for *Humphry Clinker* with another protest, "that the Letters in question . . . have no tendency to the *mala fama,* or prejudice of any person whatsoever," he persisted in the journalistic vein with current interests and public figures, more to satirize institutions and to celebrate individuals, with a sprinkling of "odd" characters with "whimsical peculiarities," such as the hack writers that gathered at Smollett's residence in Chelsea for some food and drink. The preface significantly is not in the words of Smollett, the author, but those of a fictitious editor; seldom has a novelist accomplished so much in setting the tone of his fiction as Smollett did in the masterly brief sketch of Jonathan Dustwich, and almost by style only. As the narrative advances, each of the protagonists tells his tale in his own style. At last, Smollett achieves a sympathetic caricature of a spinster in Tabitha Bramble, of a servant girl in Win Jenkins and her "Winisms," [52] of modest merit in Humphry Clinker, and Lieutenant Obadiah Lismahago, one of the more magnificent caricatures in English literature. For Lismahago there was a living person as a source, Captain Robert Stobo, though doubtless recognized by few readers then or since: the hapless soldier-adventurer in the New World with all his Scottish "deformities," though some not without distress to the English, rounded out in appearance, in action, and superbly in dialogue, the particulars chosen and imaginatively heightened and perfected.[53]

The most sustained and culminating caricature in all Smollett's prose fiction is indubitably Matthew Bramble who dominates and sets the tone in *Humphry Clinker*. Although immediately recognized and accepted ever since as a delineation of Smollett himself,[54] the caricature should not, however, confuse the identities of Smollett as an author, a narrator in several of his novels, a journalist and historian, a private citizen in his letters and *Travels*, and Smollett's imaginative creation of Bramble, in part, out of Smollett's conception of himself. Obviously there are many features and opinions recognizable as autobiographical—after all Smollett was an author of some renown—and although out of a rueful consciousness of his disabilities and deformities, he conceived Matthew Bramble, the caricature is more universal and more true than Smollett himself. From the opening line, "The Pills are good for nothing," Bramble speaks out in the heightening of a combative rationalism and emotionally charged style; in

52. See W. Arthur Boggs, "A Win Jenkins' Lexicon," *Bulletin of the New York Public Library*, LXVIII (May 1964), 323–30.
53. See Kahrl, *Smollett, Traveler-Novelist*, pp. 131–45; Robert C. Alberts, *The Most Extraordinary Adventures of Major Robert Stobo* (Boston, 1965). Captain Stobo, on his return to America, shot himself: see *N & Q*, CCIII (1958), p. 180.
54. Lewis M. Knapp, "Smollett's Self-Portrait in *The Expedition of Humphry Clinker*," in *The Age of Johnson: Essays Presented to Chauncey Brewster Tinker* (New Haven, 1949), pp. 149–58.

substance and spirit much of what Smollett had been saying and feeling for years. Yet Bramble is an entity apart and superior to his creator, a perfection not of what is rational and beautiful but irrational and incongruous, an apotheosis of the deformities of age, illness, misanthropy, sentimental attachments, and hypochondriacal apprehensions resolved not in despair, but in the aesthetic detachment of laughter—a laughter reasserting the values of the human spirit.

V

Because Smollett counted so much on an acquaintance with topical events, settings, allusions, controversies, and people, a modern reader must make the effort to repair some of the "injuries of time" in order to read him aright; yet there must be more than the topical to survive the years. If Smollett is worth the trouble, he must have a substance and meaning intelligible to us in our present frame of reference and modes of perception, more immediately perhaps in terms of the modern psychoanalytic explorations in caricature suggested by Ernst Kris and E. H. Gombrich. In retrospect the 1740's and 1750's were the golden age of English portraiture, and for two reasons: first, as remarked earlier, artists carried through analytical studies of the variations in human features and codified the multiformity, the *schemata*, as indices of human personality; secondly, artists discovered that appearance was not due so much to careful observation of nature as to the invention of pictorial effects; this resulted in caricature in the inventing of artistic devices for overcharging, in heightening features above the realities.

Gombrich notes: [55]

All artistic discoveries are discoveries not of likenesses but of equivalences which enable us to see reality in the terms of an image and an image in the terms of reality. And this equivalence never rests on the likeness of elements so much as on the identity of responses to certain relationships. . . .

55. Gombrich, *Art and Illusion*, p. 345.

It is precisely because these identities do not depend on the imitation of individual features so much as on configurations of clues that they are so difficult to find by mere looking. What we experience as a good likeness in a caricature, or even in a portrait, is not necessarily a replica of anything seen.

In prose fiction this required the perfecting of a style that was not simply a recording, a transcription, or a narrative dialogue; rather the contriving of rhetorical techniques and conventions that stimulated the acceptance of styles familiar and indigenous to diverse characters, yet unnatural as all artistic conventions are.

It is the very constitution of the psyche to be caught up in conflicts between subjective potentials and motives against human and natural limitations. There is a great heterogeneity in individual frustrations, and much human cerebration goes into the resolution of the conflicts; the more dynamic the tensions, the greater the creativity. In the anthropological sense of the word, a culture affords many resolutions, some of the most effective of all in the fine arts and literature. Readers, friends, and biographers were acutely conscious that Smollett had an almost pathological burden of frustrations and resentments. In much of his writing, in fiction and elsewhere, he relieved his exacerbated frustrations by recourse to a few modes of satire, destructive both for him and us; there is an almost conscious bitterness in his failure to approximate any sort of rational perfection. More and more, however, from caricatures [56] he learned artistically to perfect the flaws and incongruities with a skill that affords the relief of laughter; he exalts, occasionally sentimentalizes, a fault with tolerant affection. Somewhere Freud defines laughter as the aggressive acceptance of defeat. The ultimate resolution for Smollett, as for all of us, was the auto-caricature in Matthew Bramble, a cantankerous and voluble invalid whose maladies presage death. Employing the word "grotesque" in the sense of the artistry in caricature, Martin Foss, though without Smollett in mind, translates into our terms the rationale as well as the enduring literary values of Smollett:

56. See especially Robert Hopkins, "The Function of Grotesque in *Humphry Clinker*," *Huntington Library Quarterly*, XXXII (Feb. 1969), 163–77.

In times of chaos men return to a magic form of art, using the demoniac aspects of life for their stories and plays: sickness, insanity, death; but they turn them into grotesque means for laughter in order to regain their inner balance. . . . The grotesque will always appear and take hold of those ages which are under the strain of disaster, feeling the sinister and chaotic aspects of life, but advanced enough to appease the mind by laughter.[57]

57. *Symbol and Metaphor in Human Experience*, p. 143.

Eighteenth- and Nineteenth-Century Biographies of Smollett

PAUL-GABRIEL BOUCÉ

THE numerous biographies of Smollett written in the eighteenth and nineteenth centuries, although widely different in length and quality, are all marked by the same paradoxes. First of all, their number is by no means the tangible literary proof that Smollett's life was well known. Especially—but not exclusively—in the late eighteenth century, biographers readily compensated for the lack of authentic documents or reliable sources of information with pseudo-biographical data shamelessly lifted from Smollett's novels. For instance, little was—and still is—known about his childhood and adolescence in Scotland. The would-be biographer immediately culled all the anecdotes he needed to conceal his lack of genuine knowledge from the beginning of *Roderick Random* which was assumed, without much certainty, to be largely autobiographical.

The second paradox derives from the first. By a strange phenomenon of literary osmosis between Smollett's novels and life, his biography has often been abusively reconstructed from the events or characters described in his novels. Whereas usually the critics take it for granted that an author projects much of his personal experience into the composition of his novels, time and time again, Smollett's biographers have interpreted his life in the fictional terms of his novels.

In my estimate, this irritating and misleading tendency ought to be referred to as "inverted autobiography." Even during Smollett's lifetime inverted autobiography was already casting its obscuring veil over his true personality. Thus, when the Scottish historian William Robertson met Smollett for the first time in London in 1758, after a dinner at Forrest's Coffeehouse during which Smollett had appeared to his wittiest and most urbane advantage, Robertson confessed his "great surprise at the polished and agreeable manners and the great urbanity of his conversation. He had imagined that a man's manners must bear a likeness to his books, and as Smollett had described so well the characters of ruffians and profligates that he must, of course, resemble them." [1] It is only fair to add, however, that Alexander Carlyle in the following sentence comments wryly on Robertson's "rawness." But another instance, furnished by an American admirer of Smollett, Richard Smith, will help to grasp the antithetic yet complementary demands for biographical knowledge and the harmful but spontaneous recourse to inverted autobiography. Richard Smith (1735–1803) "provincial councillor for New Jersey, and later a delegate to the Continental Congress" [2] wrote to Smollett in February 1763: "Of the circumstances of your life we at this distance know little, but I should be glad to be informed whether Roderick Random or Peregrine Pickle contain any traces of your real adventures, and at what age of life, and under what circumstances they were written?" There, in an epistolary nutshell, was the legitimate craving for biographical details, and also the potentially virulent germ of much later inverted autobiography.

Before examining the biographies themselves, the reader must be forewarned and hence forearmed. None of the biographies of Smollett can be considered, in the sonorous words of Thomas Carlyle about Boswell's *Life* of Johnson, as "a revocation of the edict of Destiny." It is even doubtful whether any of them, with the possible exception of Walter Scott's "Tobias Smollett" can be ranged in the critically desirable category of "good literature," whatever the shadowy criteria of this never-laid ghost may be. A study of Smollett's biographies involves the unsettling of much

1. *The Autobiography of Dr. Alexander Carlyle of Inveresk* (London and Edinburgh, 1910), p. 356.
2. L. M. Knapp, "Smollett's Admirers in Eighteenth-Century America," *Williams Alumni Review*, XXII (1929), 114. The quotation from Richard Smith's letter is to be found on the same page, where Knapp reproduces the letter in full.

scholarly dust from volumes seldom opened now. These biographies, ranging from a few lines in a dictionary to over two hundred pages in Robert Anderson's sixth edition (1820) of Smollett's works, could not all be included in this paper, which, in the vain hope of tracing and listing all of them would have soon been doomed to degenerate into a dreary sequence of jejune bibliographical notes. And yet, in spite of the poor literary quality of some of these biographies, they are not devoid of interest for the student of Smollett's life and works. In his most informative book *Smollett's Reputation as a Novelist* (Princeton, 1947), Fred W. Boege has already shown what wealth of critical appreciation may be quarried from little-prospected fields. My concerns are understandably, more restricted in chronological and critical scope. Analysis of biographies of Smollett in the eighteenth and nineteenth centuries should enable modern students of Smollett to gain a firmer grasp of the evaluation—more often the jagged ups and downs—of the assessment of Smollett's personality as a man and a writer of the eighteenth century. And my personal hope is that such an examination will also permit successive students of Smollett to measure the debt of scholarly gratitude all Smollettians owe to the tireless research of Lewis Mansfield Knapp.

In 1764, only a year after his letter to Smollett, Richard Smith might have found a succinct answer to his biographical queries in *The Companion to the Play-House,* where in a notice of less than a page, the compiler David Erskine Baker gave probably the first sketch of Smollett's life, down to his recent departure for the South of France. The biographical data themselves are scanty and take up only eight lines of the first column to cover the period down to 1748. Baker informs his readers that Smollett is a "well-known Writer of the Present Age . . . a Native of *North Briton,* and was bred a Sea Surgeon." [3] Then, as usual with the first imprecise and anonymous biographical notices of Smollett between 1764 and 1777, the story of Smollett's life is confounded with

---

3. [David Erskine Baker], *The Companion to the Play-House* (London, 1764), no pagination. See Volume I for entry under Smollett's name. A revised edition of this book appeared in 1782 entitled *Biographia Dramatica,* edited by Isaac Reed.

the evolution of his literary career, so that the works and their relative shares of success or failure are given more attention than the author himself. Apart from the various very short biographical sketches that were published with the announcement of Smollett's death, an anonymous memoir of Smollett's life appeared in the *Westminster Magazine* (III, May 1775, pp. 225–28). It was entitled: "Some Account of the Life and Writings of the Late Dr. Smollett." There again, it is chiefly concerned with Smollett's novels rather than his life and personality, but it is not devoid of sympathy for Smollett's dour independence: "No doubt he had his failings; but still it would be difficult to name a man who was so respectable for the qualities of his head, or amiable for the virtues of his heart" (p. 228). Although it is true, as Boege remarks (p. 52), that this article was reproduced in the *Annual Register* for the same year 1775, it is nevertheless inaccurate to state that it appeared "again . . . in the 1777 edition of Smollett's *Plays and Poems*, the *Encyclopaedia Britannica,* and other places." It would be more precise to say that this biographical account of 1775 was incorporated into the first genuine life of Smollett prefixed to the 1777 edition of his *Plays and Poems*,[4] and later reproduced verbatim in the second edition of the *Encyclopaedia Britannica* (Edinburgh, 1783).[5]

Smollett's novels take pride of place in the twenty-nine pages of these "Memoirs of the Life and Writings of the Author" prefixed to the 1777 edition of his *Plays and Poems*. Furthermore, the interest in Smollett's life is closely linked with the problem of the critical evaluation of autobiographical material in the novels. The following lines, already published in the 1775 account, are typical both of the late development, as James L. Clifford[6] has shown recently, not so much of biography itself in the eighteenth century, as of any critical reflection upon this somewhat neglected genre,

---

4. The same memoir, with the same pagination, was reproduced in the second edition of the *Plays and Poems* (London, 1784).
5. There is no biographical account of Smollett in the first edition of the *Encyclopaedia Britannica* (Edinburgh, 1771).
6. James L. Clifford, "How Much Should a Biographer Tell? Some Eighteenth-Century Views," in *Essays in Eighteenth-Century Biography,* ed. Philip B. Daghlian (Bloomington, Indiana University Press, 1968), pp. 67–95.

and of the inverted autobiography that has from the start clouded the biographical and literary appreciation of Smollett's life and works:

It is a trite remark, that the lives of authors are little more than an enumeration and account of their works; they are generally so deficient in incident, that, after a compleat catalogue of their writings is produced, nothing more can be added, except the times of their births and deaths. If fame is in the least to be depended upon, this observation will not apply to Dr. Smollett. It is said, and probably with some truth, that the chief incidents in the early part of his life were given to the public in one of the first and best of his productions, *Roderick Random....*[7]

Among the reviews of this work, three deserve to be briefly analyzed and quoted for their divergent and even contradictory opinions. First of all, the *London Review* (Vol. V, March 1777, pp. 206–10) puts forward a rather curious hypothesis whereby the "Memoirs of the Life and Writings" prefacing the 1777 edition of the *Plays and Poems* might have been composed by none other than Garrick himself. Here is the judgment of the anonymous reviewer on the biographical introduction:

. . . concise and well enough written: the writer, however, appears to have had chiefly in view, not the character of Doctor Smollett, but that of Mr. Garrick; by whom it is more than probable these memoirs were manufactured. At least we conceive no other writer would be so extremely solicitous to exculpate that comedian from the charge, brought against him by Dr. S. in regard to his managerial shuffling about the author's tragedy, the *Regicide*. Whether Mr. G. be the writer of the memoirs or not, certain it is that he must have furnished the memorialist with copies of the private letters, here published, admitting them to be genuine copies of the epistolary correspondence between Dr. Smollett and Mr. Garrick (*Plays and Poems*, p. 206.).

William Kenrick, who had bitterly attacked the *Critical Review* in his pamphlet *A Scrutiny; or the Criticks criticis'd* (London,

7. *Plays and Poems Written by Tobias Smollett, M.D. With Memoirs of the Life and Writings of the Author* (London, 1777), pp. i–ii.

1759) was the editor of the *London Review*. As the review of the *Plays and Poems* is signed "W," it is not impossible to think it may have been written by Kenrick himself who still felt enough malice against Smollett to cast a slanderous slur upon the sincerity of Smollett's reconciliation with Garrick. But whoever Mr. "W" was, he failed to point out that these 1777 "Memoirs" borrowed heavily from the account of Smollett published in the *Annual Register* of 1775. The innovations of the 1777 "Memoirs" consisted chiefly in adding four letters from Smollett to Garrick, a letter from Smollett to Wilkes, a footnote on the *Travels through France and Italy* quoting Sterne's all too famous quip about "Smelfungus" in the *Sentimental Journey,* a few minor details, and the Latin epitaphs at Leghorn and Leven with the inevitable translations of both in ponderous monumental English. On the other hand, in Mr. "W's" defence, it may be advanced that his surmise did not lack psychological acumen: "From the known ingenuousness of Dr. Smollett's disposition, therefore, it is to be doubted whether his repentance was so sincere as here represented, or that he was so thoroughly convinced his censure had been illiberal or ill-grounded; as in either case we conceive he would have been just enough to have retracted it on the spot." More than a century and a half later, the same skeptical opinion is shared by Lewis M. Knapp [8] when he mentions "the supposedly complete reconciliation" between Smollett and Garrick. It is to be hoped that further research may one day solve the problem of the authorship of the 1777 "Memoirs" which remain a valuable primary source for Smollettian studies.

A short article published in July 1777 in the *Monthly Review* makes no direct reference to the *Plays and Poems* that it is supposed to examine. Instead, the critic presents a synthetic judgment of Smollett's works. In the space of fourteen lines he manages to praise Smollett's humor and his imagination as displayed in his novels, but he deplores the wretchedness of his theater and the unequal quality of his poetry. The reviewer in the August 1777 number of the *Westminster Magazine* (Vol. V, p. 435) is even

8. Lewis M. Knapp, "Smollett and Garrick" in *Elizabethan Studies and other Essays* (Boulder, Col., 1945), p. 243.

more cursorily expeditious. In five and a half lines he dismisses the *Plays and Poems* along with their biographical "Memoirs" and roundly asserts that "the private anecdotes of authors have rarely incident or instruction enough in them, to be either entertaining or edifying." But in spite of such adverse criticism and even though accuracy is unfortunately not among their qualities, these 1777 "Memoirs" remain an important biographical landmark in Smollettian studies, if only because of their chronological primacy.

For nearly twenty years, from 1778 to 1796, no new biographical account of Smollett appeared, at least none of any importance. But Smollett's novels were still very popular,[9] and a renewal of interest in the author's life was bound to make itself felt sooner or later. A reader of the *Edinburgh Magazine* in a letter to the editor, probably expressed the opinion of many Scottish gentlemen with a literary turn. He proposed that a series of Scottish portraits should be published, accompanied whenever they already existed, by graphic representations of Armstrong, Beattie, Home, Mallet, and Thomson. Among these poets, the reader does not hesitate to range Smollett: "I mention Smollet's [sic] last, because his great merit and the shocking neglect he met with, demands [sic] the particular attention of the public."[10] This request, formulated in 1786, can hardly have been satisfied four years later by the "Short Account of the Author" prefixed to the first collected edition of Smollett's works.[11] This biographical sketch is so meager that its skeletal indigence of new information prevents it from being of much value. It is mostly cribbed from the 1777 edition of Smollett's *Plays and Poems,* and it tries to conceal its dearth of factual data behind the by now general obscurity of Smollett's life: ". . . so little of these occurrences is now accurately known, that the only unerring mark of his progress through life is to be found in his

9. See Fred W. Boege, *Smollett's Reputation as a Novelist* (Princeton, 1947), pp. 45–68.
10. *The Edinburgh Magazine,* IV (Dec. 1786), p. 424.
11. *The Miscellaneous Works of T. Smollett, M.D.* (Edinburgh, 1790). For the "Short Account of the Author," see Vol. I, pp. [i]–xi. Quotation from p. [i].

writings." The fallacy of inverted autobiography was already rampant. In the following year, 1791, appeared the third edition of *The British Plutarch* which contained a "Life of Dr. Tobias Smollett," a dozen pages long, and also mostly paraphrased from the 1777 *Plays and Poems*. The general assessment of Smollett's personality strives to be impartial, without any excessive severity for Smollett's psychological faults: "He had a high spirit, and much irritability of temper, and was apt to speak of others with too great a degree of asperity. But to his particular friends and acquaintance, he was kind and generous, even beyond the reach of his abilities." [12]

With Robert Anderson (1750–1830), a Scotsman and a physician like Smollett, biographical research took a fresh start. Between 1794 and 1820, either in prefaces to Smollett's poems or novels or in separately published biographies of Smollett, Anderson proved tireless and prolific, even bordering on the verbose, in his dedication to his fellow Scotsman. Anderson made ample and often unacknowledged use of the preceding anonymous biographies of Smollett, but he is the first to have tackled the task of clearing the factual obscurities in Smollett's life with something like the exacting spirit of modern scholarship. In the constantly revised drafts of Smollett's biographies, he appears as a fervent admirer of the novelist and of his works, but he is endowed with enough impartiality not to omit his subject's human and literary failings. His first biographical sketch of Smollett was prefixed to the tenth volume of his *Complete Edition of the Poets of Great Britain* (Edinburgh, 1794): it numbered but ten pages (pp. 939–48), and some paragraphs were inserted verbatim from the 1790 edition of Smollett's works. Although such brazen plundering was rife in the eighteenth century, it is to be wondered whether Anderson did not feel free to do so for the simple but sufficient reason that he had a hand in the composition of the "Short Account" in the 1790 edition of Smollett's works. This hypothesis would at least exculpate Anderson from the heinous literary sin of plagiarism, but his connection with the 1790 edition still remains to be discovered, if it ever existed. As soon as his first separate *Life of Tobias Smollett,*

12. *The British Plutarch* (3rd ed., London, 1791), p. 127.

M.D.[13] was published in 1796, it was well received. Thus the *British Critic* (IX, March 1797, p. 333) declared that "Dr. Anderson delineates the character of the man and the author with that judgement and elegance which he usually displays." Seven years later, the *European Magazine* still thought highly of the latest edition (1803) of Anderson's biography which "does justice to the memory of Dr. Smollett, without suppressing the foibles attached to his character. The fate of this Author cannot but be lamented." [14]

Thanks to Anderson's diligent biographical zeal, the fifty odd introductory pages in his first edition of Smollett's *Miscellaneous Works* (London, 1796) had increased threefold in the sixth and last edition of 1820.[15] Apart from their chronological lack of precision, Anderson's biographies present two general characteristics. First, they insist on the part played by Scotland in Smollett's psychological and literary formation. Secondly, Anderson never balks at the autobiographical interpretation of Smollett's novels. But these biographies, despite their numerous inaccuracies, replete with enthusiastic—and even at times slightly chauvinistic—ardor for their subject, contributed largely to Smollett's popularity during the two opening decades of the nineteenth century. Boege (pp. 64–65) is perhaps unnecessarily harsh on Anderson's magpie habits. It is anachronistic to judge Anderson's heavy-handed borrowings from the preceding biographies by the rigorous standards of modern scholarship. If Anderson fell into the fallacy of inverted autobiography, at least he was aware of its dangers, as will appear from the following quotation taken from the first edition

13. Robert Anderson, *The Life of Tobias Smollett, M.D., with Critical Observations on his Works* (London, 1796; 2nd ed., 1800; 4th ed., 1803; 5th ed., 1806), apart from the first edition, all the later ones were published in Edinburgh. No copy of the third edition is to be found in the British Museum. For information about the six editions by Robert Anderson of Smollett's *Miscellaneous Works* between 1796 and 1820, see Francesco Cordasco's "Robert Anderson's Edition of Smollett," *N&Q*, CXCIII (Dec. 1948), p. 533. Cordasco's preference for the third Edinburgh edition of 1806 is questionable, since the sixth and last Edinburgh edition of 1820 is usually recognized as the best.
14. *European Magazine,* XLV (April 1804), p. 294.
15. *The Miscellaneous Works of Tobias Smollett, M.D.* (London, 1796), "The Life of Smollett," I, pp. xiii–lxvi.

of his separately published *Life of Tobias Smollett* (London, 1796, pp. 3–4):

Of the personal history of SMOLLETT, less is known than his rank in English literature might give reason to expect. It is said, and probably with some truth, that the chief incidents in the early part of his life were given to the world in his novel of *Roderick Random*. The incidents, if real, are certainly a good deal heightened by invention, and disguised by the decoration of fiction. No credit, therefore, is due to them, as authorities, in a work of truth; and they are not followed by the present writer, in this attempt to relate with the fidelity of biographical narration, what is known of his personal history and literary productions.

A much more balanced judgment than Boege's was passsed on the bulk of Anderson's biographical achievement by Mark Longaker: "Although the work of Anderson did not attain the high level of excellence that some of the Lives by Johnson reached, it illustrated a clear recognition of a form of Life-writing and a true application of the principles of that form. With such biographers as Johnson and Anderson, the sketch came into its own as an established biographical type." [16]

The only biographer who knew Smollett personally in London and then later in Paris during his 1750 stay there, was the novelist John Moore (1729–1802), the celebrated author of *Zeluco* (1786) whose subject strongly reminds the reader of *Ferdinand Count Fathom*. Moore, like Anderson, was a Scot and a physician. He was also the father of Sir John Moore, commander-in-chief in the Peninsula and the hero of Coruña where he was killed in 1809. Noyes in his edition of the *Letters of Tobias Smollett* (Cambridge, Mass., 1926) gives fourteen letters addressed by Smollett to Moore between 1750 and 1767, and Knapp in the new Clarendon Edition prints sixteen. These reveal the feeling of deep friendship that existed between the two men. It is to Moore that Smollett usually opens his heart most willingly about his declining health or his growing psychological and moral pessimism. Neither Moore nor

16. Mark Longaker, *English Biography in the Eighteenth Century* (Philadelphia, 1931), p. 491. For Robert Anderson, see pp. 486–91.

Smollett—another similitude between the two men—owes his fame to his medical profession, but to works of fiction and books of travels. Moore's edition [17] of Smollett's works was published a year after Anderson's, in 1797. It is a pity that Moore has not exploited more thoroughly his personal acquaintance with Smollett for the composition of his "Memoirs," which remain biographically vague and unhelpful. However, the lifelong friendship between the two authors enabled Moore to draw a penetrating psychological portrait of Smollett, which constitutes one of the most important direct testimonies we possess for the knowledge of Smollett's personality. Moore's affection for Smollett never blinds him to the failings of his fellow-novelist:

Free from vanity, Smollett had a considerable share of pride, and great sensibility; his passions were easily moved, and too impetuous when roused; he could not conceal his contempt of folly, his detestation of fraud, nor refrain from proclaiming his indignation against every instance of oppression . . . He was of an intrepid, independent, imprudent disposition, equally incapable of deceit and adulation, and more disposed to cultivate the acquaintance of those he could serve, than of those who could serve him. What wonder that a man of his character was not, what is called, successful in life! [18]

Moore's edition was fairly well received by the critics. The *European Magazine* [19] expresses its distaste for Moore's disquisition on romance "compiled from Warton and other writers, and contains little but what is far-fetched, and can be only with difficulty found applicable to the subject." Furthermore, the reviewer rightly complains that Moore omits to mention Smollett's *Essay on the External Use of Water*; the *British Magazine*; the *Compendium of Authentic and Entertaining Voyages*; his participation in the compilation of the *Universal History*. The *British*

17. *The Works of Tobias Smollett, M.D. With Memoirs of his Life; To which is Prefixed A View of the Commencement and Progress of Romance,* ed. John Moore, M.D. (London, 1797, I, pp. xcvii–cxcvi. Moore's life of Smollett and his *View* were both reprinted in James P. Browne's eight-volume edition of *The Works of Tobias Smollett* (London, 1872).
18. *The Works of Tobias Smollett,* ed. J. P. Browne (London, 1872), I, pp. 151–52.
19. XXXIII (Feb. 1798), p. 100.

Critic (vol. XII, July 1798, pp. 59–65) is on the whole more favorable to Moore's biographical sketch which is "agreeably written," a rather non-committal statement. But of more critical interest is the comparison between Anderson's and Moore's biographies of Smollett: "The present account is more elaborate, and contains some few materials from the personal knowledge of Dr. Moore." Anderson's criticism is a model of courtesy and canny Scotch discretion. In his own "Life of Dr. Smollett" prefixed to the sixth edition (1820) of Smollett's works, Anderson insists on the importance of Moore's personal acquaintance with Smollett, but he is astute enough to note that Moore's "Memoirs" adduce little or no new factual information. But immediately afterwards, as if to deaden the blow, Anderson stresses that Moore may be pardoned "as the undertaking was unpremeditated, and not of his own chusing, and he was engaged in it when his health was declining, and the infirmities of age were increasing fast upon him, he may be supposed to have employed the materials which were at hand, rather than such as might have been provided by diligence and premeditation." Anderson's last sentence about Moore's edition was probably intended as something of a Parthian shaft: "This edition of his *Works*, as it is improperly entitled, has not been reprinted." "Sic transit gloria. . . ."

Anderson, in his various biographies of Smollett had gathered—or perhaps garnered—the best and (for the period) most complete factual information on Smollett's life. Moore, although he failed to add significant new biographical data in spite of his personal knowledge of Smollett, had provided Smollett's readers with a valuable assessment of his friend Smollett's complex personality. But it remained for a third Scotsman, whose literary fame dwarfed that of his two predecessors in the field of Smollettian biography, to write the most popular account of Smollett's life in the early nineteenth century: such was Sir Walter Scott's role.

The "Prefatory Memoir" composed by Scott on Smollett's life was used in 1821 as an introduction to the second volume of John Ballantyne's *Novelist's Library*. Fifty years after Smollett's death, Walter Scott brings no new elements to the chronological knowledge of his subject's life. On the contrary, Scott begins his life of Smollett by paying full, if not fulsome, homage to Moore and especially Anderson whose "careful research . . . leaves to us little except the task of selection and abridgement." [20] But the forty-odd pages of his biographical sketch contain much subtle psychological penetration stemming not only from Scott's admiration of Smollett as a novelist, but also from his own checkered experience as a writer, so that a sort of biographical empathy flows between Scott and Smollett. Scott is right in stressing Smollett's sometimes haughty awareness of his lineage: "Our author was descended from an ancient and honourable family; an advantage to which, from various passages in his writings, he seems to have attached considerable weight, and the consciousness of which seems to have contributed its share in forming some of the peculiarities of his character." [21] It is hardly surprising that Scott, as a romantic poet almost professionally in love with the wild scenery of his native country, should stress the influence of Smollett's early environment on his sensibility. That "Smollett was in the highest degree sensible of the beauties of nature, although his fame has chiefly risen upon his power of delineating human character," [22] may be a *post hoc ergo propter hoc* type of biographical fallacy, as Smollett's feeling for the romantic scenery of Scotland appears rather late in his career, chiefly in *Humphry Clinker*. Another defect in Scott's life of Smollett lies in his resolutely autobiographical interpretation of *Roderick Random*, although Scott seems aware of the ludicrous dangers of systematizing the process: "It was generally believed that Smollett painted some of his own early adventures under the veil of fiction; but the public carried the spirit of applying the characters of a work of fiction to living personages much farther perhaps than the author intended." [23] Scott probably exaggerates Smollett's "intimate knowledge of the nautical world" [24] displayed in the same novel. He is also the originator of a hard-dying biographical legend concerning Smollett's haphazard and high-pressure method of composing the monthly installment of *Launcelot Greaves* for the *British Magazine*:

20. Walter Scott, *The Lives of the Novelists* (London, [1910]), p. 71.
21. *Ibid.* p. 71.
22. *Ibid.* p. 72.
23. *Ibid.* p. 77.
24. *Ibid.* p. 75.

Smollett appears to have executed his task with very little premeditation. During a part of the time he was residing at Paxton, in Berwickshire, on a visit to the late George Home, Esq., and when post-time drew near, he used to retire for half an hour or an hour, to prepare the necessary quantity of *copy*, as it is technically called in the printing-house, which he never gave himself the trouble to correct, or even to read over.[25]

This was repeated *ad nauseam* by most biographers after Walter Scott until Lewis M. Knapp[26] conclusively demonstrated that there was no foundation for this statement—doubly so, as Paxton House was not built in 1760! More or less consciously, Scott probably viewed Smollett through the distorting prism of his own romantic genius, especially when he wrote of Smollett as "a searcher of dark bosoms [who] loved to paint characters under the strong agitation of fierce and stormy passions."[27] In September 1826, the *Quarterly Review* published a long article on the 1825 Galignani edition of the *Lives of the Novelists*, which was on the whole highly laudatory of Scott, but showed scanty sympathy for Smollett and his lifelong difficulties: "The unhappiness to which Smollett's violent and misanthropical temper through life condemned him, may in like manner afford an useful lesson to those who have been sympathizing with his hot headed and cold hearted heroes."[28] Obviously, Smollett's literary image was becoming unpopular even before the apparently rigorous dawn of the Victorian era.

Such were the three great biographers of Smollett at the close of the eighteenth and at the opening of the nineteenth centuries. Even more than Anderson and Moore, Scott contributed largely to Smollett's popularity, but, as Boege remarks, he may also unwittingly have caused the quasi-oblivion into which Smollett's life and works receded during the greater part of the same century. Boege accuses Scott of having "inadvertently helped to remove Smollett from the list of widely read authors by being so much more popular himself."[29]

25. Scott, *Lives*, p. 92.
26. Lewis M. Knapp, *Tobias Smollett Doctor of Men and Manners* (Princeton, 1949), p. 229.
27. Scott, *Lives*, pp. 109–10, n. 20.
28. *Quarterly Review*, XXXIV (Sept. 1826), 370.
29. Boege, *Smollett's Reputation*, p. 69.

It would be unfair not to mention some of the minor biographies that appeared during the same period as the greater ones of Anderson, Moore, and Scott, and down to the middle of the nineteenth century. Although they added little to the knowledge of Smollett's life, in their humble way they vulgarized the work of Anderson, Moore, and Scott. The third edition of the *Encyclopaedia Britannica* (Edinburgh, 1797) reproduced the same article on Smollett as the second edition of 1783,[30] slightly revised and enlarged. The article remained identical in the fourth (1810), fifth (1817), and sixth (1823) editions. A four-page entry (pp. 47–51) also figured in the 1798 London edition of *A New and General Biographical Dictionary* (Vol. XIV). In spite of certain chronological inaccuracies then common, such as Smollett's birth date as 1720, *Ferdinand Count Fathom* as 1754, and the beginning of the *Critical Review* as 1755, the short sketch ends with a most sympathetic appraisal of Smollett's human and literary personality: "Upon the whole, this unfortunate man, for such he certainly was, was yet a man of virtue as well as abilities; possessed of good as well as great qualities; was under many lights amiable, as well as respectable; and who seems to have deserved a better lot" (pp. 50–51). The third edition of Jeremiah Whitaker Newman's *The Lounger's Common-Place Book* (London, 1805)[31] devotes nine pages (pp. 191–99) of enthusiastic criticism to Smollett's novels, but is little concerned with the biography as such. Newman manages to convey the impression that he takes pleasure in recording the enjoyment of his youth over *Peregrine Pickle*. He is also one of the few critics who ever found anything to praise about the *Regicide*: "This piece of Smollet's [sic] excels in language, situation, and the dramatic requisites, most of the wretched things which were presented to the public at that period, but are now forgotten" (p. 199).

The early nineteenth century is well known for its ponderous addiction to large complete editions of the British poets in monumental collections that adorned the bookshelves of the rising bour-

30. Boege, *Smollett's Reputation*, p. 75, is misguided in assuming that the third edition of the *Encyclopaedia Britannica* was the first one in which a notice of Smollett appeared. The first inclusion of Smollett's life was in the second edition of 1783.
31. The first edition, which I have not seen, appeared in 1792, according to Boege, *Smollett's Reputation*, p. 59. Boege demonstrates, p. 64, that Anderson cribbed from Newman.

geois class. Most probably their criteria were more the yards of occupied shelf space than the ounce of sterling genius. Among such collections, some biographical notices of Smollett may be mentioned. Alexander Chalmers—whose Scottish origins, surgical training, and indefatigable hackwork in London bear some marked similitudes to Smollett's life—published a biographical sketch of Smollett in the fifteenth volume of *The Works of the English Poets* (London, 1810, pp. 541–53). This was reproduced in abridged form (with or without Chalmers's consent?) by Robert Walsh in his fifty-volume collection of *The Works of the British Poets*.[32] Chalmers is more concerned with passing a severe moral judgment on Smollett's works than with his subject's life. He is a forerunner of Victorian reprobation, but at the same time he expresses admiration for the poetic talents that Smollett failed to cultivate. Chalmers brings in a few new elements of Smollett's biography. He identifies "Paunceford," the character in *Humphry Clinker*, thanks to the indications that Hamilton, the printer of the *Critical Review*, gave him. Smollett's slashing reply to the Reverend Thomas Comber's pamphlet—*A Vindication of the Great Revolution in England* . . . (London, 1758)—in the *Critical Review* for September 1758 is quoted, and Chalmers mentions Smollett's episodic feuds with John Shebbeare, Dr. John Hill, Ralph Griffiths and his spouse, all of whom Smollett treated as "little inconsiderable curs barking at the moon." But as Smollett himself learnt from bitter and jading experience, the venomous bite of these curs often proved as bad as their bark. Among the short biographical notices included in collections of poets, may be mentioned Thomas Campbell's (1819), Samuel Weller Singer's (1822), and the Reverend George Gilfillan's (1855). In Campbell's *Specimens of the British Poets*,[33] a few interesting reservations are expressed concerning the autobiographical interpretation of Smollett's novels, especially *Roderick Random*: "In the characters of a work, so compound [sic] of truth and fiction, the author alone could have estimated the personality which he intended, and of

32. *The Works of the British Poets*. ed. Robert Walsh, Jr. (Boston, Mass., 1822), XXXIII, pp. 325–36.
33. Thomas Campbell, *Specimens of the British Poets* (London, 1819), VI, pp. 218–24, on Smollett's life.

that intention he was not probably communicative." The life written by Singer for the *British Poets* [34] consists chiefly of a righteous moralizing commentary on Smollett's novels, and like Chalmers, Singer admires Smollett's poetry: his verses are "few, but they are excellent; they breathe inspiration" (p. 213). This highly favorable judgment is not endorsed today by most readers of Smollett's poetry. The Reverend George Gilfillan—another Scottish polygraph—also pays more critical attention to Smollett's works than to his life in his *Poetical Works of Johnson, Parnell, Gray and Smollett* (Edinburgh, 1855).[35] Gilfillan admires Smollett's originality, his "invention," but condemns his laxity of style and the coarseness of his novels, among which only *Roderick Random* and *Humphry Clinker* are praised. The Reverend's moral preoccupations obviously biased his critical estimate of Smollett's human and literary personality.

Meanwhile some editions of Smollett's works, other than Anderson's, were being published with biographical introductions. Professor Knapp has been kind enough to send me a photocopy of a life of Smollett found in an hitherto unrecorded, 1816 Dublin edition of Smollett's works that he recently acquired.[36] Unfortunately, this is not a biographical treasure trove, as the life of Smollett is, but a rapid summary of Anderson's work. The twelve-volume London edition of 1824 also includes (Vol. I, pp. [vii]–xi) an extremely skimpy biographical sketch replete with chronological errors and such peremptory and hostile affirmations as: "He married in 1747, a lady with whom he expected a good fortune, of which, however, he received very little, and the expensive style in which he set out in life brought him very soon into serious trouble" (p. viii).

More important, in quantity and in biographical quality, is Thomas Roscoe's memoir of Smollett for the one-volume *Miscellaneous Works* first published in London in 1841 and reprinted at

---

34. *The British Poets,* ed. Charles Whittingham (Chiswick, 1822), LXVI, pp. 197–214. Singer's life of Smollett was reproduced, somewhat abridged, in the editions of the *British Poets* published by Routledge (London, 1853, 1881).
35. See the "Life of Tobias Smollett," pp. 211–17. This book was reprinted with the same pagination in *Cassell's Library Edition of British Poets* (London [1878]).
36. *The Miscellaneous Works of Tobias Smollett, M.D.* (Dublin, 1816), I, pp. [i]–xvi.

least a dozen times during the nineteenth century. Roscoe devotes some thirty pages (pp. [vii]–xl) to the "Life and Works of Tobias Smollett," in which he sums up or very occasionally supplements the biographies of Anderson, Moore, and Scott. He relates the usual anecdotes of sometimes dubious authenticity but always piously repeated by the biographers even to our day: the snowball thrown by the young apprentice Smollett on an irate Glasgow surgeon,[37] perhaps the "Crab" of *Roderick Random*; Gordon's blunt fondness for his apprentice, which, according to Scott, the master once expressed thus: ". . . my own bubbly-nosed callant with the stane in his pouch;" [38] the seventh stanza added to "The Tears of Scotland" in spite of the frightened entreaties of his friends; [39] the trick played on his mother when he visited her again in Scotland after a fifteen years' absence, trying to pass off as a gentleman just returned from the West Indies, but quickly detected by his mother because of "his old roguish smile;" [40] and finally the all too famous jibe of Sterne at "Smelfungus" Smollett in the *Sentimental Journey*. Roscoe is incapable of quoting his predecessors—which he indulges in frequently and at length—without heaping hyperbolical eulogies on their heads. His favorite is Scott whom he dubs Smollett's "most recent and enlightened biographer" (p. xiii), or "the immortal author of Waverley" (p. xxxii), or "his inimitable countryman, equally celebrated for humour and pathos." Roscoe, however, is conscious of bolstering Smollett's popularity, and with a touch of personal "puff oblique," declares that "owing to the cheap form in which they appear, the works of Smollett are now, for the first time, given to the world." Roscoe, into the bargain, probably gave quite a few headaches *to the world*, as the very fine type used for the double column pages constitutes an exquisite ocular torture.

Biographies of Smollett are also to be found in lexicographical works and miscellaneous writings. In France, Michaud's *Biog-*

37. Moore's *Works* (1797), I, pp. cxii–cxiii and Roscoe, *Miscellaneous Works* (1841), IX.
38. Cf. Scott, *Lives*, p. 73 and Roscoe, *Miscellaneous Works*, X.
39. Cf. Anderson (1820 ed.), I, p. 22 and Roscoe, *Miscellaneous Works*, XI.
40. Cf. Moore, *Works*, CXXXVI and Roscoe, *Miscellaneous Works*, XX.

raphie Universelle, Ancienne et Moderne contained an article on Smollett's life by Lefebvre-Cauchy as early as 1825 (Vol. XLII, pp. 494–98), which was reprinted in the second edition (1854–65). The author is familiar with the biographies of Anderson and Scott, with whom he respectfully begs to disagree, as he finds Scott too lenient with Smollett's faults. After a fairly accurate summary of Smollett's life, Lefebvre-Cauchy attempts to delineate Smollett's moral character: "Il était irascible, jaloux, vindicatif, présomptueux" (p. 492). Poor Smollett! How dearly he had hated the French, but now they were paying him back in his own coin. The article in Charles F. Partington's *British Cyclopaedia of Biography* (London, 1838) is unblushingly made of paragraphs and snippets thieved from Scott's life, with a few minor alterations in the phrasing. Philip Prince's *Parallel Universal History* (London, 1838) also contained a very short biographical sketch of twenty-two lines (p. 438) which was much enlarged in the second edition of 1842–43 (Vol. II, pp. 548–9). Prince is less harsh than his Victorian predecessors on Smollett, whom he judges "a highly upright man in private character" (p. 549). He sympathizes with Smollett's checkered life: "He must be added to the number of those who, after contributing to the amusement, the improvement and the intellectual pleasures of others, find vexation, disgust, and neglect, the reward for mental exertion." For the first time since the third edition in 1797, the *Encyclopaedia Britannica* offered a new article on Smollett in its seventh edition (Edinburgh, 1842). [41] More details on Smollett's family background are given, and for the first time his birth is correctly dated 1721. The author advances 1746 as the date of Smollett's return to London from the West Indies. But the dates of the *Compendium*, of Smollett's libelous article in the *Critical Review*, and of *The Present State* are erroneous. As usual, most of the article is made up of critical considerations on the novels which are analyzed with warm approbation, even *The History and Adventures of an Atom*, which is rather surprising for the times. At the close of the article, the author presents a balanced view of Smollett's personality, impartially encompassing his irascibility and sociability, personal prejudices

41. See XX, pp. 425–28. For the 8th edition (1860), see XX, pp. 360–63.

and patriotism, improvidence and generosity. The same article, with the addition of a few notes, was reprinted in the following edition in 1860.

The Reverend Henry Francis Cary, a former assistant keeper of printed books at the British Museum over whom Panizzi was promoted to the headship of the library in 1837, had contributed to the *London Magazine* a series of lives of the English poets which were published in book form after his death, in 1846. In his *Lives of English Poets*, the shy recluse devoted some thirty-five pages to Smollett's more adventurous and boisterous existence. The only originality in Cary's not unfavorable examination of the man and his works is the rather strange theory according to which *Ferdinand Count Fathom* was conjectured to have been "hastily translated from another language,"—from French. Cary buttressed this extraordinary contention with his analysis of a number of patent gallicisms scattered in the novel. Of scant biographical value too, Eugene Lawrence's *Lives of the British Historians* (New York, 1855) offers no startling revelation on Smollett's life (pp. 385–95), because the author, whose style is light and pleasant, relies mostly on Anderson, Moore, and Scott.

But after the middle of the nineteenth century there are signs of a critical and biographical renewal of interest in Smollett's life and works. Thackeray's famous and often quoted pages on Smollett in his *English Humourists* published in 1853 may have induced James Hannay, five years later, to write a long and important article on Smollett in the *Quarterly Review*.[42] James Hannay was another Scot among the biographers of Smollett, and perhaps even more relevant to his understanding of the novelist, an ex-officer in the Navy who had been court-martialed and dismissed from the service as he could not bear the rigors and harshness of naval discipline. James Hannay—who should not be confounded [43] with his son David Hannay, the author in 1887 of a full-length biography of Smollett—insists on the importance of Smollett's Scottish background about which he offers new information. Hannay, in spite of his critical acumen is sorely tempted by the dangerous sirens of autobiographical interpretation: ". . . to this day the reader of

42. *Quarterly Review*, CIII (Jan.-April 1858), pp. 66–108.
43. Boege, *Smollett's Reputation*, p. 109, obviously makes the mistake.

Roderick Random cannot divest himself of the idea that he is reading about Smollett. So much is this the case, that both Smollett
himself, and his friends for him, had a good deal to do afterwards
to persuade people that he had not intended the ruffianly old
judge in the story to be a picture of his own grandfather; nor the
pedagogue to be Mr. Love of Dumbarton; nor Potion the apothecary to be worthy Mr. Gordon of Glasgow." But Hannay succumbs
to the Victorian critical habit—already latent in the eighteenth
century—of comparing Smollett with Fielding, only to enhance
the latter's putative superiority. His appreciation of Smollett's
personality does not suffer from any "lues Boswelliana," as he takes
care to underline Smollett's misanthropic irritability: "He was a
more querulous Swift, with less of ferocity and professing about the
same estimate of human nature . . . Yet, with all this, there was
much in him that was likeable. His misanthropy was in great
measure, the effects of ill-health. What would have been weakness
in his complaints of ill usage was saved from that character by the
pugnacity with which he returned the supposed insults; and no
one who knew him doubted his generosity."

Another harbinger of the revival of interest in Smollett was
Joseph Irving—still another Scot!—not properly speaking a biographer of Smollett, but an annalist, heraldist, and an authority on
Scottish history. In 1859 he published, for private circulation, his
now very rare book *Some Account of the Family of Smollett of
Bonhill* (Dumbarton, 1859) whose twenty-four pages were
crammed with useful genealogical information on Smollett's an-
cestry and parentage.[44] For the first time since Anderson's biographies, new letters of Smollett were published in Irving's book.

The work of James Hannay and Joseph Irving were followed in
the last four decades of the nineteenth century by three important
biographies that—*mutatis mutandis*—played the same role as those
of Anderson, Moore, and Scott over half a century before. These
three biographies by Robert Chambers (1867), David Hannay

---

44. By the same author, see also *The History of Dumbartonshire* (2nd ed:
Dumbarton, 1860), especially pp. 334–55 on Smollett's family; the same genealogical material he used again in his *Book of Dumbartonshire* (Edinburgh
and London, 1879), II, pp. 175–208.

(1887), and Oliphant Smeaton (1897) will be examined separately, but should not be considered as the only literary signs of renascent interest in Smollett: biographical introductions to editions of Smollett's works will also be analyzed briefly. Even the French seem to have shared a modicum of biographical curiosity about Smollett. In *L'Intermédiaire des Chercheurs et Curieux*—the worthy French equivalent of *Notes and Queries*—there was a query (Vol. I, 20 Nov 1864, p. 308) about Smollett and his *Travels through France and Italy:* "En 1766, cet Anglais fait un voyage en France, et dans son récit, prédit la Révolution. Quel était ce Tobie Smollett? Quel est le titre de son ouvrage?" This reader should have consulted Michaud's biographical dictionary and his query shows that he is somewhat confused about the *Travels* and the posthumous, perhaps apocryphal "Prophecy" attributed to Smollett.[45] But it is interesting to note that a month later the query had received five answers, which tends to prove that Smollett was not wholly forgotten in France even then. Anyhow, a year later, an article figured in Hoeffer's *Nouvelle Biographie Générale* (Paris, 1865, Vol. XLIV, pp. 82–84), signed by E. J. B. Rathery, which in a concise form gives most of the information then available on Smollett's life.

Robert Chambers, as well as Hannay and Smeaton, was a Scot. He published his *Smollett: His Life and a Selection from his Writings* (Edinburgh, 1867) as the last of his printed productions, but had already dealt several times before with Smollett in various books.[46] His book marks the beginning of a new phase in the field of Smollett biographies. He brings to the composition of his biography the care of a minute scholar and the enthusiasm of a Scotsman for the literature and history of his country. Furthermore, his biography, which still reads well today, revealed new facts about Smollett's life, especially about the Scottish, earlier part

---

45. See Lewis M. Knapp, "The 'Prophecy' Attributed to Smollett," *The Review of English Studies* XVI (May 1965), 177–82.
46. See Robert Chambers, *Traditions of Edinburgh* (Edinburgh, 1825); I, pp. 270–80 on Mrs. Smollett's house; *Reekiana. Minor Antiquities of Edinburgh* (Edinburgh, 1833), pp. 231–33, on the house of Smollett's relations; *A Biographical Dictionary of Eminent Scotsmen* (Glasgow, 1832–35), IV, pp. 268–78, on Smollett. Revised editions of this work were published in 1870 and 1875.

of it, Smollett's struggles and friendly connections in London and his work on the less known books or periodicals such as the *Universal History*, the *British Magazine*, or the *Briton*. Chambers is among the first of Smollett's biographers to react against the insidious autobiographical interpretation of *Roderick Random*: "The strange irregular manner in which Roderick Random gets into the Navy, as well as the most of his adventures in London, is probably pure fiction. The actual Random was not without friends both able and willing to help him in this branch of the public service" (p. 38). Chambers's analysis of Smollett's works is imbued with a chuckling sense of sparkling enjoyment, but his patent critical fondness for the novels does not prevent Chambers from pointing out Smollett's failings. His psychological diagnosis about the unfortunate polemical fray between Wilkes and Smollett is still valid today: "Most unluckily for one who was a master of satire, and fond of using the weapon, he [Smollett] was sensitive to the rebuke and satire of others to a pitiable degree" (p. 122). Last but not least, Chambers's was the first systematic study in which Smollett's life did not disappear behind the critical appraisal of his novels.

Twenty years after Chambers's *Smollett*, David Hannay's *Life of Tobias Smollett* (London, 1887) constitutes an important stage in the biographical study of Smollett. Hannay, a journalist and a specialist of British naval history, was the first one to examine closely the maritime period in Smollett's life, especially the ill-fated expedition to Carthagena (1740–1). Thanks to his knowledge of British naval history, Hannay draws a vivid, accurate and concise picture of Admiral Vernon's ships and sailors at Carthagena. Hannay, instead of dismissing contemptuously the *Regicide* as the abortive but perversely cherished child of Smollett's never-quite-fulfilled theatrical ambition, saw the biographical value of the unfortunate tragedy: "What value it has is purely biographical, but in that respect it is not unimportant. It shows at least that Smollett was early resolved to be a writer, and to do the best work in literature if trying would help him." Finally, the bibliography by J. P. Anderson of the British Museum was the first attempt—understandably incomplete and at times even inaccurate—to compile a biographical and critical documentation on Smollett. Hannay's book was well received by the critics. In the *Athenaeum* (8 December 1888, pp. 767–69), it was epitomized as "readable, interesting, and interesting to a high degree," while J. P. Anderson's bibliography was somewhat extravagantly reckoned "perfect as usual."

Oliphant Smeaton's *Tobias Smollett* (Edinburgh, 1897) poses many problems for the modern student of Smollett. Smeaton, a journalist and a novelist who died in 1914, may have had access to now unavailable documents on Smollett, or else his fertile imagination may have blithely filled the factual gaps. Boege is unnecessarily harsh on a popular biography that is pleasantly written, if at times with too much stylistic claptrap. Knapp's opinion [47] shows more impartiality: "A sympathetic but undocumented account, possibly based in part on material still unpublished or possibly, in places, the product of the author's undisciplined imagination." For instance, Smeaton is the only one among Smollett's biographers, past and present, to give Smollett's exact birthdate. The following paragraph is fairly typical of Smeaton's breezy way and flippant disregard for the minutiae of precise scholarship: "In one of the unpublished letters of John Home, author of *Douglas*, which it was recently my fortune to see, he mentions a walk which Smollett and he had taken together. . . . During the course of the walk Smollett mentioned the fact that his birthday had been celebrated two days before. The date of their meeting was the 18th March 1750. If reliance can be placed on this roundabout means of arriving at a fact, Smollett's birth took place on the 16th March 1721." Countless question marks can be penciled in the margins of Smeaton's biography. Thus Smeaton advances without the faintest trace of documentary proof—at least for his discerning readers—that Smollett's father, Archibald, died in 1721; that "during the first two years of his intellectual seedtime he was committed to the care of a worthy dame in the neighborhood," a formulation redolent with memories of Wordsworth; that Mr. Gordon, the Glasgow surgeon to whom Smollett was apprenticed "gave him a room in his house, and a cover was already laid for him at the good old surgeon's table;" and finally—to take only a few examples among a score of other possible ones—that Smollett, during his 1750 stay in

47. Knapp, *Tobias Smollett*, p. 340, note 26.

Paris wrote, "To live in Paris . . . is to live in heaven." No such letter is known to this day. But in spite of his faults, Smeaton's biography has the merit of presenting a sympathetically intuitive analysis of Smollett's sometimes contradictory and ambiguous psychological motivations. His initial contention—debatable perhaps, but certainly not negligible in the light thrown upon Smollett by a close characterological analysis [48]—is that the "poetic stimulus" forms the true key to unlock the otherwise elusive and self-centered character" of Smollett. Finally, Smeaton, like Hannay and Chambers, also protests against the abusive facility of autobiographical interpretation and those biographers "who have been smitten with the mania for reading the facts of a man's life into his works."

Another sign of the renewal of interest in Smollett was the appearance of several new editions of his works between 1870 and the end of the nineteenth century. Despite the importance of their introductions tracing the history of Smollett's reputation as a novelist, less space will be devoted to them than to the books of Chambers, Hannay, and Smeaton, since the purpose of those introductions is usually more critical than purely biographical. David Herbert wrote a forty-page "Life of Tobias Smollett" for the one-volume edition of the author's works published (Edinburgh, 1870) by William P. Nimmo, the publisher. Although it is not devoid of factual and chronological errors, it presents a thoughtful, unbiased analysis of Smollett's personality, for instance, when the young Scot entered the Navy in 1740: ". . . Smollett was not born to call any man master. And he certainly was not of a temper to endure the worse than brutal treatment to which many of the fine old tars of the jolly times agone, reduced such a landscum as educated gentlemen whose office it was, to lessen their sufferings in many other ways than by lopping off their limbs." Herbert is at times bluntly honest about the gaps in the knowledge of Smollett's biography, such as the length of his stay in the West Indies or the circumstances of his wooing and winning Miss Lascelles. From bluffness Herbert occasionally indulges in piques of scholarly gruffness, for instance, against Chambers's "unsuccessful

48. This idea is developed in a chapter entitled "La personnalité de Smollett: Essai d'analyse" of my book, Les Romans de Smollett (Paris, Didier, 1971).

attempt to fill up this blank in Smollett's biography with a vague guess at one solitary fact, *viz.*, that Mr. Thomas Bontein, a second cousin to Smollett, who was at that time in Jamaica, would probably be friendly to the youth, [which] is one of those knowing and showy feats of research which decoy and damage excellent and honourable biographers, studious of facts and fame." Apparently, the internecine "petite guerre" among modern scholars is no startling novelty. Herbert was possessed of enviable felicity in his concise summing up of events or books. Thus, he calls the year 1746 "a busy year for judges, juries, hangmen, headsmen, and Smollett," or *The History and Adventures of an Atom* a political and satirical romance "in which Japanese names are but a thin japan" laid over the names of British political leaders.

Typical of Herbert's no-nonsense honesty, and at times even slightly cantankerous straightforwardness, is the following debunking of the romantic fallacy over some blanks in the knowledge of Smollett's childhood and adolescence: "The surroundings of the old house of Dalquhurn seem to have been very romantic in the first quarter of the eighteenth century, when George I was king. They supplied the earlier biographers—especially Dr. Moore, whose life, at this stage, is about Dr. Smollett, and as many other people and places as he could find and find room for—with some rather superfine padding, to relieve the tedium of stating facts. The passage in praise of the Vale of Leven quoted hereabouts by Anderson, Scott, and Roscoe (Dr. Moore quotes lines of his own in praise of the Clyde), can be read in its proper connexion in *Humphry Clinker*." As far as can be ascertained, it was David Herbert who first tried to annotate systematically *Roderick Random, Peregrine Pickle*, and *Humphry Clinker*.

James P. Browne's 1872 reissue of Moore's edition with a preface of his own does not add anything significant to the knowledge of Smollett's biography, although Browne's preface (Vol. I, pp. v–xxxviii) displays great cordiality both towards the man and his works. From a critical point of view, the next two editions are much more important,[49] but again, show no trace of fresh biographical research. George Saintsbury's general introduction and

49. For George Saintsbury's critical writings see Boege, *Smollett's Reputation,* pp. 134–36; on W. E. Henley's edition, see Boege, *Smollett's Reputation,* pp. 136–37.

critical prefaces to *The Works of Tobias Smollett* (London, 1895) were often reprinted in later editions (for instance 1916 and 1925). Saintsbury barely devotes ten pages to Smollett's life, followed by a rather ambiguous summary of his personality chiefly concerned with its literary rather than human aspects. At least Saintsbury has the merit of freshening up the battered and inevitable parallel drawn between Fielding and Smollett. For once, the two authors' *biographies* are compared and their "very curious similarity" is underlined. Saintsbury then dwells on Smollett's national and personal pride, the "low flashing point" of his temper, his cantankerousness antithetically coupled with his improvident generosity. But in Saintsbury's Victorian eyes, Smollett's chief and unpardonable fault was his lack of delicacy: "To delicacy, indeed, in any of its forms, Smollett appears to have been an utter stranger. He is admittedly one of the nastiest writers in English. . . ." Saintsbury's statement is ambiguous because it is not clear whether he most resents Smollett's supposed indelicacy as a man or as a writer. Or perhaps, Saintsbury bases his severe judgment of Smollett the man on Smollett's works and a few coarse incidents narrated with enough comic gusto to absolve their author from the subtle gloating intentions of Sterne. Saintsbury then was yet another victim of the erroneous deductions of inverted autobiography.

But W. E. Henley's case is even more flagrant. His long introduction (pp. v–xlviii) to an edition of *The Works of Tobias Smollett* (Westminster and New York, 1899–1901) is a strange mixture of admiration for Smollett's doughty pugnacity and of downright hatred and loathing for other aspects of his life and works. Henley, with a kind af aggressive flippancy, after citing the names of Moore, Scott, David Hannay, Robert Chambers, warns his readers that his purpose is "to give but the briefest outline of the career, and to keep as close to the man—the humorous, arrogant, redheaded, stiff-necked, thin-skinned, scurrilous, brilliant Scots hack of genius—as his novels will let [him]." It is something of a minor literary mystery to consider how Henley, who exerted his brilliant critical gifts to the best of his capricious and fiery abilities in favor of Fielding, treated Smollett so shabbily. It is also something of a wonder that the readers of Henley's introduction should have persevered and tackled Smollett's works themselves after the hot broadsides of sarcasms, jeers, condemnations, sneers, and reproaches Henley delighted to fire into Smollett's poor hulk. Here is a typical slighting note to *The Regicide*: "It is called *The Regicide*, and deals in a lofty, high-sniffing, perfunctory way with the murder of James I. They may read it who can in the Twelfth volume of the present Edition." It would be besides the point to try and defend here *The Regicide*, but Henley was totally blind even to the biographical value of Smollett's long rejected tragedy, a personal tragedy in itself. Near the end of his curious introduction, Henley, who certainly must not have considered his edition as a labor of love, admits: "I have said what I believe to be the worst that can be said of Smollett." This, indeed, was biography in a new key, and with a vengeance! A critic in *Blackwood's Edinburgh Magazine* (Vol. 167, May 1900, pp. 688–99) at the end of his review article thanked Henley "for the final edition of a great English classic" (p. 699), a description which most unfortunately is almost still true today, as Henley's edition, with its grave textual defects, omissions, and all too frequent unreliability remains—at least until the *Bicentennial Edition of Smollett's Works* appears—the most complete, or rather the least incomplete one available. The same critic reproaches Henley on two apparently antithetic heads, but perhaps closely connected ones in depth: Henley insists "more strongly than is necessary upon Smollett's coarseness" and on the other hand, his "puritanism now and again seems to get the better of him" (p. 698). Another critic in *The Dial* (Vol. xxxiii, 1 February 1902, pp. 81–83) noticed how Henley had savaged Smollett, and sought to slash back "ad hominem" for being "just now in the public eye because of his churlish, curious exhibition of bad taste in attempting to throw disillusionment upon his old-time fellow in life and literature, R. L. Stevenson. Trenchant critic and true poet Mr. Henley is, however; and this bit of criticism is in his familiar jerkily brilliant and bookish style."

If Mabel E. Wotton's *Word-Portraits of Famous Writers* (London, 1887) [50] adds strictly nothing to Smollett's biography, an article published in the same year by William Minto, Professor of English Language at the University of Aberdeen, in the ninth edition of the *Encyclopaedia Britannica* (Vol. XXII, pp. 183–85), shows on the whole a favorable appreciation of Smollett's fiction, although it is half as long as the precedent one, first published in

50. See the article on Smollett, pp. 289–90.

1842, in the seventh edition. Minto gives a quick summary of Smollett's childhood, quotes Walter Scott frequently and still commits such chronological errors as placing the *Compendium* in 1757 or assuming that Smollett "obtained a medical degree from a German university about 1752." Far more reliable is Thomas Seccombe's article in the *DNB* (Vol. 53, 1898, pp. 174–84), which is grounded on undeniably original biographical research. Seccombe cites his manuscript sources in the British Museum and appends a critical bibliography that is still useful today for nineteenth-century criticism. In 1907, Seccombe edited Smollett's much neglected *Travels through France and Italy* for the "World's Classics," with his usual critical and scholarly thoroughness. Although Seccombe was on the whole more than sympathetic to Smollett's harrowing plights both as a man and a writer, he dwells on another hard-dying legend, propagated by Saintsbury too, namely that Smollett was not so much irreligious as a-religious, a dour pagan: "The religious point of view never occurred to him." This blunt statement needs to be somewhat qualified, in the light of Knapp's biographical discoveries.[51] Furthermore, his religiosity, if any, may have been a sort of faint undercurrent flowing deeply beneath the boisterous surface of his novels: it certainly may be guessed at in several of his more pessimistic letters.

Closing a study of Smollett's biographies at the end of the nineteenth century may appear arbitrary. But, in fact, there is practically a quarter of a century's biographical gap in Smollettian studies before their vigorous renascence about 1925 under the scholarly impulse of such American students of the Johnsonian period as H. S. Buck, A. Whitridge, E. S. Noyes, an impulse acted upon later by E. Joliat, C. E. Jones, L. L. Martz, G. M. Kahrl and, last but certainly not least, L. M. Knapp, to name the authors of *books* on Smollett. The British biographical contribution proved singularly slender and of more than dubious quality. Lewis Melville's *Life and Letters of Tobias Smollett* (London, 1926) is a most unreliable medley of grossly erroneous dates, garbled quotations, and flippant statements, unfortunately reprinted in 1966 by the Kennikat Press.

51. L. M. Knapp, *Tobias Smollett*, p. 113, on Smollett's participation in parish affairs in Chelsea about 1759.

Much then remained to be done in the field of Smollettian biography. Between 1867 and 1897 biographies of Smollett had contributed to spur some fresh interest in the man and the novelist, and thus to retrieve him from the semi-oblivion into which the preceding generation had let him slip. A sort of approximate pattern of biographical interest may be surmised from the general survey of Smollett's biographies throughout the nineteenth century. It looks as though a binary rhythm existed regulating the interest in Smollett's biography. After his death, a first generation between 1796 and 1821 expressed its admiration for the man and the novelist in well-meaning, but often under-documented and over-laudatory works. Then, the following generation showed only lukewarm interest in Smollett and his life. Finally, during the last four decades of the nineteenth century, Smollett's biographers took a keen interest in an author whom their fathers had somewhat forgotten. In spite of their factual inaccuracies, Smollett's nineteenth-century biographers discerned in him "un homme de coeur" beneath his gruff and irascible husk. And perhaps, most important of all, they were critical enough of the biographical legends and traditions to challenge and sometimes eschew the lures of inverted autobiography that tended to assimilate Smollett to his less recommendable fictional creations. If autobiography may be schematized as an outgoing creative movement from the author to his novels, inverted autobiography may be finally summed up as the more or less total biographical assimilation of the author to his characters, thus offering a strange, but by no means infrequent, case of destructive literary cannibalism. To prevent this abusive assimilation of the young Scot arriving in London, for instance— the raw, needy, and friendless Roderick—much factual research was necessary. The biography published in 1949 by Lewis M. Knapp was the result of long years of dedication to a labor of literary love and scrupulous honesty. With characteristic modesty, he could write, at the end of his biography: "There has usually been a tendency, *not justified by what is now known of his character*, to attribute to Smollett the vices of the unheroic Roderick, Peregrine, and Fathom." [52]

52. The italics are mine.

Smollett's Traveler

ROBERT D. SPECTOR

THE time has passed when Smollett's travel book can any longer be considered merely an autobiographical record of his actual journey through France and Italy. Louis Martz and George Kahrl, marking the beginning of a second major stage in the twentieth-century reassessment of Smollett's work, clearly suggested the ways in which *Travels Through France and Italy* was an artistic production to be distinguished from what Thomas Seccombe had considered a loose collection of letters, "pretty much" as Smollett had originally written them during his trip and cast together with the "deliberate intention of making as much money as possible out of [them]." [1]

---

1. Louis Martz, *The Later Career of Tobias Smollett* (New Haven, 1942); George Kahrl, *Tobias Smollett, Traveler-Novelist* (Chicago, 1945); Thomas Seccombe, Introduction to *Travels Through France and Italy* (London, 1907), p. xii. Although Seccombe's introduction and edition were an attempt to resurrect Smollett's reputation, interest in Smollett lagged until the 1920's, at which time there appeared: Howard S. Buck, *A Study in Smollett: Chiefly "Peregrine Pickle"* (New Haven, 1925) and *Smollett as Poet* (New Haven, 1927); Arnold Whitridge, *Tobias Smollett, A Study of His Miscellaneous Works* (New York, 1925); *The Letters of Tobias Smollett*, ed. Edward S. Noyes (Cambridge, Mass., 1926); and the Shakespeare Head edition of the novels (Oxford, 1925–26), 11 vols. In addition to the studies by Martz and Kahrl in the 1940's, see Claude E. Jones, *Smollett Studies* (Berkeley and Los Angeles, 1942); Fred W. Boege, *Smollett's Reputation as a Novelist* (Princeton, 1947); Lewis M. Knapp's biography, *Tobias Smollett, Doctor of Men and Manners* (Princeton, 1949) and many of his important articles. For a recent discussion of the question of the *Travels*, as autobiography, see John F. Sena, "Smollett's Persona and the Melancholic Traveler: An Hypothesis," *ECS*, I (1968), 353–69.

To be sure, no one would care to argue that Smollett's original letters to his correspondents in Britain did not provide the core of his published work or that Smollett's actual circumstances, let alone his peculiar personality, were not significant in shaping his travel volume. To ignore that relationship would be all but impossible. Not only did such contemporaries as Philip Thicknesse and Laurence Sterne insist upon the relationship; [2] Smollett himself, in a letter to his friend, Dr. John Moore, provided a tie between his travel work and autobiography:

The observations I made in the course of my travels through France and Italy I have thrown into a series of Letters, which will make two volumes in Octavo. They are now printing, & will be published in the spring. I will not answer for their success with the Public; but as I have given a sort of natural History of Nice, with my remarks upon that climate, and a register of the weather, I hope the Performance may be useful to other valetudinarians who travel for the Recovery of their Health. [3]

Indeed, Smollett's remarks superficially suggest the appropriateness of the old biographical approach to his *Travels*.

And yet, even Smollett's words, carefully read, should have warned against a simple biographical interpretation. His first sentence distinguishes between a process of merely gathering his original letters and one of recasting from experience to final form. His concluding comment suggests an artistic purpose at one with the frequently professed aim of art in the eighteenth century: the high regard for *utile*, the more important member of the Horatian twofold dictum of *dulce et utile*. Smollett's expressed concern for usefulness, in fact, is hardly limited to "other valetudinarians who travel for the Recovery of their Health." The *Travels* itself stands

2. Whitridge, *Tobias Smollett*, p. 90, notes Thicknesse's mock title for Smollett's *Travels: Quarrels Through France and Italy for the Cure of a Pulmonic Disorder;* see Philip Thicknesse, *Useful Hints to those who make the Tour of France* (London, 1768), Letter I, p. 5, and Philip Gosse, *Dr. Viper: The Querulous Life of Philip Thicknesse* (London, 1952), p. 317; and Noyes, *Letters*, p. 217.
3. Noyes, *Letters*, p. 96.

as a kind of guidebook—more personal than the ordinary guidebooks, but as insistent as any upon serving a useful purpose. For
that purpose Smollett required an effective design, a particular
kind of persona, and a careful selection of material—all of which
account for the artistry of his *Travels*.

That artistry has been observed by recent critics, who have
learned to balance the autobiographical detail and Smollett's
craftsmanship. However, even the best discussions have generally
been limited to a particular aspect of Smollett's art in the *Travels*.[4]
Both Martz and Kahrl are intent on demonstrating what they consider to be the development of Smollett's style from his earlier
picaresque novels to the major achievement of *Humphry Clinker*.
They provide interesting analyses of Smollett's use of source materials and even of his development of the *Travels* within the genre
of the fictionalized, familiar letters.[5] To Ronald Paulson, concerned mainly with the satiric tendencies in Smollett's art, the
Travels serves mainly to illustrate the connection between Smollett's techniques and the art of Juvenalian satire. Paulson notes as
well the relationship of Smollett's work to the tradition of "imaginary visits" of Montesquieu and Goldsmith, and he perceives the
way in which Smollett uses sickness and evil and filth as a part of
his moral design. However, Paulson is more concerned with the
Travels as a reflection of Smollett's mind or with its suggestiveness
of Smollett's themes in his novels than he is with it as a work of art
in itself.[6]

Recently, in an article on "Smollett's Persona and the Melancholic Traveler: An Hypothesis," John F. Sena has attempted a
more full-scale analysis of the *Travels* as art than has any earlier
commentator.[7] For Sena, Smollett's traveler "would have been
easily recognized by a contemporary reader as the type of splenetic

4. My own recent discussion of the *Travels* (*Tobias George Smollett*, New
York, 1968, pp. 35–36) is concerned with showing its relationship to the novelist's career and hence its biographical value.
5. See Kahrl, *Tobias Smollett*, Chapter 8; Martz, *The Later Career of Tobias
Smollett*, Part II, Chapter 1.
6. Ronald Paulson, *Satire and the Novel in Eighteenth-Century England* (New
Haven, 1967), pp. 191–94; 201.
7. Sena, "Smollett's Persona," *ECS*, I (1968), 353–69.

or melancholic man found in numerous literary and medical works of the period." [8] Sena traces the characteristics of the persona throughout the work, demonstrating how the details of travel and occupation, diet, exercise, and climate, all relate to the particular development of the persona.[9] Tentative though it is, Sena's analysis of the *Travels* comes closest to explaining Smollett's artistic achievement in the work.

Nevertheless, Sena's reading *is* tentative, and it misses an over-all design in the work, a design to which the persona, his ailments, and his observations are contributory and not Smollett's primary object. That design would seem to be the most plausible point at which to begin an analysis of the *Travels*, but oddly enough, though it appears most obvious, critics—sometimes perhaps because of the remaining concern with the autobiographical character of the work—have tended to ignore or minimize it. Certainly, the persona's remarks upon leaving England are in direct contrast to those upon his return, and yet no one has seen fit to emphasize the fact or to relate it to the *Travels* as a whole.

The opening letter of the *Travels* presents an unhappy Briton who describes the situation that has led to his decision to go abroad. The terms suggest self-imposed exile: [10] "traduced by malice, persecuted by faction, abandoned by false patrons, and overwhelmed by the sense of a domestic calamity, which it was not in the power of fortune to repair," [11] psychologically, he would appear to have no alternative but to flee. The country itself is described in the most unfavorable terms "as a scene of illiberal dispute, and incredible infatuation, where a few worthless incendiaries had, by dint of perfidious calumnies and atrocious abuse, kindled up a flame which threatened all the horrors of civil dis-

8. *Ibid.* p. 355. As Sena indicates, his analysis of the persona is indebted to the discussion of Thomas R. Preston, "Smollett and the Benevolent Misanthrope Type," *PMLA* LXXIX (1964), p. 51–57.
9. *Ibid.* pp. 360–66.
10. Paulson, *Satire and the Novel*, p. 191, describes this departure as the "prototypical exile of the Juvenalian idealist" and sees only the physical illness as setting off the persona from the "conventional Juvenalian."
11. The text used for the *Travels* is Volume X in *The Miscellaneous Works of Tobias Smollett, M.D.* (London, 1824), 12 vols. Hereafter all single references, designated by the number of the letter, will appear in the text. Multiple or additional references will appear in the notes.

sension." He adds, as well, his own poor health, the "weak state of my lungs," and his wife's grief as motives for his journey, but, despite the fact that so much of his later comment concerns matters of health, these appear less consequential than his disaffection for his country and his countrymen. These matters operate, to be sure, to account for his particular journey and to explain partially his splenetic point of view, but the major change effected through his travels, a change to which his health is a contributory factor, concerns his attitude toward England.

The journey serves to alter his view of his homeland. England may not be paradise, but by comparison with France and Italy, it is a heavenly country on earth. No weak romantic, no wild enthusiast, Smollett's persona insists that he is not blinded by fantastic patriotism; nevertheless, he summarizes the significance of his travels in the most patriotic terms, finding his fellows and their way of life worthy to be put upon a pedestal compared with what he has found abroad:

I am at last in a situation to indulge my view with a sight of Britain, after an absence of two years; and indeed you cannot imagine what pleasure I feel while I survey the white cliffs of Dover at this distance [from Boulogne]. Not that I am at all affected by the *nescia qua dulcedine natalis soli* of Horace. That seems to be a kind of fanaticism founded on the prejudices of education, which induces a Laplander to place the terrestrial paradise among the snows of Norway, and a Swiss to prefer the barren mountains of Solleure to the fruitful plains of Lombardy. I am attached to my country, because it is the land of liberty, cleanliness, and convenience: but I love it still more tenderly, as the scene of all my interesting connexions, as the habitation of my friends, for whose conversation, correspondence and esteem, I wish alone to live. (XLI)

This change in the persona is the main business of the design of the *Travels*. Such an over-all view of the work focuses on the persona, his character, his attitudes—both general and particular— toward his experiences abroad, and his reasons for writing to those at home. The purpose is didactic, and Smollett needs a character capable of representing the probable attitudes of the "normal" Englishman and the likely effects upon him of a journey to the

Continent. At the same time, the persona must be someone with sufficiently impressive characteristics so that the readers will be willing to accept his authority; and yet, he must be different enough from them so that he will be interesting in himself. For the first, Smollett offers the persona's range of knowledge—in "history, sociology, art criticism, archaeology, and natural history" [12]— together wtih his careful concern for gathering facts to make his judgment. For the latter, his very crotchetiness, his physical ailments, and his strong personality, as Kahrl suggests,[13] give animation to the *Travels*, turning it from a tedious parade of learning into a work of art.

To begin with, Smollett isolates his persona to keep the focus of the *Travels* deliberately upon him. Although the traveler is accompanied on his journey by his wife and two young ladies, the women play so negligible a role as to be inconspicuous for the major portion of the work. They exist solely to provide necessary motivation at points along the way or to emphasize the strength and masculine courage of the persona. The women—those delicate creatures—suffer from fright, sea-sickness, various discomforts, and Smollett uses their weakness and timidity to emphasize the hardships of the journey in a way that ennobles the fortitude and fearlessness of the persona.[14]

This heightening of the character of the persona is necessary for Smollett to gain the required respect for him from his audience. It

12. Kahrl, *Tobias Smollett*, p. 113. See, too, Seccombe, *Travels*, pp. xviii and xxi. Demonstrating Smollett's unacknowledged use of various sources, Martz, *The Later Career of Tobias Smollett*, p. 73ff., successfully challenges "the assumption that the large fund of learning distributed throughout the *Travels* comes straight from Smollett's own knowledge." Kahrl, p. 111, refutes what he sees as Martz's charge of "plagiarism" by arguing that an eighteenth-century writer could not be bothered with notes and citations in such a work, and that Smollett's practice does not take away from, but rather adds to, his scholarship. Both arguments, however, are concerned not with the persona, but with Smollett himself. The point is that Smollett creates a persona whose *personal* knowledge is intended to impress the reader. Too much citation of sources would weaken the sense of the persona's authority. When Smollett seeks to demonstrate the persona's scrupulous concern for exact information or his learned background, the letters *do* indicate his familiarity and use of authorities.

13. Kahrl, *Tobias Smollett*, p. 113.
14. *Travels*, XXV XXXIV, XXXV.

is one of many examples. For the traveler's servant of some twelve years' standing to refuse to leave his service becomes, as Seccombe notes, "a good testimonial . . . to a temper usually accredited with such a splenetic sourness. . . ." (I).[15] That sourness, too, seems more than a product of his various ailments or a natural bent; continually Smollett attributes it to some nobler cause. When a postmaster acts unfairly to his servant, the persona cannot stand idly by (VIII). Treated without respect by a land-lord, cheated on a bill, he makes ready to mete out "manual chastisement" (XIII).[16] Who can blame him for objecting to bed-bugs (XXV), preferring the peace and quiet of the countryside to "the tumult of a populous commercial city" (XXVII)? If his artistic judgments reject received opinion, it is due to his honesty rather than his arrogance, for it is, after all, a most modest man who apologetically promises his correspondent further details on antiquities, since it is "a subject, upon which I am disposed to be (perhaps impertinently) circumstantial" (XXXI). His charity is described quietly in his aid to "a young Irish recollect" who has been treated shabbily by the French clergy (XII).

Even the persona's physical ailments may serve to make his character seem more admirable. If they lead to a continual harping on the details of health—full of Smollett's characteristic use of strong physical imagery to create verisimilitude—they also remind the reader that the persona has friends interested in his well-being, ready to advise him on remedial measures, worried by his condition, awaiting word of his progress (XXV). He himself shows a generous concern for others—as his letter to Moore about "other valetudinarians who travel for the Recovery of their Health" suggests. That, he says, is the reason for his remarks on the climate of Nice and a register of its weather. But it is not merely Nice and its climate that he describes in these terms. His didactic purpose in this respect covers Boulogne, "the boasted air" of Montpellier and the effect of Lyons on "pulmonic disorders" (IX); it leads to a discussion of remedies, treatments, and the reputations of doctors, a discussion running throughout the work. For Smollett the state of health of his persona becomes a means of humanizing him, a man-

15. Seccombe, *Travels,* XXXV.
16. See, too, *Travels,* XXXV.

ner of providing motivation, and one aspect of his over-all didactic purpose in his *Travels*.

That over-all didactic purpose is directed at showing his countrymen British superiority, teaching them how to travel abroad, warning them not to be taken in by foreign practices and foreign affectation. That is the hard core of the *Travels*, to which the search for health is truly dedicated. Here Smollett's persona is admirably suited to his purposes and functions consistently throughout the work. Seccombe long ago recognized the fundamental character of the persona, but unfortunately confused it with Smollett himself and consequently only vaguely understood its use. Talking about Smollett, where he should have spoken of the persona, Seccombe compares him with Hogarth, a "sturdy and true-born patriot." He characterizes him as a "Typical Briton, perfervid Protestant of Britain's most Protestant period, and insular *enragé*. . . ." On Smollett's treatment of the French, Seccombe concludes that it is grossly unfair, "written in the most insular period of our manners, and during a brief lull in a century of almost incessant mutual hostility between the two nations." As for Smollett on Italy, "we perceive at every turn how completely the Protestant prejudice of his 'moment' and 'milieu' had obtained dominion over him." To mitigate somewhat Smollett's responsibility, Seccombe notes that his attack on the French was "written partly . . . to suit the English taste of the day," as indicated by the frequent reprinting of these passages in contemporary periodicals; moreover, Seccombe concludes, the "race-portrait" of the French was fairly common at the time.[17]

Much of Seccombe's comment is appropriate to a description of Smollett's persona. Smollett himself, though he obviously shares most of the attitudes of his persona, never resembles the full-blooded Englishman that Seccombe portrays—his *The Tears of Scotland* and his outsider's attack on British society in his novels mark the difference.[18] Here in the *Travels*, however, a major concern is to demonstrate to his audience, through the change in his persona, from the beginning of the book to its conclusion, the superiority of the British to their continental neighbors. For that purpose his criticism of the religious, social, and political customs

17. Seccombe, *Travels*, pp. xiii, xxviii–xxix, xlix.
18. See Spector, *Tobias George Smollett*, especially Chapter 1.

of the French and Italians and his denigration of the veneration shown for their art are essential.

Both Seccombe and, more recently, Sena have argued that Smollett attacks the Englishman as well as the French and Italians, but that is a distorted picture of what Smollett actually does in the *Travels*. To be sure, in his depressed mood upon leaving England, his persona complains about conditions on the road and in Dover (I). However, his intent is clear when he calls for corrective action, as he is aware of the impression made upon foreigners and the need to protect "the honour of the kingdom . . ." (I). His later treatment of the faults of Englishmen abroad—cited by both Seccombe and Sena as "no less severe in criticism of his own countrymen than he was with his pronouncements against the French and Italians" [19]—is equally concerned with the honor of the British. He castigates the "number of raw boys, whom Britain seemed to have poured forth on purpose to bring her national character into contempt" (XXIX). Nevertheless, their conduct is attributed to their youth and ignorance and is by no means presented as a measure of the English character. They are, instead, to be contrasted with the taciturn "good man, mild, charitable, and humane," whose character is "truly British" (XXXV). The callow youths are more than balanced by the hospitable English families at Montpellier (X). To be sure, the faults in the English character—extravagance or a foolish desire to be thought connoisseurs—leave them prey to the dishonesty of the cheats who abound on the Continent,[20] but the faults are less those of the deceived than those who are doing the deceiving. Moreover, part of Smollett's purpose is to educate his countrymen so that they will not be bilked by foreigners.

Treatment of the French in the *Travels* is clearly designed to celebrate the superiority of the British character, both in itself and in what it produces. Even when the persona has started out disgusted with his own countrymen, they are made out to be not nearly so bad as the French (I). At all levels of society, the fundamental character of the French, compared with the British, is marked by "idleness and dissipation" (VI). French wine is inferior, "neither so strong, nourishing, nor (in my opinion) so

19. Sena, "Smollett's Persona," p. 368; Seccombe, *Travels,* p. lvii.
20. *Travels,* X, XXIX.

pleasant to the taste as the small-beer of England" (XXXIX).[21]
English porcelain surpasses the French (VIII); English bridges
overshadow the French in construction, beauty, and utility; [22] the
much-prized bridge over the Rhône would hardly be boasted of by
"a common mason in England . . ." (IX). As for "posting" on
English roads, it is "much more easy, convenient, and reasonable"
than in France, and carriages, roads, and postillions are better at
home than abroad (XLI).

This British superiority is naturally reflected in the institutions
and manners of the two countries. By comparison with British
conditions, mores, and manners, those of the French are unsan-
itary, indecent, pompous, and dishonest.[23] Smollett's persona uses
the occasion of the seizure of his books by French customs officers
to ridicule the French reputation for "politeness and hospitality."
It is a closed society in which there is a lack of concern for the
individual (II). The openness of English society, the sense of competition, provides for better road conditions (XLI). In response to
a question about whether the French people are more taxed than
the British, the persona compares conditions in the two countries,
making England a terrestrial paradise by comparison. The poor
pay for the luxuries of the rich and the military; the king himself
is a proper object of ridicule and contempt; and revolution itself
seems inevitable (XXXVI). The sight of galley slaves at the Villa
Franca, outside Nice, draws the comment, it is "a sight which a
British subject, sensible of the blessing he enjoys, cannot behold
without horror and compassion" (XIV).

No French institution suffers more under the pen of Smollett's
persona than French Roman Catholicism. Here he is altogether,
in Seccombe's words, the "perfervid Protestant of Britain's most
Protestant period." In fact, as he describes it, the religious conflict
between the French and British reflects the over-all antagonism
between the two nations. French law, after all, makes it a capital
crime for Protestant ministers to perform their functions (XII),
and the practice at French schools in Boulogne deliberately sub-
verts Protestantism by teaching foreign students to hate their own

21. See, too, *ibid*. VIII.
22. *Ibid*. IX, XXIX.
23. *Ibid*. V, VII, XII, XXII, XL.

religion and by returning "enthusiastic converts to the religion of Rome" (III). As for the French religion itself, it is a parcel of "bigotry and fanaticism" (III), a farce of superstitions, ludicrous miracles, and nonsense, responsible for impoverishing the people in mind and body.[24]

Not surprisingly, the Italians fare no better than the French, as Smollett's persona regards them under the same light of nationalistic comparison. To be sure, the military competition that existed between the British and French was absent in the relationship to the Italians, and no memory of the hatred generated by the fairly recently concluded Seven Years' War entered into the account of the Italians as it had with the French. Nevertheless, religious differences and ordinary national competitiveness move Smollett's persona against the Italians with the same didactic purpose that motivated his account of the French.

Once more, English superiority can be demonstrated in the architecture of its bridges: "I have not seen any bridge in France or Italy, comparable to that of Westminster, either in beauty, magnificence, or solidity; and when the bridge at Black-Friars is finished, it will be such a monument of architecture as all the world cannot parallel" (XXIX). Compared with the Thames, even the Tyber is "no more than an inconsiderable stream . . ." (XXIX). Italian gardens cannot match the beauty of those in Stowe, Kensington, and Richmond, for while "The Italians understand, because they study, the excellencies of art . . . they have no idea of the beauties of nature" (XXXI). A public room at St. Remo is "so dirty and miserable, that it would disgrace the worst hedge alehouse in England" (XXV). Of public houses on the road from Rome to Florence, the persona announces, "I will venture to say that a common prisoner in the Marshalsea or King's-Bench is more cleanly and commodiously lodged than we were in many places . . ." (XXXIV).[25] Even the legacy of classical antiquity in Rome is not to be compared with English achievements in creating the "conveniences of life" (XXIX).[26]

24. *Ibid.* IV, V, XIII, XVII, XX. See E. Joliat, *Smollett et la France* (Paris, 1935), pp. 111–57.
25. *Ibid.* XXX, XXXV.
26. *Ibid.* XXXII.

Italian Catholicism comes under the same attack as the French and is linked with it by Smollett's persona (XXVII). The antagonism between the Italians and English may be attributed in part to the religious differences between them, and, as the persona describes it, universal Roman Catholicism binds countries in what appears a plot designed to subvert the Protestant leader of European nations (XXXIV). As for the religion itself, under its domination "no country was ever known to prosper" (XXIX) and its pernicious influence undermines the very taste and art of nations (XXXI).

Italians themselves are simply not to be trusted—they do not measure up to English standards of honesty (XXXV). "Treacherous and cruel" (XXIX), "villainously rapacious" (XXXIV), from the common people to the nobility—or at least anyone "who has any pretensions to family" (XXVII)—they offer the Englishman a sense of the superiority of his own common-sensical Protestant society.

The pride in his society that allows the traveler to return happily to England two years after his dismal departure is the point that the didacticism of the *Travels* offers. Through France and Italy Smollett's persona sees and reports on events from a Briton's point of view, evaluating these European nations to come to a conclusion that whatever its faults, his country is superior to any on earth. Even as he investigates foreign military defenses, he measures British superiority. The Genoese would have been wiser to look to England rather than France for their protection, for "a resolute commander might, with a strong squadron, sail directly into the harbour, without sustaining much damage . . ." (XXVI); "popes will do well to avoid misunderstandings with the maritime protestant states, especially the English, who being masters of the Mediterranean, and in possession of Minorca, have it in their power at all times . . . to take the city, without opposition" (XXX). Smollett's persona looks at the weakness of the defenses at Toulon or at the "dreary commerce" in Marseilles and is pleased to note what the triumph of British military force has meant to the European balance of power and trade (XXXIX). Why, the British military power is such that it makes inglorious even the celebrated battles of classical antiquity: "I do believe . . . that half a dozen

English frigates would have been able to defeat both the contending fleets at the famous battle of Actium . . ." (XXXII).

With such an eye and such values and intentions, no wonder
Smollett's persona approaches the criticism of art as he does. He is
the ordinary Briton, no "connoisseur," determined to offer his
judgment of art in personal terms. He is not to be taken in by all
that has been said before. He is the common-sensical, intelligent
observer, all too well aware of the affectations of others, all too
conscious of those countrymen of his who are duped in one way or
another by continental guides and guidebooks, country-men who
profess a knowledge that is not theirs and consequently allow
themselves to look and be ridiculous. In the same way that those
English travelers expose themselves to continental predators because of their display of extravagance, they become vulnerable to
art dealers and tourist guides because they do not allow their own
good sense to tell them what to make of a work of art.

Judgments about Smollett as art critic generally miss the point
of what he is doing with such material in the *Travels*. Whether he
was, as Sterne said, a "choleric Philistine"; [27] whether his comments "on pictorial art are absurd"; [28] whether—which seems
highly improbable—"his descriptions of the buildings and works
of art he saw are intrinsically tedious and jejune," [29] these matters
ignore what Smollett attempts to do with the art criticism in the
Travels. Seccombe, here as elsewhere, finally misses the point because he so thoroughly identifies the persona with Smollett himself; but Seccombe also understands what Smollett is about in the
work. He notes accurately the criticism of false taste, the affectations of the "connoisseurs," the dependence on "good sense and
sincere utterance." [30]

Talking about his artistic judgments, Smollett's persona declares, "I am used to speak my mind freely on all subjects that fall
under the cognizance of my senses . . ." (XXVIII). And so he does,
depending upon his *own* sense of decorum and his *own* standards

27. Osbert Sitwell, Introduction to *Travels Through France and Italy* (London, 1949), p. ix.
28. Robert E. Moore, *Hogarth's Literary Relationships* (Minneapolis and
London, 1948), p. 166.
29. Sitwell, Introduction to *Travels,* p. viii.
30. Seccombe, *Travels,* pp. liii–lv.

of artistic propriety. Of Michelangelo's "famous statue of the dead Christ in his mother's lap" to be found in St. Peter's, he complains that Christ is "emaciated" and that "there is something indelicate, not to say indecent, in the attitude and design of a man's body, stark naked, lying upon the knees of a woman" (XXXI). Raphael's Madonna de la Seggiola appears to him "defective in dignity and sentiment. It is the expression of a peasant rather than of the mother of God" (XXVIII). He describes a Gothic abbey as "affected, unnatural, and desultory . . ." (VI), and similarly rejects "the modern taste of architecture [with its] churches and palaces . . . crowded with pretty ornaments which distract the eye, and by breaking the design into a variety of little parts, destroy the effect of the whole" (XXX). His principles may be disputed, but they are not to be dismissed without consideration, for they represent an independent judgment based on open-mindedness and common sense and intelligence. It is a judgment capable of accepting the tribute to "the celebrated Transfiguration, by Raphael [at the church of St. Peter in Montorio]," and, at the same time, questioning the relationship of its parts, its failure to keep the attention focused on it as a whole (XXXIII).

Smollett's persona, writing to those who want *his* opinion and *his* judgment, emphasizes that point to his audience:

If I was silly enough to make a parade, I might mention some hundreds more of marbles and pictures, which I really saw at Rome; and even eke out that number with a huge list of those I did not see: but, whatever vanity I may have, it has not taken this turn; and I assure you, upon my word and honour, I have described nothing but what actually fell under my own observation. As for my critical remarks, I am afraid you will think them too superficial and capricious to belong to any other person. . . . (XXXIII)

A single letter is replete with such phrases as "I chiefly admired," "I was charmed with," "I was attracted by," "I admired a" (XXXIII). He refuses to repeat what has "been circumstantially described by twenty different authors of travels" (XXVII) or those "much better qualified than I . . ." (XXXI). But neither will he allow himself to be bullied by their judgments. He is unafraid to declare that although he had heard much of the *ponte Carignano*, it "did not at all answer my expectation" (XXVI). His most frequently ridiculed judgment comes out of his disappointment in what he had been led to expect: "I was much disappointed at sights of the pantheon, which after all that has been said of it, looks like a huge cockpit, open at top" (XXXI). He places himself before his audience as an intelligent, informed Englishman, offering comments based on common-sense principles that they were likely to share if not deluded by "connoisseurs." His emphasis on decorum, regularity, simplicity, and naturalness is aimed at appealing to such taste.[31]

According to Smollett's persona, those who follow him to the Continent would do well to eschew the misleading judgments of connoisseurs (XXVIII). The very word itself—together with *virtuosi*—stands as a warning against affectation, bad taste, and spurious judgment. Connoisseurs are to be distinguished from the "common spectator" (XXVIII).[32] But he writes for the latter and emphasizes common sense, although he does not deny that something more is "required to discover and distinguish the more delicate beauties of painting" (XXVIII). The value of rejecting the judgment of connoisseurs, however, becomes most apparent in his ironic comments on the Leaning Tower of Pisa:

... I should never have dreamed that this inclination proceeded from any other cause, than an accidental subsidence of the foundation on this side, if some connoisseurs had not taken great pains to prove it was done on purpose by the architect. Any person who has eyes may see that the pillars on that side are considerably sunk. ... I think it would have been a very preposterous ambition in the architects, to show how far they could deviate from the perpendicular in this construction; because in that particular any common mason could have rivalled them. ... (XXVII)

In his art criticism as in his other descriptions of France and Italy, Smollett's persona is a man of authority, making judgments that come out of his own extraordinary common sense and intended as advice for his readers. He emphasizes the need to judge art without being unduly impressed by received opinion, for just as English travelers are gulled by continental innkeepers and

31. *Travels,* VI, XXVIII, XXX, XXXI, XXXIII.
32. *Ibid.* XXIX, XXXIII.

coachmen, they are duped by the pretentious artistic judgments of "connoisseurs" and "virtuosi" and become innocent victims of unscrupulous guides and salesmen of "art." He is always conscious of his audience, having deliberately made clear that what he writes is for a society larger than his particular correspondent:

... I considered all the letters I have hitherto written on the subject of my travels, as written to your society in general, though they have been addressed to one individual of it; and if they contain anything that can either amuse or inform, I desire that henceforth all I send may be freely perused by all the members . . . (VIII)

He carefully researches his material; he methodically sets himself up as a reliable and concerned observer. What he does not know, he either checks in books or raises as questions for those most likely to provide the correct answers; but in any event, he seeks to verify whatever he offers, even if that means making "a second excursion to these antient ruins, and measur[ing] the arena of the amphitheatre with packthread" (XVI).[33] It is important that he be accurate because he is performing a service for his countrymen. He details costs, prices, routes, and conveniences so that those of his fellow citizens who follow after him will not be abused by the variety of cheats and deceits that await them abroad.[34] His purpose is didactic, in the best tradition of the art of his period, and the over-all design of the *Travels*, like Goldsmith's *The Traveller*, is to convince his audience—even as he has become convinced—that for all its faults, England offers the best prospect for happiness on earth.

33. The *Travels* offers many more such examples. See, for instance: IX, X, XX, XXI, XXIV, XXVI, XXVII, XXIX, XXX, XXXIII. Some sample comments: ". . . as far as I can judge from information. I have perused a Latin manuscript"; "Upon further inquiry"; "I was strangely misled by all the books consulted"; "Mr. Webb's criticism on this artist is certainly just."
34. Examples are too numerous to cite, but see, for example: *Travels,* I, IV, V, VI, VIII, IX, X, XII, XIX, XXIII, XXIV, XXV, XXVII, XXIX, XXXV. Some sample comments: "I mention these circumstances to give you an idea of the imposition to which strangers are subject in this country"; "I would advise every traveller who consults his own ease and convenience, to be liberal of his money to all that sort of people; and even to wink at the imposition . . ."; "Their imposition on us . . ."; "To give you an idea of the extortion of those villainous publicans . . ."; "a post-master, whose house I would advise all travellers to avoid."

PUBLICATIONS OF LEWIS M. KNAPP

1929
"Smollett's Admirers in Eighteenth-Century America," *Williams Alumni Review,* Williams College, Williamstown, Massachusetts, XXII, 114–15.

1930
"Ann Smollett, Wife of Tobias Smollett," *PMLA,* XLV, 1049.

1931
"Smollett's *Roderick Random,*" *TLS,* Jan. 8.
"Smollett's Verses and their Musical Settings in the Eighteenth Century," *MLN,* XLVI, 224–32.
"A Rare Satire on Smollett," *TLS,* Oct. 8.

1932
"Smollett and Le Sage's *The Devil Upon Crutches,*" *MLN,* XLVII, 91–93.
"Smollett's Early Years in London," *JEGP,* XXXI, 220–27.
"Elizabeth Smollett, Daughter of Tobias Smollett," *RES,* VIII, 312–15.
"A Sequel to Smollett's *Humphry Clinker,*" *TLS,* Oct. 6.
"Smollett's Works as printed by William Strahan, with an unpublished Letter of Smollett to Strahan," *The Library, The Transactions of the Bibliographical Society,* 282–91.

1933
"More Smollett Letters," *MLN,* XLVIII, 246–49.
"Letter by Colley Cibber to his Daughter," *N&Q,* Aug. 5, CLXV, 80.

1934
"The Naval Scenes in *Roderick Random,*" *PMLA,* XLIX, 593–98.

1935
"The Publication of Smollett's *Complete History* . . . and *Continuation,*" *The Library, The Transactions of the Bibliographical Society,* 295–308.
"Smollett and the Case of James Annesley," *TLS,* Dec. 28.

1936
"An Important Smollett Letter," *RES,* XII, 75–77.

1939
"Ralph Griffiths, Author and Publisher, 1746–1750," *The Library, The Transactions of the Bibliographical Society,* 197–213.

1943
"Smollett's Friend Smith," *TLS*, Oct. 9.

1944
"Smollett and the Elder Pitt," *MLN*, LIX, 250–57.

"Rex versus Smollett: More Data on the Smollett-Knowles Libel Case," *MP*, XLI, 221–27.

"Smollett's Letter to Philip Miller," *TLS*, June 24.

"Dr. John Armstrong, Littérateur, and Associate of Smollett, Thomson, Wilkes, and other Celebrities," *PMLA*, LIX, 1019–58.

1945
"Smollett and Garrick," *University of Colorado Studies*, II, 233–43.

1948
Review of *Smollett's Reputation as a Novelist* by Fred Boege, *Princeton Studies in English*, No. 27. Princeton, Princeton University Press, 1947, in *JEGP*, XLVII, 98–100.

1949
"Smollett's Self-Portrait in the *Expedition of Humphry Clinker*" in *The Age of Johnson: Essays Presented to Chauncey Brewster Tinker*, New Haven, Yale University Press, 1949, 149–58. Reprinted 1964 by Yale University Press.

Tobias Smollett Doctor of Men and Manners, Princeton, Princeton University Press, 1949. Reprinted in 1963 by Russell & Russell, Inc., New York.

1951
Review (Lewis M. Knapp and Lillian De La Torre) of Francesco Cordasco's *Letters of Tobias George Smollett A Supplement* to the *Noyes Collection with a Bibliography of Editions of the Collected Works*, Madrid, 1950, *PQ*, XXX, 289–91.

1952
"Smollett and Fizès (?)" and "Rejoinder" (Lewis M. Knapp and Lillian De La Torre), *MLN*, LXVII, 69–70, 71.

"Fielding's Dinners with Dodington, 1750–1752," *N&Q*, 20 December 1952, CXCVII, no. 26, 565–66.

1953
"Forged 'Smollett' Letters," *N&Q*, 163.

"Specialist Collecting," *Antiquarian Bookman*, XI, 11.

1954
"Smollett, Tobias George," *New Century Cyclopedia of Names*, 1954, Vol. III.

"Abridgements of Smollett for Children," *N&Q*, 475.

Review of James R. Foster's "Smollett and the *Atom*" (in *PMLA*, 1953), *PQ*, XXXIII, 298–99.

1956
"Smollett's Letter to Samuel Mitchelson," *N&Q*, June 1956, New Series III, 262.

1957

"Smollett's Translation of 'Don Quixote': Data on its Printing and its Copyright," *N&Q*, 543–44.

1958

Review of Smollett's Hoax: "Don Quixote" in English, by Carmine Rocco Linsolata, Stanford, California: Stanford University Press, 1956, *JEGP* LVII, 553–55.

1959

"Dr. John Armstrong's 'Of Benevolence'," *N&Q*, June 1959, New Series VI, 218–19.

1960

"Another Letter from Smollett to Dr. William Hunter," *N&Q*, 299–300.

1961

"A Rare Set of Smollett's Novels," in "Notes from the Rare Books Room," 412 Norlin Library, The University of Colorado, no. 10.

1963

"Smollett, Mac Kercher, and the Annesley Claimant" (Lewis M. Knapp and Lillian De La Torre), *ELN*, I, 28–33.

1964

"The Keys to Smollett's *Atom*," *ELN*, II, 100–102.

1965

"The 'Prophecy' attributed to Smollett," *RES*, XVI, 177–82.
"Comments on Smollett by the Rev. Dr. Thomas Birch," *N&Q*, 218–21.
"Smollett's Translation of Fénelon's *Telemaque*," *PQ*, XLIV, 405–7.

1966

"Early Scottish Attitudes toward Tobias Smollett," in *Essays in English Neoclassicism*, University of Iowa, *PQ*, XLV, 262–69.
Review of Radical Doctor Smollett by Donald Bruce, Boston, Houghton Mifflin Company, 1965, *MLQ*, XXVII, 226–28.
An edition of *The Expedition of Humphry Clinker*, London, Oxford University Press.

1968

"Smollett and Johnson, Never Cater-Cousins?" *MP*, LXVI, 152–54.

1969

A review of André Parreaux's edition of *Humphry Clinker* published in *Études Anglaises*, XXII, No. 2, April-June 1969, 197–98.

1970

The Letters of Tobias Smollett, Oxford, Clarendon Press.

1971

An essay in *Student Guides to the Novel*, Oxford, Clarendon Press.
"Tobias Smollett" in *Cambridge Bibliography of English Literature*.

INDEX

"A Collection of 10 Tracts on Mary Taft, the celebrated pretended Breeder of Rabbits," 87

Addison, Joseph, 105

Aiken, John, *Critical Essay*, 104

Akenside, Mark, 193-95

Alberts, Robert C., *The Most Extraordinary Adventures of Major Robert Stobo*, 197

Aldrovandus, 96

Alemán, Mateo, *Guzmán de Alfarache*, 112

Allan M., *The Tradescants: Their Plants, Gardens and Museums 1570-1662*, 99

Allen, Ralph, 102-3

Amherst, Alicia, *A History of Gardening in England*, 99

Amherst College, 4

Ananas, 80-109

Anderson, J. P., 223-24

Anderson, Robert, 203, 208-15, 217-21, 226

An Essay on the New Species of Writing Founded by Mr. Fielding, 135

A New and General Biographical Dictionary, 215

Annual Register, 204, 206

Anson, George, *Voyage round the World*, 14

Ansley, Louise, 4

Anstey, Christopher, *The New Bath Guide*, 20

Antal, Frederick, *Hogarth and His Place in European Art*, 174

Antwerp, 120

Apicius Coelius, 194

Aquinas, St. Thomas, 126-27

Arbuthnot, John, *The Anatomist Dissected: or The Man-Midwife finely brought to Bed*, 88

Aristotle, 80, 83-84, 126-27, 137, 179; *De Generatione et Corruptione*, 83; *Nichomachean Ethics*, 126; *The Experienced Midwife*, 83

Armstrong, Dr. John, 207; *The Art of Preserving Health*, 103-4

Athenaeum, 224

A Treatise of All Sorts of Foods, Both Animal and Vegetable, 105

Augustine, 126

Ault, Norman, *Minor Poems of Alexander Pope*, 87

Austin, Jane, *Pride and Prejudice*, 77-78

autobiography, inverted, 201-2

Baker, C. H. Collins, *The Life of James Brydges First Duke of Chandos*, 101-2

Baker, David Erskine, 203

Baker, M. I., *The Life of James Brydges First Duke of Chandos*, 101-2

Ballantyne, John, *Novelist's Library*, 212

Baltimore, Frederick Calvert, Baron, 23

Barbadoes, 99

Baretti, Giuseppe Marc' Antonio, 23

Barnes, Harry Elmer, 26

Bartel, Max, "The Longings of Pregnancy," 84

Bartel, Paul, "The Longings of Pregnancy," 84

Bartholin, Thomas, 91

Bastard, William, "On the Cultivation of Pine-Apples," 104

Bastille, The, 15

Bath, Bishop of, 41

Bath, England, 10, 14, 21, 159-60, 163-66, 168

Bathurst, 1st Earl, 101

Battestin, Martin C., 73, 134

Battie, Dr. William, 18

Bayne-Powell, Rosamond, 160

Beattie, James, *An Essay on Laughter and Ludicrous Composition*, 169, 179, 193-94, 207

Beaumont, Cyril W., *The History of Harlequin*, 188

Bellet, Isaac, 92-93; *Letters on the Force of the Imagination in Pregnant Women*, 92

Belloc, Hilaire, 35
Berkeley, Bishop, 93
Bernini, Giovanni Lorenzo, 170, 172
Besant, Sir Walter, 160
Bestiary, The, 73
Blackwood's Edinburgh Magazine, 228
Blanchard, Frederic T., 135
Bloch, Tuvia, 135, 143, 158
Blondel, James Augustus, 81, 89-92, 94
Blount, Martha, 102
Boege, Fred W., *Smollett's Reputation as a Novelist,* 135, 203-4, 207, 210, 214-15, 220, 226, 231
Boggs, W. Arthur, 197
Bolingbroke, Henry St. John, 1st Viscount, 43
Bond, Donald, 105
Bonhill, Scotland, 221
Bontein, Thomas, 226
Boswell, James, 3, 54, 127; *Life of Johnson,* 134, 202
botany, eighteenth-century, 98-107
Boucé, Paul-Gabriel, 225
Boulger, G. S., 99
Boulogne, 237, 240
Bover, John, 191
Boyce, Benjamin, *The Benevolent Man: A Life of Ralph Allen,* 103
Boydell, John, 172-73
Boyle, Robert, 91
Bradley, Richard, 100-101
Brady, Robert, 27
British Critic, 209, 211-12
British Magazine, 17, 211, 213, 223
The British Plutarch, 208
Brown, Edward, 105
Brown, John R., "A Chronology of Major Events in Obstetrics and Gynecology," 94
Brown, Tom, *Amusements Serious and Comical,* 99
Browne, James P., 96, 211, 226
Brydges, James, 102
Buck, Howard Swazey, 194, 229; *Smollett as Poet,* 231; *A Study in Smollett: Chiefly "Peregrine Pickle,"* 57, 135, 190, 231
Bunbury, Henry William, 180
Burke, Joseph, ed., *William Hogarth, Analysis of Beauty,* 175
Burlington, 3rd Earl of, 102
Burnet, Gilbert, Bishop of Salisbury, 43
Bute, John Stuart, 3rd Earl of, 53-55, 173
Butler, Samuel, 125
Butlerian verse, 91
Byron, George Gordon, Lord, 151

Caesar, Julius, 141
Caillois, Roger, *Man, Play, and Games,* 114-17, 125
Cambridge, University of, 100
Campbell, Thomas, 216
Canterbury, Archbishop of, 41
caricature, theory of, 179-90
Carlyle, Alexander, 140, 181, 202
Carlyle, Thomas, 202
Carracci, Annibale, 170, 172, 175
Carracci, Augustin, 170
Carroll, John, 66
Carte, Thomas, 27
Carter, Elizabeth, 134
Carthagena, expedition to, 14, 181, 191, 223
Cary, The Reverend Henry Francis, 220
Caryll, John, 86
Cervantes, Miguel de, *Don Quixote, The History and Adventures of,* 18, 57, 65, 179
Chalmers, Alexander, 216-17
Chambers, Ephraim, 99, 104-6
Chambers, Robert, 221-23, 227
Chandos, Duke of, 101
Charing Cross, London, 97
Charles I, 99
Charles II, 99-100
Charleton, Walter, 105
Chaucer, Geoffrey, *The Reeve's Tale,* 13
Cheselden, William, *Anatomy of the Humane Body,* 97
Chester, Bishop of, 87
Cheyne, George, *An Essay on Regimen,* 106
Chichester, Bishop of, 41
Chichester, Lake of, 42
Church of England, 48, 53
Churchill, Charles, 176
Cibber, Theophilus, 184, 188, 191
Cicero, 103, 179
Clarendon, Edward Hyde, 1st Earl of, 35
Clayborough, Arthur, *The Grotesque in English Literature,* 178
Cleland, John, *Memoirs of a Woman of Pleasure,* 132; *Memoirs of Fanny Hill,* 132; review of *Peregrine Pickle,* 131
Clifford, James L., 204
Cocchi, A., *The Pythagorean Diet, of Vegetables Only, Conducive to The Preservation of Health,* 105
Cohn, Albert M., *Bibliographical Catalogue of the Printed Works Illustrated by George Cruikshank,* 180
Cole, William, 100
Collins, J. L., *The Pineapple,* 99

Colorado College, 5

Comber, the Reverend Thomas, 216

Compendium of Authentic and Entertaining Voyages, 211, 219, 229

Congreve, William, *Love for Love,* 11; *The Double Dealer,* 137; Maskwell, 137

Conway, Henry Seymour, 46, 51

Cooper, M., *Pica,* 84

Cordasco, Francesco, 209

Corneille, Pierre, *Le Cid,* 117

Corsica, 145

Courteen, Sir William, 99

Coypel, Charles-Antoine, 179

Cozens, Alexander, *Principles of Beauty, Relative to the Human Head,* 175, 179, 185

Crawford, Earl of, 41

Crawley, Pitt, 56

Critical Review, 16-17, 92, 109, 215-16, 219

Cromwell, Oliver, 38-39, 99

Cruikshank, George, 176, 180

Culpepper, Nicholas, 80-84; *Directory for Midwives,* 83-84; *The Experienced Midwife,* 83-84; *The English Physitian,* 83-84, 104-5

Cyprianus, Charles, 91

Daghlian, Philip B., 204

Dalquhurn, Scotland, 226

Danckerts, Henry, *Rose, The Royal Gardener, presenting to Charles II the first pine-apple grown in England,* 98-99

Darly, Mary, 172

Darly, Matthew, 172

Darly, Mary and Matthew, *A Political and Satyrical History,* 172

Davies, Mary, *The Accomplish'd Rake,* 66

Davis, Robert Gorham, 156

de Beer, E. S., 99

Decker, Sir Matthew, 100-101

Defoe, Daniel, 67-68, 72, 166; *Robinson Crusoe,* 67-72; *Roxana,* 124

della Porta, G. B., *De Humana Physiognomonia,* 171

de Neuhoff, Théodore, 145

Derrick, Samuel, 23

Dettingen, 11

Dewhurst, Kenneth, *John Locke (1632-1704) Physician and Philosopher: A Medical Biography,* 106

Dial, The, 228

Dickens, Charles, 10-17; *Nicholas Nickleby,* 17; *Oliver Twist,* 10; *The Old Curiosity Shop,* 10

Dictionarium Botanicum, 100

Digby, Sir Kenelm, 91

Digeon, Aurélien, *Les Romans de Fielding,* 66

Dodsley, Isaac, 103

Dolben, Mr., 48

Douglas, James, 97

Drouvert, Michael Anne, 97

Drummond, Sir Jack, *The Englishman's Food,* 105

East India Company, 100

Edinburgh, Scotland, 21, 163, 166

Edinburgh, University of, 104

Edinburgh Magazine, 207

Ehrmann, Jacques, 114

Ellison, Ralph, *Invisible Man,* 112

Encyclopaedia Britannica, 204, 215, 219, 228

England, 11, 19, 156, 167, 173, 235

Episcopalians, 41

Esdras, The Book of, 88

European Magazine, 209, 211

Evans, David L., 156

Evelyn, John, *Diary,* 99-100

Farquhar, George, *The Beaux' Stratagem,* 188-89, 191

Father Malebranche's Treatise Concerning the Search after Truth, 89

Feversham, Lord, 33

Fielding, Henry, 9, 57-60, 65-70, 73-76, 78, 133, 134-36, 148, 155, 158, 175, 183, 195, 221, 227; *Amelia,* 57, 74-75, 78; *Don Quixote in England,* 58; *Jonathan Wild,* 58; *Joseph Andrews,* 9, 58, 65, 73-75, 134, 175; *Tom Jones,* 57-61, 64-75, 78, 106, 135

Fisher, William, 174

Fitzsimons, M. A., 26

Fleet Prison, 15

Flying Post, 87

Foord, A. S., 54

Foote, Samuel, 188

Forrest's Coffeehouse, 202

Forster, John, *Life of Dickens,* 17

Fortescue, William, 102

Foss, Martin, *Symbol and Metaphor in Human Experience,* 170, 195, 199-200

Foxon, David, 132

Fraser, Alexander Campbell, 106

Frederick, Prince of Wales, 54

Freud, Sigmund, 199

Friedman, Arthur, 160

Gainsborough, Earl of, 101
Gardener's Dictionary, The, 100
Gardener, William, "Botany and the Americas," 99
Garrard, Sir Samuel, 48
Garrick, David, 171, 178, 188-89, 191, 205-6
Garrison, Fielding H., An Introduction to the History of Medicine, 83, 85, 94
Gentili, Dr. Giovanni, 5
Gentleman's Magazine, The, 57, 93-95, 98
George I, 87
George, Mary Dorothy, 26, 173; English Political Caricature to 1792, 176; Hogarth to Cruikshank, 173
Ghezzi, Pier Leone, 172-73, 175-76
Gibbon, Edward, 28-29, 35
Giddings, Robert, The Tradition of Smollett, 112
Giles, John, Ananas, a Treatise on the Pine Apple, 80-81
Gilfillan, the Reverend George, 216-17
Girard, René, Desire, Deceit, and the Novel, 74
Glasgow Medical School, 98
Gloucester, Bishop of, 42
Godalming, 85, 89
Goffman, Erving, Interaction Ritual, 119
Goldberg, M. A., Smollett and the Scottish School, 118, 139, 156
Goldsmith, Oliver, 26, 106, 160, 233; She Stoops to Conquer, 78; The Traveller, 246; The Vicar of Wakefield, 77-78
Gombrich, E. H., Art and Illusion, 170, 185, 198
Gombrich, E. H., and Ernst Kris, Caricature, 170, 198
Gordon, Dr. John, 221, 224
Gosse, Philip, Dr. Viper: The Querulous Life of Philip Thicknesse, 232
Gough, Richard, 100
Grand Tour, satire on, 193
Granger, James, A Biographical History of England, 171
Gray, Thomas, 173
Greek romances, 13
Green, John Richard, 29
Greene, D. J., 53
Grey, Lord, 50
Griffiths, Ralph, 132, 216
Grignion, Charles, 176
Grose, Francis, Rules for Drawing Caricaturas, 178-79
Groton, Massachusetts, 4

Reni, Guido, 187
Guilford, 86
"Gulliver, Lemuel," The Anatomist Dissected: or The Man-Midwife finely brought to Bed, 88
Guthrie, William, 26

Habbakkuk Hilding, 57
Hadfield, Miles, Gardening in Britain, 99-101, 103
Hake, Henry M., "Pond's and Knapton's Imitations of Drawings," The Print Collector's Quarterly, 173
Halsband, R., 100
Hamilton, Archibald, printer, 216
Hannay, David, 27, 220-25, 227
Hannay, James, 220-21
Hanover, Elector of, 100
Hartley, David, Observations on Man, 107
Hay, D., 105
Hayman, Francis, 180
Haymarket, the, 188
Hazlitt, William, 168
Heliodorus, 91
Henley, W. E., 226-28
Henry VIII, King, 36-37, 48
Herbert, David, 225-26
Herbert, Lord, 2nd Earl of Pembroke, 37
hermaphrodites, 97
Hertford, Francis Seymour Conway, 1st Marquess of, 46
Hesiod, 91
Hill, G. B., 134
Hill, Dr. John, 57, 95, 216; The Adventures of George Edwards, A Creole, 95; The History of a Woman of Quality: or The Adventures of Lady Frail, 95; Lucina sine Concubitu, 95; and Smollett's Peregrine Pickle, 95
Hilles, F. W., ed., The Age of Johnson, 66
Hind, Arthur M., Engraving in England in the Sixteenth and Seventeenth Centuries, 171
History Today, 99
Hoadly, Benjamin, Bishop of Winchester, 49
Hobbes, Thomas, 139
Hoefer, Jean-Chrétien, 222
Hofmann, Werner, Caricature: from Leonardo to Picasso, 170
Hogarth William, 172-76, 179-80, 185, 187-89, 193-96, 238; Analysis of Beauty, 175, 185-86; The Bench, 175; The

Bruiser, 176, 179; *Characters and Caricaturas,* 175; *The Gate of Calais or The Roast Beef of Old England,* 176, 179; *Gulielmus Hogarth,* 176; *John Wilkes Esq.,* 177; *Laughing Audience,* 174; *A Midnight Conversation,* 174; *Scholars at a Lecture,* 174; *Simon Lord Lovat,* 176; *Tailpiece to the Catalogue,* 176; *Taste in High Life,* 174
Home, George, 214
Home, John, 207, 224
Hope, John, 104
Hopkins, Robert, 163-67, 199
Horace, 189, 235
Hore, Captain Daniel, 191
Horstius, Jacobus, 91
Howard, John, 86
Howe, P. P., 168
Huizinga, Johann, *Homo Ludens,* 114, 125
Hume, David, 28-33, 35-37, 46, 48, 50-51, 54, 56; *Treatise on Human Nature,* 107
Hunt, William, 26, 28
Hunter, Dr. John, 46, 127
Hunter, Dr. Richard, 18
Hunter, Dr. William, 91, 93
Hunterian Museum, Glasgow, 98
Huntingdonshire, 39

Ibsen, 7
"Imaginationists," the, 89-91
Ireland, 11
Irving, Joseph, 221

Jamaica, 5, 10
James, Henry, 155; *The Ambassadors,* 157
James II, King, 31-32, 41, 43, 46, 48
James, Robert, *A Medicinal Dictionary,* 99, 104-5
Jefferson, D. W., "Tristram Shandy and The Tradition of Learned Wit," 108
Jesuits, 48
Jesus College, Oxford, 174
Jewish Naturalization Bill, 1753, 143
Johnson, George W., *A History of English Gardening,* 99
Johnson, Samuel, 3-4, 45, 54, 133, 136, 189, 210; *Life of Mr. Richard Savage,* 66; *The Rambler,* 9, 28; *Rambler no. 4,* 132, 134; *Rasselas,* 28, 67
Joliat, E., 229; *Smollett et la France,* 241
Jones, C. E., 229; *Smollett Studies,* 231

Jonson, Ben, 191
Joyce, James, 32, 34

Kafka, Franz, *Amerika,* 10
Kahrl, George M., 229; *Tobias Smollett: Traveler-Novelist,* 156, 191, 194, 197, 231, 233, 236
Kenrick, William, 57, 205-6
King, Sir Peter, 48
King's Bench Prison, 18, 149
Knapp, Helen June Heath, 4
Knapp, Lewis M., 3-8, 27-30, 181, 202, 206, 210, 217, 222, 229, 247-49; characterized, 3-8; "Early Scottish Attitudes toward Tobias Smollett," 177, 249; "The Publication of Smollett's *Complete History . . . and Continuation,*" 26, 247; "Smollett's Self-Portrait in *The Expedition of Humphry Clinker,*" 156, 197, 248; *Tobias Smollett: Doctor of Men and Manners,* 6, 28, 57, 93, 140, 149, 181, 189, 214, 224, 229-31, 248
Knapp, Louise Ansley, 4
Kris, Ernst, *Psychoanalytic Explorations in Art,* 170, 172-73, 198

Landa, Louis A., 82
Lassells, Ann, 5
Last, Sarah, 98
Lawrence, Eugene, 27, 46, 220
Lazarillo de Tormes, 112, 124
Le Brun, Charles, *Traité sur les passions,* 171
Lecky, William Edward Hartpole, 29-30
Le Cour, M., 99
Lefebvre-Cauchy, 219
Leghorn, Italy, 5, 206
Le Glay, André, 145
Lemery, M. L., *A Treatise of All Sorts of Foods,* 105
Lemnius, 85
LeSage, Alain René, 112; *Gil Blas,* 9-10, 18
Letters to the Reverend William Cole, 100
Leven, Scotland, 206, 226
Lewis, John, 189
Lewis, Wilmarth S., 3, 100
Leyden, 99
Linnaeus, 104
L'Intermédiaire des Chercheurs et Curieux, 222
Locke, John, *An Essay Concerning Human Understanding,* 106
Lockwood, Thomas, 135

London, 4, 5, 22, 89, 155, 159-61, 163-68, 172, 183, 186-87, 194, 202, 210, 216, 219, 223
London Magazine, 220
London Review, 205-6
Longaker, Mark, 210
Longinus, *On the Sublime*, 183
Love, John, 221
Lucian, 49
Lynch, Bohun, *A History of Caricature*, 170

MacKercher, Daniel, 5, 190
McCue, Lillian, 7
McKillop, Alan Dugald, 135, 158

Macalpine, Ida, 18
Macaulay, Thomas Babington, 1st Baron, 25, 28-31, 34-35, 45-46, 50-51
Macksey, Richard A., 76
The Magazine of Magazines, 135
Mahon, Lord, 29
Malebranche, 89
Malins, Edward, *English Landscaping and Literature: 1660-1840*, 103
Mallet, David, 54, 207
Mandeville, Bernard de, 139, *Fable of the Bees*, 101
Mann, Sir Horace, 177-78
Mann, Thomas, *Felix Krull*, 112
Manningham, Sir Richard, 87
Martz, Louis L., 229; *The Later Career of Tobias Smollett*, 156, 166, 231, 233, 236
Marxist history, 35
Mary II, Queen, 40, 42, 52
Maubray, John, *The Female Physician, Containing all The Diseases Incident to that Sex, in Virgins, Wives and Widows*, 84-85
Mauclerc, John Henry, *Dr. Blondel confuted: or . . .*, 91-92
Medical History, 86
Melville, Lewis, 229
Memoirs of Martinus Scriblerus, 76
Methodists, 21, 164
Michaud, Joseph François, 218-19, 222
Michelangelo, 244
Millay, Edna St. Vincent, 45
Miller, Philip, *The Gardener's Dictionary*, 100
Milton, John, 67-68; *Paradise Lost*, 69, 139
Minto, William, 228-29
Molyneux, Samuel, 86-87

Monro, Dr. Alexander, *primus*, 91, 93
Montagu, Lady Mary Wortley, 100, 135
Montesquieu, Charles de Secondat, Baron de la Brede et de Montesquieu, 233
Monthly Review, The, 94, 132, 206
Montpellier, 237, 239
Moore, Dr. John, 210-12, 214-15, 218, 220-21, 226-27, 232, 237
Moore, Sir John, son of Smollett's editor, 210
Moore, Robert E., 136, 180, 239
Morrell, Thomas, 186
Moses, 141
Mossner, E. C., 45-46

Namier, Sir Lewis Bernstein, 29, 35
Nangle, Benjamin Christie, 132
Napoleon, 45
Newcastle, Duke of, Thomas Pelham-Holles, 20, 164
Newman, Jeremiah Whitaker, 215
Newton, Isaac, 88
Nice, 232, 237, 240
Nicolson, Marjorie Hope, 88
Nimmo, William P., 225
Non-jurors, 48
Northcote, James, *The Life of Sir Joshua Reynolds*, 177
North Parade, Bath, 21
Notes and Queries, 222
Novelist's Magazine, 95
Nowell, C. E., 26
Noyes, Edward S., 46, 127-28, 210, 229, 231-32

Oesterreich, M., 173
Oldmixon, John, 27
Origen, 126
Orwell, George (Eric Blair), 45
Ould, Fielding, *A Treatise of Midwifery*, 94
Oxford, England, 15, 174
Oxford English Novels, 4

Palmer, Sir James, 99
Panizzi, Sir Anthony, 220
Pantheon, the, 245
Paré, Ambroise, 91
Pares, Richard, 54
Park, William, 131, 135
Parker, A. A., 124
Parkinson, Thomas, 105
Partington, Charles F., 219
Patch, Thomas, *A Caricature Group*, 178; *A Gathering at Sir Horace Mann's*

House, 178; *The Musical Party*, 178; *The Punch Party*, 177
Paulson, Ronald, 74, 135, 146-47, 174, 194, 233-34
Pechey, John, *Complete Midwife's Practice Enlarged*, 98
Pennant, Thomas, 166
Pennicott, William, 100
Peterborough, 42
Pharmacopaeia Universalis, 105
"philosophical history," 33
Philosophical Transactions of the Royal Society of London, 87, 93-94, 97, 104
physicians, satires on, 84-90, 105
pineapples, 98-108
Pisa, Leaning Tower of, 245
Pitt, William, 1st Earl of Chatham, 55
Plato, 126, 152
Ploss, Hermann Heinrich, "The Longings of Pregnancy," 84
Plotinus, 126
Pond, Arthur, 172
Pope, Alexander, 39; activities as a gardener, 101-3; *The Correspondence of Alexander Pope*, ed. George Sherburn, 86, 102-3; "The Discovery: Or, The Squire turn'd Ferret," 86-87; *The Dunciad*, 15, 149; *Epistle to Burlington*, 101; *Essay on Criticism*, 6
Portland, 2nd Duke of, William Bentinck, 101
Potter, Stephen, 122
Pottle, Frederick A., 3
Powell, L. F., 134
Present State of All Nations, 104, 166, 172, 188, 219
Preston, John, 60
Preston, Thomas R., 234
Prince, Philip, 219
Pump Room, the, in Bath, 21
Pundt, A. G., 26

Quarterly Review, 214, 220
Quevedo, Francisco, *La Vida del Buscón*, 124
Quin, James, 163, 191
Quincy, John, *Complete English Dispensatory*, 80, 105
Quintilian, 179

Rabelais, 49
Rahner, Hugo, *Man at Play*, 126-27
Raphael, Rafaelo Sanzio, 175, 187, 244
Rathery, E. J. B., 222

Reid, B. L., 153, 156
Revolution, the English, 51-52
Reynolds, Sir Joshua, 176-77; *School of Athens*, 177
Rich, John, 188
Richardson, Samuel, 65-67, 69, 76, 78, 133-34, 136, 152, 155, 162; *Clarissa*, 66-67, 69, 71-72, 77-78, 159; *The History of Charles Grandison*, 133; *Pamela*, 9, 65, 78, 134
Richardsonian view of the novel, 135
Robertson, J. L., 103
Robertson, William, 28-29, 202
Rohde, E. S., *The Story of the Garden*, 100
Roman Catholic history, 35
Rome, Italy, 173, 177, 241, 244
Roscoe, Thomas, 217-18, 226
Rose, John, 99-100
Rosenbach, A. S. W., *A Catalogue of the Works Illustrated by George Cruikshank and Isaac Cruikshank*, 180
Ross, Thomas W., 6
Rousseau, G. S., 18, 57, 63, 82, 88, 93, 95
Rowlandson, Thomas, 176, 180
Royal College of Physicians, London, 81, 105
Royal Society of Medicine, London, 87-88, 91

Sacheverel, Henry, 48
Sadler's Wells, 21, 160
St André, Nathaniel, 86-88; *A Short Narrative of an Extraordinary Delivery of Rabbits*, 87-89
St. Giles's, parish of, London, 23
St. James's, parish of, London, 23
Saintsbury, George, 155-56, 226-27, 229
Sale, William M., Jr., 66
Schenkius, Johann, 91
Scipio, Publius Africanus, 141-42
Scotland, 11, 19, 23, 156, 166-67
Scott, Henry, 102-3
Scott, Sir Walter, 10, 14, 15, 20, 202, 212-15, 218-21, 226-27, 229
Scott, William, 95
Scriblerian satires, 86-88
Seccombe, Thomas, 229, 237-39, introduction to *Travels Through France and Italy*, 229, 231, 236, 238, 240, 243
Selby-Bigge, L. A., 107
Seligman, S. A., "Mary Toft: the Rabbit Breeder," 86
Sena, John F., 231, 233-34, 239
Serle, John, 102

Shakespeare, William, 28, 83, 191, 193; *Henry V*, 11; *Measure for Measure*, 83; *Richard III*, 137

Sharp, Samuel, 23

Shaw Hall, Berkshire, 101

Shebbeare, Dr. John, 216

Sherburn, George, 60, 86, 102

Singer, Samuel Weller, 216-17

Sitwell, Osbert, Introduction to *Travels Through France and Italy*, 243

Sloane, Sir Hans, 87

Smale, Thomas, 191

Smeaton, Oliphant, 222, 224-25

"Smelfungus," 165, 218

Smellie, William, 82-83, 93, 108; *Treatise on the Theory and Practice of Midwifery*, 82-83, 97

Smith, Richard, 202

Smollett, Anne Lassells, 5, 225

Smollett, Tobias: action in works of, 186; agonistic structure of novels of, 122-24; allusive techniques, 187; architecture, opinions about, 241; as art critic, 243-46; and Augustan satirists, 74; autobiography, 231; biblical echoes, 73; *Bicentennial Edition of the Works of Tobias Smollett*, 4, 6; biography, 6; biography, first full-scale, 6; biographies of, eighteenth- and nineteenth-century, 201-28; borrowings from Fielding, 65; British history, 53; caricature techniques in works of, 170-95; character sketches, 35; characterization of, 160-61; characters compared to Fielding's, 57-61; and the Christian myth, 69-72; city life described in works of, 165; comic characters, 80-83, 129; as comic novelist, 45; contemporaries' view of, 243; correspondence, 6, 46; corruption in society as theme in works of, 146; dedications, 151; delinquency as theme in works of, 124; diction, 151; didacticism, 133; early editions of works of, 210-12; Edwardian estimates of, 227-29; emotions of fear in works of, 137; England, image of in works of, 141-43; English law, 143; English revolution, ideas on the, 52-53; English xenophobia as theme in works of, 140; episodic structures in novels, 133; evil characters in prose of, 137; family as theme in works of, 58-65; father-son relations in works of, 63-66; forgeries of letters of, 3; and the grotesque, 169-95; hermaphrodites in satirical works of, 97; heroes of novels, 131; as historian, 25-50; historiography, 29; human nature in works of, 134; humanitarianism, 47; hyperbole, 149; imitation in novels of, 131-40; intellectual shallowness, 30; irony in works, 149, 158; Italian theories of caricature as an influence, 181-96; Jamesian estimate of fiction of, 155; journalism, 32; and Juvenalian satire, 233; and latitudinarianism, 49; as letter writer, 6, 46; liberalism, 49; literary games in works of, 113-14; low life characters, 135; manners in novels of, 12; medical controversialist, 88-92; medical satire, 81-108, 195; and medicine, 80-108; mimicry in works of, 118-20; mock-heroic techniques, 149; mother-son relations in novels of, 63, 66; myths about, 5; nationalism, 139-40, 151; observations on mankind, 11; obstetrical theories, contributions to, 97; obstetrics, 93-95; pantomime in prose of, 188; Paris in estimate of, 225; patriotism, 139-40; philosophical depth, 35; picaresque, 65; picaresque games in fiction of, 111-28; picaresque fiction, definition of, 112-15; the picaresque journey, 115; picaros in fiction of, 115, 129; the pilgrimage theme in works of, 65-77, 156; plagiarism, charges of, 236; plan of works, 137; plots, 22, 132; point-of-view techniques, 163; political career, 55-56; politics in life and works of, 45-46, 50-51, 54-55; Pope and Smollett, 39; pregnancy, theories of, 81-90; and psychoanalytical criticism, modern, 198-229; realism, 45; religion, opinions about, 242; reputation as novelist, 214-22; revolution, ideas about, 53; rhetorical techniques, 129; romance as element in works of, 18, 138, 144; satire in works of, 138-39; satiric habit of mind, 97; science in works of, 108-9; significance of Scottish lineage, 213; the stage, influence of, 188; and Sterne's *Tristram Shandy*, 76; structure in novels of, 66-67, 157; style, 30-32, 45, 156-58, 199; Swift, literary relation to, 39; Swift, view of, 49; Tory partisanship, alleged, 29; Tory versus Whig in writings of, 46-47; tragedy, attempts to write, 9; and travel literature, 166; travels in France, 20; uncle-nephew relations in Fielding and his works, 64; Victorian estimates of works of, 218-21; war, views of, 42; wit in works of, 63, 81-82; writing habits, 17, 28-29

WORKS: CREATIVE

The Adventures of Ferdinand Count Fathom (1753), 16-19, 58, 103, 115-16, 136-53, 183, 201, 210, 215, 220, 230, evil characters in, 137-38, Major Macleaver, 145, moral purpose of, 138, satanism, 139, Sir Mungo Barebones, 145, sex and violence in the world of, 147; *The Adventures of Peregrine Pickle* (1751), 4, 11, 14-16, 18, 20, 26, 30, 57-58, 61-65, 69-96, 98, 101, 107-8, 115-21, 128-31, 135-36, 152, 158-59, 162, 182, 190-96, 202, 215, 226, 230, Emilia Gauntlet, 14-16, 69-70, 72, 78, Fleet Prison, 15, form of the novel, 190-91, Grizzle, 61-64, 79-82, 101, 104, 108; medical satire, 84-93, picaresque games in, 117-22, Mr. Pickle, 61-62, 64, 71, 79, Mrs. Pickle, 61-64, 71, 80-83, 108, Commodore Trunnion, 11, 61-65, 70, 72, 81, 98, voyages and expulsion of Peregrine, 69, wit in, 79-84; *The Adventures of Roderick Random* (1748), 5, 9, 11-14, 17-20, 26, 30, 57-58, 65, 72, 106, 113-20, 121-24, 128-30, 134-36, 139, 147-48, 152, 158-59, 181-89, 196, 201-2, 205, 210, 213, 216-18, 221, 223, 226, 230, "Apologue" to Dublin edition, 181, Banter, 11, Bragwell, 11, Chatter, 11, Launcelot Crab, 11, Cringer, 11, Lavement, 13, 106, Melopoyn, 14, Narcissa, 186-87, Strap, 13, 57, Dr. Wagtail, 13, 120, Miss Williams, 13, 57; *The Adventures of Sir Launcelot Greaves* (1760-61), 12, 17-19, 58, 115, 149, 196, 213, Ferret, 19; *Advice: A Satire* (1746), 96; *The Briton* (1762-63), 52-53, 55, 223; *A Complete History of England* (1757-58), 17, 25, 27-28, 30, 32, 35, 45, 48, 50, 52, 53-56; *Continuation of the Complete History of England* (1760-65), 25, 50, 57; *An Essay on the External Use of Water* (1752), 211; *The Expedition of Humphry Clinker* (1771), 6, 19, 21-23, 58, 65, 77, 115, 130, 148, 152-57, 159-68, 182, 196-99, 213, 216-17, 226, Brambleton-hall, 167, Jery Melford, 20, 161-67, Lismahago, 20, 22, Lydia Melford, 20, 22, 160-62, 164-66, Mary Jones, 21, Matthew Bramble, 19-20, 22, 24, 77,

115, 160-68, Micklewhimmen, 20, multiple point of view in, 158-63, "Paunceford," 216, Tabitha Bramble, 20, 22, 161-62, 166, Winifred Jenkins, 20-21, 77, 159-62; *The History and Adventures of an Atom* (1769), 28, 55, 57, 219, 233; *The Regicide* (1749), 205, 215, 223, 228; "The Tears of Scotland" (c. 1746), 218, 238; *Travels Through France and Italy* (1766), 20, 45, 58, 156, 165, 197, 206, 222, 230-46, design of, 234, didactic purpose in, 235, 238, persona, 233-37, treatment of foreigners, 238-39

TRANSLATIONS TRADITIONALLY ASSIGNED TO SMOLLETT

The History and Adventures of the Renowned Don Quixote (1755), 17, 149

COLLECTED WORKS REFERRED TO

Plays and Poems (1777), 204-8; *The Miscellaneous Works of Tobias Smollett, M. D.* (various editions), 207, 209, 217, 234; *Works*, ed. John Moore (1797), 96, 211

Spain, 144

Spectator, 105

Spector, Robert Donald, 27, 46, 52-53, 115, 238

Spilsbury, Francis, *Free Thoughts on Quacks*, 106

Stephens, F. G., *Catalogue of Prints and Drawings in the British Museum*, 173

Sterne, Laurence, 45, 108, 155, 165, 206, 227, 232, 243; *A Sentimental Journey*, 23, 165, 206, 218; *Tristram Shandy*, 58, 75-76, 82; novels compared to Smollett's, 108

Stevens, George Alexander, 95-96; *Dramatic History of Master Edward*, 95

Stevenson, R. L., 228

Stobo, Captain Robert, 197

Strauss, Albrecht B., 183

Suetonius, 30

Sussex, England, 14

Swift, Jonathan, 39, 49, 88, 103, 221; *Gulliver's Travels*, 88, 192

Sydenham, Dr. Thomas, 83

Tacitus, 30, 35

Talbot, Catherine, 134

tar water, 93

Taylor, A. J. P., 45

Taylor, T., 89

Tellende, Henry, 100-101
Tertullian, 126
Thackeray, W. M., 25, 28, 30, 220
Thicknesse, Philip, 23, 232; *Quarrels Through France and Italy for the Cure of a Pulmonic Disorder*, 232; *Useful Hints to those who make the Tour of France*, 232
Thomas, K. Bryn, *James Douglas of the Pouch and his pupil William Hunter*, 86, 88, 97
Thompson, J. W., 26
Thomson, James, 54, 207; "Summer," 103; Smollett's friend, 103; and *Ferdinand Count Fathom*, 103
Thucydides, 35
Titian, Tiziano Vecelli, 187
Tofts, Mary, 85-89, 91, 96
"Toryism," 47-48
Townshend, Marquis of, 173
Toynbee, Paget, 173
Tradescant, John, the younger, 99
Trevelyan, George Macaulay, 25, 29
Trevelyan, Sir George Otto, 29-30
Tudor and Stuart Club, of the Johns Hopkins University, 76
Tully, *see* Cicero
Turner, Dr. Daniel, 82, 89-90, 91-92, 94; quarrel with Dr. Blondel, 88-90; and the "Imaginationists," 89-91
Twickenham, 101-3

Universal History, 211, 223

Van Dyck, Anthony, 17
Vane, Frances Anne, Vicountess, 16, 70, 134, 190
Vauxhall Gardens, 22, 161
Victorian journalism, 32
Vinci, Leonardo da, 170, 175

Wager, The, 14
Wales, 11, 19, 23

Walpole, Horace, 4th Earl of Orford, 3, 34, 46, 51, 100
Walpole, Sir Robert, 1st Earl of Orford, 39, 51
Walsh, Robert, 216
War of the Austrian Succession, 42
Waugh, Evelyn, 126
Webb, Daniel, 246
Wells, Bishop of, 42
Westminster Hospital Dispensary, London, 87
Westminster Magazine, 204, 206-7
Whibley, Leonard, 173
Whig history, 46, 52-53
Whiston, William, *The Opinion of the Rev'd Mr. William Whiston concerning the Affair of Mary Toft . . .*, 88
White, T. H., 73
Whitridge, Arnold, 28, 229, 231-32
Whittingham, Charles, 217
Wilbraham, Anne, *The Englishman's Food*, 105
Wilkes, John, 206, 223
William III, King, 40-42, 52
Williams College, 4
Willis, Thomas, 83
Winchester College, 15
Wolf, Edward C. F., *Rowlandson and His Illustrations of 18th Century English Literature*, 180
Woman: An Historical and Anthropological Compendium, 84
Wood, John, 160
Woodward, Henry, 188
Woodward, John, 105
Wordsworth, William, 224
Work, James A., 76
Wotton, Mabel E., 228

Yale French Studies, 114
Yale University, 3-4
Yonge, Sir William, 43